Justice

Other New and Forthcoming Titles from
HACKETT
READINGS IN PHILOSOPHY

Justice

Edited, with an Introduction, by
Jonathan Westphal
Idaho State University

Hackett Publishing Company, Inc.
Indianapolis/Cambridge
1996

02   01   00   99   98   97   96   1   2   3   4   5   6   7   8   9

For further information, please address

Hackett Publishing Company, Inc.
P.O. Box 44937
Indianapolis, Indiana 46244-0937

Cover design by John Pershing

Text design by Dan Kirklin

Library of Congress Cataloging-in-Publication Data

Justice/edited, with an introduction, by Jonathan Westphal.
    p. cm.—(Hackett readings in philosophy)
    Includes bibliographical references.
    ISBN 0-87220-346-8 (cloth). ISBN 0-87220-345-X (pbk.).
    1. Justice (Philosophy) I. Westphal, Jonathan, 1951– .
II. Series.
B195.J87J87 1996   96-30268
172'.2—dc20   CIP

The paper used in this publication meets the minimum requirements of American National Standard for Information Sciences—Permanence of Paper for Printed Library Materials, ANSI Z39.48-1984.

Contents

Acknowledgments

This volume owes much to others, especially to Governor William Weld, a Pnin in the world of politics, or at least more of a Pnin *manqué* than his political opponents or he himself might admit, though for different reasons. I am very grateful to Peter Lubin for his suggestions and advice, and to Deborah Wilkes, surely the nicest and most amusing of possible philosophy editors, and to Carol Scott. I also wish to thank Justin Broackes, Russell Wahl, Chris Cherry, Alexei Westphal, Dorothy Emmet, Steve Richert, and Wayne Gabardi for their comments and advice.

For Stephanie

Justice

"Do justice, love mercy and walk humbly with thy God" is the inspiring injunction of the Old Testament prophet Micah (6:8). To most people, whether or not they are theists or religious believers, the second and third parts of the injunction are clearer and easier to understand than the first. Mercy or mercifulness is simply undeserved forgiveness. Humility is thinking that one is of less worth or importance than one actually is. It is the opposite of pride, which is thinking too much of oneself. But what is justice, and what is it to do justice? This simple but surprisingly difficult question is addressed by the essays and selections in this volume.

Part of the difficulty of this question is a significant ambiguity in the word "justice." For example, it can refer to the whole administration and application of the law to society. "A justice" in Britain and America, meaning a judge or magistrate, embodies and reflects this usage. Again, when an innocent person is blamed and sent to prison for a crime which he or she has not committed, what has occurred is a "miscarriage of justice" in this sense. So "justice being done" means the impartial, equal, fair, and successful application of the law. This kind of justice can also denote a correction of the law, in particular to an existing but defective law which tends to promote injustice, perhaps by being out of date or perhaps by being morally wrong. This introduces a wider moral sense of "justice" and its applications.[1]

In addition to justice in a legal sense, there is also distributive justice.[2] If one contemplates the organization of society as a whole, especially the overall distribution of goods and benefits including income and money as well as offices and opportunities, one notes that some people have more than others, and some very much more. One is bound to ask whether such a state of affairs is just, and if so, why. Each selection in this anthology offers a clear and direct answer to the question: What are the principles of "distributive justice"? All of the selections also illuminate the concept of justice itself.

The arrangement of the selections is primarily chronological, working forward from two excerpts from the *Republic* of Plato, written early in the

---

1. See the helpful discussion of justice and law in John Stuart Mill, selection 10, beginning at paragraph 13.

2. Following the distinctions made by Aristotle in selection 5.

fifth century B.C., to an address given by the international jurist Hans
Kelsen in the twentieth century. There are two pairs of exceptions to the
chronological arrangement. The volume opens with a literary piece by the
Argentinian writer Jorge Luis Borges and closes with an excerpt from a
novel by the Russian-American writer Vladimir Nabokov. The Borges
piece is followed by extracts from the twentieth-century Harvard political philosophers Robert Nozick and John Rawls. The justification for the
contemporary starting point is that justice is not only an academic and historical concept, though it is properly discussed by academic scholars,
among others, and it does have a history. Justice is also a concept that has
meaning today outside the universities.

1. The enigmatic plot of Borges's "The Lottery in Babylon" involves a
society in which a secret lottery determines justice, including punishments and the arrangements of life in general. When a crime is committed, someone gets punished, but what the punishment is and to whom it
is given are decided by a lottery. So the connection between what the
Babylonians do and what they receive as a matter of justice is entirely broken. It may seem obvious that a system of random punishment is the exact opposite of justice. Ordinarily, there is a connection between what is
done and what is received as a result, but part of the interest of Borges's
metaphysical fable is that this is not such an obvious idea, for it is not obvious that an ordinary state lottery, with a multimillion dollar prize, is
unjust or unfair. It may be unjust or unfair because it is unfairly con-
ducted, not because of the huge resulting inequality of wealth. It is fair,
suggests Borges, precisely when it is random. Indeed, it could be that for
this reason a distribution of jobs, income, and prestige by lottery is in the
end the only just one![3] Or perhaps a socioeconomic lottery will as a matter
of fact produce the most desirable and beneficial outcome for all. But the
question still arises whether this beneficial or preferred distribution is a
just one. Part, though of course only part, of what is wrong or unjust about
the practice of reprisal shootings of randomly chosen prisoners in wartime
is that the victims are chosen randomly, as by a lottery.

There is a hidden recognition of this point in Borges's nightmare parable. The group which organizes the lottery, known as "the Company,"
"with divine modesty, avoids all publicity. Its agents, as is natural, are

---

3. A recent work by Barbara Goodwin has taken Borges's idea as its inspiration.
In *Justice by Lottery* (Hemel Hempstead, Harvester, 1993), Goodwin argues that
jobs, income, and prestige will be most justly distributed by lottery.

secret. . . . The silent functioning, comparable to God's, gives rise to all sorts of conjectures." Some say that the Company has not existed for centuries, others that it is eternal, and another, "in the words of masked hierarchs, *that it has never existed and will not exist.*" If this is so, and here is the culmination of Borges's dark conception, then the world, with all its obvious unfairnesses, is just, no matter what its organization, for it is the outcome of a "natural" lottery of history and biology.

2. Robert Nozick writes in *Anarchy, State, and Utopia*, however, that "we are not in the position of children who have been given portions of pie by someone who now makes last minute adjustments to rectify careless cutting. There is no *central* distribution, no person or group entitled to control all the resources, jointly deciding how they are to be doled out." The Company does not exist. Nozick says guardedly that "the term 'distributive justice' is not a neutral one." He is writing within a tradition of conservative political thought which is suspicious of this term. The bias of the term, from the conservative point of view, is that it sanctions apparently unlimited use of law and the coercive powers of government to make social and economic changes. Yet this goes against freedom, according to Nozick. "There is no more a distributing or distribution of shares [of resources] than there is a distributing of mates in a society in which persons choose whom they shall marry."

Nozick's arguments against anything more than the minimal state he desires, the state limited to negative activities (policing and enforcing contracts are his examples), do raise the question, which he does not discuss in the selection taken from his book, of the justice of the original holding of the resources, if indeed there was any such "original" holding. Critics will be reminded of the story of the hobo trespassing on the field of the great landowner.

Landowner: Hey, get out of this field!
Hobo: Why should I?
Landowner: Because it's my field.
Hobo: Where did you get it?
Landowner (in superior tones): I inherited it from my father.
Hobo: Where did he get it?
Landowner (with increasing annoyance and increasing superiority): He inherited it from his father.
Hobo: Where did *he* get it from?
Landowner (with very great superiority): Why, he fought for it!
Hobo (unimpressed): All right, I'll fight you for it.

Whether the transfer of holdings is just cannot be separated from the justice of the original holdings. The difficulty then for Nozick is that there is probably no way of unravelling history and finding out to what everyone is actually entitled. Historical inquiries of this sort, for example, in connection with stolen works of art, often lead to contradictory results, requiring, in the interests of justice, negotiations or even a straight redistributive decision.

3. The selection by Nozick's Harvard colleague John Rawls is a classic of liberal political philosophy. Published in 1971, *A Theory of Justice* has received an enormous amount of detailed discussion, criticism, and commentary. The book's central claim is a conception of justice, which Rawls spells out in two "principles of justice." These principles, found on p. 302 of his book, are, in the final formulation, in order of precedence: (1) that each person in a just society is to have the greatest liberty consistent with a similar liberty for others, and (2) that social and economic inequalities are justified to the extent that they provide the greatest benefit to the least advantaged group in society. (This final version of the second principle includes Rawls's preferred interpretation of the *everyone* of the earlier version given in the text below.)

How are the two principles established? Rawls's fascinating answer is that they are those principles which would be chosen by reasonable parties in something he calls "the original position." Roughly, this is a hypothetical situation of equality, prior to society, in which "no one knows his place in society," his wealth, class, abilities, intelligence, age, or sex (though Rawls does not mention the last). "The principles of justice," he writes, "are chosen behind a veil of ignorance." The original position is thus a device for explaining how people would arrange justice if they were not biased by their actual wealth, class, and abilities. Rawls's theory is a version of what is known as the contract theory. Those in Rawls's original position *contract* out of it by committing themselves to principles of justice. But among contract theories, Rawls's version

has the unique merit of disentangling from the criticisms to which it has been rightly subjected the valid insight at the heart of contract theory—the insight that to give meaning to a plea for justice it is necessary to get behind the formation of vested interests. If a person claims that an inequality to which he is subject is unjust, he must be able to give an affirmative answer to the question: 'Is this claim based on a principle to which you would have subscribed even if, as far as you knew, you were as likely to be a loser as a gainer by its implementation?"[4]

In this sense, Rawls's method is a way of asking both what justice itself is and what principles of distribution it requires. One attractive feature of his answer to the first question—that justice is fairness—is that, if true, it illuminates the relation between distributive justice and justice in the "legal" sense mentioned earlier, for they are both applications, though to different areas, of fairness and impartiality.

In spite of what some critics of Rawls have said, his original position is a psychologically and historically realistic place to start. For the most part, questions about what is just arise from the experience of *injustices*, in which there is a conflict between the demands of individuals acting, as it were, from a particular place or "interest" in society. What is certainly needed is unbiased judgement or fairness, and this is what is encapsulated in the original position.

To some critics, what happens in Rawls's original position may not have any particular moral significance. Why, they ask, does it produce principles which are principles of justice and not merely the converging of agreement or opinions? If what determines principles of justice is merely *agreement* in the original position about the distribution of anticipated spoils, then we would be bound to look elsewhere for their *moral* justification. Agreement and consensus do not make justice. If I *agree* to be killed, that by itself cannot make the killing just or right.

The criticism seems to miss the commonsense moral point of Rawls's conception of the original position and makes the original position into a sort of metaphysical quasi-*place* located behind a veil of ignorance. Why should what is agreed in the original position behind a veil of ignorance be of any more moral interest than what is decided in the town square behind the railway station? The criticism distorts the character of Rawls's conception as a device for removing everything which would influence decisions in a non-moral direction. Everyone is familiar with situations in which one is well advised to "put yourself in the other fellow's shoes." This is not just a matter of sympathy, of being able to see things from the point of view of another person, but rather of actually adopting a position or point of view in which one forgets or is willing and able to ignore *which* of the parties one actually is and of making a decision without being af-

---

4. W. G. Runciman, *Relative Deprivation and Social Justice*, London, Routledge, 1966, p. 253.

fected by what one stands to lose or gain personally. What one decides in such a position is then free from the special bias resulting from the injustices of one's actual position. It could be compared to the position of an international team of Olympic judges who are prevented from knowing the nationalities or identities of the competitors to whom they are awarding points. The awards are impartial and disinterested; and the point is that these are *moral* awards.

4. The passage from the first book of Plato's dialogue, the *Republic*, pits Thrasymachus against Socrates. Thrasymachus proposes a startlingly cynical and un-Rawlsian definition of justice which says in effect that there is no original position. Justice, Thrasymachus says, is what is to "the advantage of the stronger." ("Might makes right" is the ugly modern formulation.) Thrasymachus is saying in effect that we suffer from what Karl Marx and the communists called "false consciousness," in which our understanding of principles of social justice is necessarily distorted and made partial by our own position in society. There is some psychological plausibility to this because people do find it difficult to see political and social questions unaffected by their own beliefs and desires. But they can also make altruistic decisions about political and social questions.

By the end of Book I, Socrates, who represents Plato's own point of view in the dialogue, has managed to dislodge Thrasymachus (though by irritatingly longwinded arguments) and he proceeds to show how justice can work as something which is not the property of a particular group, such as the mighty, as Thrasymachus had argued. This may seem axiomatic in the liberal democracies of today, but in anti-democratic societies, it can be much less obvious that what is right does not emanate from those who in some sense "contribute" most to society, namely those who are "full of power" and willing to use it. In the course of developing a picture of an ideal society in Book IV of the *Republic*, Socrates gives us his own definition of justice as minding your own business and avoiding involvement in military, socioeconomic, and political classes other than your own. He *accepts* Thrasymachus' starting point. *Since* justice is not a tug-of-war between different classes and interests, it must be the opposite, a harmony of classes. "Meddling and exchange between the three classes, then," says Socrates, "is the greatest harm that can happen to the city and would rightly be called the worst thing its citizens could do to it." "Exactly," replies Thrasymachus. "And wouldn't you say that the worst thing that someone could do to his city is injustice?" asks Socrates. "Of course," agrees Thrasymachus.

5. Translators of Plato's *Republic* often note that the word *dikaiosune* has a much wider sense than the English word "justice" which is used to translate it, so that Plato is not just talking about a just city or society but about one which is also right or good. "The opposite, *adikia*, then has the sense of general wrongdoing," notes G.M.A. Grube in a footnote to his translation of the text.[5] Aristotle was Plato's pupil, and his special gift lay in logical analysis rather than in the development of imaginative pictures of an ideal society. The excerpted chapters from Book V of the *Nicomachean Ethics* deal in turn with different kinds of justice, which Plato, unable to see beyond what Aristotle calls "general justice" or decent treatment in general, had not distinguished. Aristotle's own general conception of justice is that it is law, but that there is a distinct part of it, "special justice," which is the same as fairness. In his discussion of distributive justice, Aristotle develops this concept as a kind of ratio of goods, similar to his account of the other kinds of justice. The unjust character wants too much of "goods" in his relations with others, e.g., of honor or social position and wealth, and the opposite vice is possible too. Distributive justice is not satisfied, according to Aristotle, "whenever equals receive unequal shares, or unequals equal shares, in a distribution," and, he notes, drily, "that is the source of quarrels and accusations."

Aristotle is confident enough of his concept of distributive justice not to feel obliged to decide what counts as an equal person here or when people are of equal worth.

> For everyone agrees that what is just in distribution must fit some sort of worth, but what they call worth is not the same; supporters of democracy say it is free citizenship, some supporters of oligarchy say it is wealth, others good birth, while supporters of aristocracy say it is virtue.

6. St. Thomas Aquinas, the medieval Christian theologian and philosopher, was, it has been said, the first Whig (though this is regularly said of many others, including Aristotle), i.e., someone who believes in constitutional government and inevitable resulting progress. ("Whig" is also the acronym for "We Hope In God.") In philosophical matters, Aquinas was the faithful follower of Aristotle, referring to him in the first paragraph of selection 6, as he always does, just as "the Philosopher," as if there were no other. He immediately defends Aristotle's definition of justice, in

---

5. Plato, *Republic*, trans. G.M.A. Grube, revised C.D.C. Reeve, Indianapolis, Hackett, 1992, p. 5, n. 8.

which "justice is a habit [that is, a disposition, a state] whereby a man renders to each one his due by a constant and perpetual will." He follows Aristotle in first attempting to understand what a just *man* is, as opposed to a just act, and in taking justice to be the virtue which one has in relationship with others. It is not, as Plato had thought, "about the entire matter of moral virtue," but, Aquinas says, again following Aristotle, only about "external actions and things, under a certain aspect of the object, in so far as one man is related to another through them." Aristotle's account of distributive justice remains in Aquinas' hands a form of the entitlement theory: "The proper act of justice is nothing else than to render to each his own." But what makes things "his own?" As Nozick says, there is surely a variety of *different* ways in which a person can come to "own" something. (Later in the *Summa*, in Question 66, "Of Theft and Robbery," Aquinas discusses whether it is "natural" and "lawful" to possess external things, and why.)

7. Leibniz was a distinguished philosopher, courtier, diplomat and political adviser, librarian, historian, theologian, physicist, mathematician, and logician who was appointed Professor of Law at the University of Altdorf at the very early age of twenty-one, though he declined the position. He had written a doctoral thesis on the legal topic of hard cases, "De Casibus Perplexis" ("On Perplexing Cases"). "Reflections on the Common Concept of Justice" reflects his wide interests and experiences. For example, he brushes aside the view of "a certain Thrasymachus" with the immaculate skill of the highly trained lawyer and logician.

> That is just, [Thrasymachus] says, which suits or pleases the most powerful. If this were true, the sentence of a sovereign court or a supreme judge would never be unjust, nor would an evil but powerful man ever deserve condemnation. What is more, the same action could be just and unjust depending on the judges who decide, which is ridiculous. It is one thing to *be* just, another to *pass* for just and to take the place of justice.

Like Rawls, Leibniz argues that justice itself requires us to do good in addition to what is "strictly" just, and that "[t]his is the rule of reason and of our Master. Put yourself in the place of another, and you will have the true point of view to judge what is just or not."[6] This proposal implies, as

6. The "rule of reason and of our Master" to which Leibniz is referring is the so-called golden rule, "As ye would that men should do to you, do ye also to them likewise" (Luke 6:31).

Leibniz puts it, that "one cannot be just without being charitable." He also expresses this by saying what justice requires positively as well as negatively. He argues, on entirely orthodox Rawlsian grounds, "not only that men ought to abstain from doing evil but also that they ought to prevent evil from being done and even to alleviate it." "I can remove that obstacle without pain [to me]," he continues. "Would you not think it right to ask me to do so and to remind me that I would ask it of you if I were in a similar plight? I complain, and you would complain in the same circumstances; therefore, I complain with justice." Here Leibniz is discussing what economists call "Pareto optimality," which occurs, as Rawls puts it, whenever an arrangement of things is such that "it is impossible to change it so as to make some persons (at least one) better off without at the same time making other persons (at least one) worse off.[7] Leibniz is arguing for Pareto optimality as a component of justice on the basis of something very like Rawls's original position. His final definition of the "common" concept of justice which we all share, or should share, is shaped by this point of view. Justice is "the constant will to act as far as possible in such a way that no one can complain of us if we would not complain of others in a similar situation." Leibniz's concept of charity and Rawls's second principle of justice demand as far as possible that we should benefit those (Rawls's "least advantaged") whom we would wish to be so benefited if we were among them. Yet this does not imply a strict and unworkable egalitarianism.

8. David Hume put his finger on the weakness of egalitarianism. He noted that people are very different from one another, and he predicted that "the most rigorous inquisition" would result from an effort to make them the same.

> Render possessions ever so equal, men's different degrees of art, care and industry will immediately break that equality. Or if you check these virtues, you reduce society to the most extreme indigence; and instead of preventing want and beggary in a few, render it unavoidable to the whole community. The most rigorous inquisition is requisite to watch every inequality on its first appearance; and the most severe jurisdiction, to punish and redress it.

Hume, then, was a conservative. He was also a utilitarian, in fact a founder of utilitarianism, the theory that the basic ethical notion is *ben-*

---

7. John Rawls, *A Theory of Justice*, Cambridge, Mass., Harvard University Press, 1971, p. 67.

efit, to be understood in terms of well-being or happiness. This is the doctrine that pronounces an action right if it produces "the greatest happiness for the greatest number." So Hume is bound to claim that "public utility is the *sole* origin of justice." His arguments need careful thought. For example, he claims that if everyone had enough of everything, there would be no *need* for justice. He also states that when there are public emergencies, justice is suspended in favor of utility. "The public, even in less urgent necessities, opens granaries without the consent of proprietors; as justly supposing, that the authority of magistracy may, consistent with equity, extend so far." Yet even in a famine, legal ownership is not *denied*, but merely overridden by considerations of public interest, for the owner can subsequently seek appropriate compensation.

One might think that the consequences of Hume's theory would be very radical, in the sense that they would demand a complete reordering of society in line with the principle of utility, but here Hume takes a surprising position. "These reflections," he writes, "are far from weakening the obligations of justice, or diminishing anything from the most sacred attention to property." His remarks about the "sacred attention to property" apply equally to justice. "For when a definition of *property* is required, that relation is found to resolve itself into any possession acquired by occupation, by industry, by prescription, by inheritance, by contract, &c. . . . These words too, inheritance and contract, stand for ideas infinitely complicated; and to define them exactly, a hundred volumes of laws, and a thousand volumes of commentators, have not been found to be sufficient." Thus the idea of property is "infinitely complicated," but its aim and result are simple: utility or benefit. At this point, one wants to unravel Hume's theory to see where, if anywhere, an overall concept of justice is to be found. (One difficulty to be borne in mind, often remarked, and already noted by Thomas Reid in the eighteenth century, is the extraordinary narrowness of Hume's discussion, which is entirely restricted to property, ignoring universal or "natural" rights.)

9. The German philosopher Kant says that the question "'What is justice?' can be every bit as perplexing for a jurist as the well-known question 'What is truth?' is for a logician, assuming, that is, that he does not want to lapse into mere tautology or to refer to the laws of a particular country at a particular time," as Hume did. (Hume might have responded that to frame the idea of truth, a hundred scientific volumes and a thousand volumes of commentary are required. This would, however, miss the point of looking for a definition or theory of truth.) With Kant, we return

to that strand in political philosophy which comes to the forefront in Rawls's twentieth-century universal liberalism. Both for Kant and for Rawls, the first and universal rule of justice is: "Act externally in such a way that the free use of your will is compatible with the freedom of everyone according to universal law." Rational beings must act from *principle* if they are to act ethically, and the principle on which they act must be entirely *a priori*, a universally binding *ought* derived from reason, not from experience. If it is wrong for governments to imprison people indefinitely without trial, for example, it is wrong absolutely, at all times and in all places and in all circumstances.

10. John Stuart Mill was, like Hume, a utilitarian, and this view affords the greatest contrast with Kant's absolutism. Utilitarianism claims that what is right is not right necessarily and in itself, but is right only to the extent that it produces the maximum benefit. For Mill and Hume, the question arises what the relationship is between what is "useful and beneficial" and in the public interest, and justice as such. For justice does not seem to be something which can legitimately be traded against social benefits, no matter how great. "In all ages of speculation," writes Mill, "one of the strongest obstacles to the reception of the doctrine that Utility or Happiness is the criterion of right and wrong has been drawn from the idea of Justice." What is just is distinct, as Leibniz had observed, from what is expedient. Mill is bound, as a utilitarian, to say that justice is a *sort* of utility. But what sort? He locates the distinction between generalized utility and justice in particular in the existence of a *right*. "Wherever there is a right, the case is one of justice . . ." he says.

> Thus, a person is said to have a right to what he can earn in fair professional competition; because society ought not to allow any person to hinder him from endeavouring to earn in that manner as much as he can. But he has not a right to three hundred a-year, though he may happen to be earning it; because society is not called on to provide that he shall earn that sum. On the contrary, if he owns ten thousand pounds three per cent stock, he *has* a right to three hundred a-year; because society has come under an obligation to provide him with an income of that amount.

Mill has a ready answer for any critic who wants to know what this "right" is. His answer is that it is something which society ought to protect. "If the objector goes on to ask, why it ought? I can give him no other reason than general utility." His explanation of the absoluteness of justice is also that it derives from the most basic of utilities, which is "security," and that it must not be "intermittent." The feelings which grow around this requirement are so strong that *"ought* and *should* grow into *must,* and recognized indispensability becomes a moral necessity. . . ." For Mill, justice is "a name for certain classes of moral rules, which concern the essentials of human well-being more nearly, and therefore of more absolute obligation, than any other rules for the guidance of life. . . ," the name, that is, for the *higher* social utility.

Mill's comments on Kant are therefore very interesting. Mill does not deny justice's requirement of rational impartiality, but adds that "we ought to shape our conduct by a rule which all rational beings might adopt *with benefit to their collective interest.*" One would hesitate to add this rider to the original biblical formulation of the golden rule for fear of blasphemy, but it is instructive and even amusing to see Mill appropriating the more astringent Kantian moralism in the name of general welfare.

Does justice demand a flat equality of goods, benefits, and incomes, or strict egalitarianism, as it is known? Should the distribution be determined by the quantity, quality, or difficulty of the work that men and women do? Should it also be determined by need, so that those who are unable to contribute also benefit as a matter of justice? Or is justice simply a matter of legal entitlement? If so, what principles determine which entitlements the law should protect? Here, Mill surveys the range of answers to these questions:

> Some Communists consider it unjust that the produce of the labour of the community should be shared on any other principle than that of exact equality; others think it just that those should receive most whose wants are greatest; while others hold that those who work harder, or who produce more, or whose services are more valuable to the community, may justly claim a larger quota in the division of the produce. And the sense of natural justice may be plausibly appealed to in behalf of every one of these opinions.[8]

11. The maxim given by the revolutionary communist theorist Karl Marx is a variant of the second of these principles stated by Mill. Marx's formulation in the *Critique of the Gotha Program* states that "a higher phase of communist society" will "inscribe on its banner: From each according to his ability, to each according to his needs!" This was a traditional socialist maxim, but Marx's innovation was to apply it only to the

---

8. John Stuart Mill, selection 10.

pure communist phase of society. Marx makes a bitter criticism of the first of Mill's principles, equal right. "Equal right is still in principle—*bourgeois right*," Marx says, meaning by "bourgeois" that it serves the interest of the class of capitalists, those who hold capital, against the proletariat, or working class, those who do not hold capital and earn their living by daily wages.

Marx detected "bourgeois right" even in the socialist writing of his time, particularly that of the "vulgar socialist" thinker Ferdinand Lasalle, against which the *Critique of the Gotha Program* is partly directed. Marx proposed a stunning argument against this "bourgeois right." Since "one man is superior to another physically or mentally and so supplies more labour in the same time . . . [t]his [supposed] *equal* right is an unequal right for unequal labour"! Since "one worker is married, another not; one has more children than another . . . [to] avoid all these defects, right instead of being equal would have to be unequal." Echoing this passage in Marx, Lenin, the man who led Russia into the Communist Revolution of 1917, wrote in *State and Revolution*, Ch. V, "The Economic Base of the Withering Away of the State," "Every right is an application of the *same* measure to *different* people, who, in fact, are not the same and are not equal to one another; this is why "equal right" is really a violation of equality, and an injustice."[9]

Lenin and Marx believed that the "inequality of equality" would be removed in the "higher" phase of communist society, when the machinery of the post-revolutionary political state would "wither away" and labour would become "not only a means of life but life's prime want," as Marx puts it. There is disagreement among scholars and commentators about whether Marx is *for* true justice, against the false justice of bourgeois society, or *against* justice, because justice and "equal right" are functions of bourgeois society. (Lenin is much quicker to claim injustice.) For whichever reason, Marx does not on the whole use the word "justice," but his view is recognizably a philosophical view about distributive justice.

12. The measured and rational treatment of justice by philosophers like Aristotle, Leibniz, and John Stuart Mill did not continue without interruption through the twentieth century. The treatment of justice by the respected international jurist Hans Kelsen is precise and carefully argued, but it is entirely relativistic. Kelsen also believes that there is no ordering principle for *any* ethical values, not even political ones. Which is better,

9. V. I. Lenin, *State and Revolution*, New York, International Publishers, 1943.

freedom or equality? "The answer," according to Kelsen, "has always the character of a subjective, and therefore only relative, judgement of value." Value, he asserts confidently, is a "social phenomenon," whatever exactly this means.

Why should relativism be such a distinctively twentieth-century view? One cause, perhaps, is that the technologies of communications and of war have weakened and confused the belief in the objective and enduring value of justice. The hopes for political progress have also been disappointed over and over again by irruptions of the irrational.

> Man's external behavior is not very different from that of animals. The big fish swallow the small ones, in the kingdom of animals as well as in that of men. But if a human fish, driven by his instincts, behaves in this way, he wishes to justify his behavior before himself as well as before society, to appease his conscience by the idea that his behavior in relation to his fellow man is right.

Kelsen examines the theories of Aristotle, Kant, and others, including Jesus, and concludes that "absolute justice is an irrational ideal, or, what amounts to the same, an illusion—one of the eternal illusions of mankind." Yet he cannot resist describing his own vision of justice. "Since science is my profession . . . 'my' justice, then, is the justice of freedom, the justice of peace, the justice of democracy—the justice of tolerance."

Kelsen's purpose was to separate moral philosophy from the pure or "positive" theory of law. The "science" to which he is referring in the passage above is a quasi-sociological theory which would give an account of the functioning of law as an institution distinct from its philosophical justification. A legal system rests on a *Grundnorm*, or basic directive (e.g., "Obey the constitution"), which summarizes all the aims of the community, but this norm itself is a hypothetical construct which has no reality outside the theory of law. Such a perspective raises the terrifying question of what is to be said to those who do not accept what could be called the ethical *Grundnorm* of the rest of humanity and whose own "postulate" is deliberately anti-human. What—what then—is justice?

13. And so we come to Mira Belochkin. Mira appears in Vladimir Nabokov's delightful novel *Pnin* in the memory of Timofey Pnin, a Russian emigré who is also America's oldest assistant professor. Pnin is involuntarily remembering his youthful love for Mira.

In order to exist rationally, Pnin had taught himself, during the last ten years, never to remember Mira Belochkin—not because, in itself, the evocation of a youthful love affair, banal and brief, threatened his peace of mind (alas, recollections of his marriage to Liza were imperious enough to crowd out any former romance), but because, if one were quite sincere with oneself, no conscience and hence no consciousness, could be expected to subsist in a world where such things as Mira's death were possible. One had to forget—because one could not live with the thought that this graceful, fragile, tender young woman with those eyes, that smile, those gardens and snows in the background, had been brought in a cattle car to an extermination camp and killed by an injection of phenol into the heart, into the gentle heart one had heard beating under one's lips in the dusk of the past. And since the exact form of her death had not been recorded, Mira kept dying a great number of deaths in one's mind, and undergoing a great number of resurrections, only to die again and again, led away by a trained nurse, inoculated with filth, tetanus bacilli, broken glass, gassed in a sham shower bath with prussic acid, burned alive in a pit on a gasoline-soaked pile of beechwood.

What does justice mean "in a world where such things as Mira's death are possible?" How can the abstract arguments of the philosophers about Aristotle's special justice pay their dues to "this graceful, fragile, tender young woman" as described by Nabokov, to whom general justice or decent treatment and also life have been denied? Mira Belochkin can remind us how important justice is, because it protects what is most important to us. There is a moral duty to understand the philosophical theory of justice, because of the potentially lethal consequences of misunderstanding it.

Note: Unbracketed footnotes in the texts are those of the authors. Bracketed notes are those of the translators.

1

Jorge Luis Borges,
"The Lottery in Babylon,"
from *Labyrinths*

Jorge Luis Borges of Argentina (1889–1986), poet, novelist, librarian, author, and literary critic, has a worldwide reputation as the author of the fantastic, or metaphysical, short stories collected in Ficciones *(1945) and* El Aleph *(1949). According to his editor, James Irby, "Borges created a work like no other. Perhaps the most striking characteristic of his writings is their extreme intellectual reaction against all the disorder and contingency of immediate reality, their radical insistence on breaking with the given world and postulating another."*

Like all men in Babylon, I have been proconsul; like all, a slave. I have also known omnipotence, opprobrium, imprisonment. Look: the index finger on my right hand is missing. Look: through the rip in my cape you can see a vermilion tattoo on my stomach. It is the second symbol, Beth. This letter, on nights when the moon is full, gives me power over men whose mark is Gimmel, but it subordinates me to the men of Aleph, who on moonless nights owe obedience to those marked with Gimmel. In the half light of dawn, in a cellar, I have cut the jugular vein of sacred bulls before a black stone. During a lunar year I have been declared invisible. I shouted and they did not answer me, I stole bread and they did not behead me. I have known what the Greeks do not know, incertitude. In a bronze chamber, before the silent handkerchief of the strangler, hope has been faithful to me, as has panic in the river of pleasure. Heraclides Ponticus tells with amazement that Pythagoras remembered having been Pyrrhus and before that Euphorbus and before that some other mortal. In order to remember similar vicissitudes I do not need to have recourse to death or even to deception.

I owe this almost atrocious variety to an institution which other republics do not know or which operates in them in an imperfect and secret manner: the lottery. I have not looked into its history; I know that the wise men cannot agree. I know of its powerful purposes what a man who is not versed in astrology can know about the moon. I come from a dizzy land where the lottery is the basis of reality. Until today I have thought as little about it as I have about the conduct of indecipherable divinities or about my heart. Now, far from Babylon and its beloved customs, I think with a certain amount of amazement about the lottery and about the blasphemous conjectures which veiled men murmur in the twilight.

My father used to say that formerly—a matter of centuries, of years?—the lottery in Babylon was a game of plebeian character. He recounted (I don't know whether rightly) that barbers sold, in exchange for copper coins, squares of bone or of parchment adorned with symbols. In broad daylight a drawing took place. Those who won received silver coins without any other test of luck. The system was elementary, as you can see.

Naturally these "lotteries" failed. Their moral virtue was nil. They were not directed at all of man's faculties, but only at hope. In the face of public indifference, the merchants who founded these venal lotteries began to lose money. Someone tried a reform: The interpolation of a few unfavorable tickets in the list of favorable numbers. By means of this reform, the buyers of numbered squares ran the double risk of winning a sum and of paying a fine that could be considerable. This slight danger (for every thirty favorable numbers there was one unlucky one) awoke, as is natural, the interest of the public. The Babylonians threw themselves into the game. Those who did not acquire chances were considered pusillanimous, cowardly. In time, that justified disdain was doubled. Those who did not play were scorned, but also the losers who paid the fine were scorned. The Company (as it came to be known then) had to take care of the winners, who could not cash in their prizes if almost the total amount of the fines was unpaid. It started a lawsuit against the losers. The judge condemned them to pay the original fine and costs or spend several days in jail. All chose jail in order to defraud the Company. The bravado of a few is the source of the omnipotence of the Company and of its metaphysical and ecclesiastical power.

A little while afterward the lottery lists omitted the amounts of fines and limited themselves to publishing the days of imprisonment that each unfavorable number indicated. That laconic spirit, almost unnoticed at the time, was of capital importance. *It was the first appearance in the lottery of nonmonetary elements.* The success was tremendous. Urged by the clientele, the Company was obliged to increase the unfavorable numbers.

Everyone knows that the people of Babylon are fond of logic and even of symmetry. It was illogical for the lucky numbers to be computed in round coins and the unlucky ones in days and nights of imprisonment. Some moralists reasoned that the possession of money does not always determine happiness and that other forms of happiness are perhaps more direct.

Another concern swept the quarters of the poorer classes. The members of the college of priests multiplied their stakes and enjoyed all the vicissitudes of terror and hope; the poor (with reasonable or unavoidable envy) knew that they were excluded from that notoriously delicious rhythm. The just desire that all, rich and poor, should participate equally in the lottery, inspired an indignant agitation, the memory of which the years have not erased. Some obstinate people did not understand (or pretended not to understand) that it was a question of a new order, of a necessary historical stage. A slave stole a crimson ticket, which in the drawing credited him with the burning of his tongue. The legal code fixed that same penalty for the one who stole a ticket. Some Babylonians argued that he deserved the burning irons in his status of a thief; others, generously, that the executioner should apply it to him because chance had determined it that way. There were disturbances, there were lamentable drawings of blood, but the masses of Babylon finally imposed their will against the opposition of the rich. The people achieved amply its generous purposes. In the first place, it caused the Company to accept total power. (That unification was necessary, given the vastness and complexity of the new operations.) In the second place, it made the lottery secret, free and general. The mercenary sale of chances was abolished. Once initiated in the mysteries of Baal, every free man automatically participated in the sacred drawings, which took place in the labyrinths of the god every sixty nights and which determined his destiny until the next drawing. The consequences were incalculable. A fortunate play could bring about his promotion to the council of wise men or the imprisonment of an enemy (public or private) or finding, in the peaceful darkness of his room, the woman who begins to excite him and whom he never expected to see again. A bad play: mutilation, different kinds of infamy, death. At times one single fact—the vulgar murder of C, the mysterious apotheosis of B— was the happy solution of thirty or forty drawings. To combine the plays was difficult, but one must remember that the individuals of the Company were (and are) omnipotent and astute. In many cases the knowledge that certain happinesses were the simple product of chance would have diminished their virtue. To avoid that obstacle, the agents of the Company made use of the power of suggestion and magic. Their steps, their maneuverings, were secret. To find out about the intimate hopes and terrors of each individual, they had astrologers and spies. There were certain stone lions, there was a sacred latrine called Qaphqa, there were fissures in a dusty aqueduct which, according to general opinion, *led to the Company*; malignant or benevolent persons deposited information in these places. An alphabetical file collected these items of varying truthfulness.

Incredibly, there were complaints. The Company, with its usual discretion, did not answer directly. It preferred to scrawl in the rubbish of a mask factory a brief statement which now figures in the sacred scriptures. This doctrinal item observed that the lottery is an interpolation of chance in the order of the world and that to accept errors is not to contradict chance: it is to corroborate it. It likewise observed that those lions and that sacred receptacle, although not disavowed by the Company (which did not abandon the right to consult them), functioned without official guarantee.

This declaration pacified the public's restlessness. It also produced other effects, perhaps unforeseen by its writer. It deeply modified the spirit and the operations of the Company. I don't have much time left; they tell us that the ship is about to weigh anchor. But I shall try to explain it.

However unlikely it might seem, no one had tried out before then a general theory of chance. Babylonians are not very speculative. They revere the judgments of fate, they deliver to them their lives, their hopes, their panic, but it does not occur to them to investigate fate's labyrinthine laws nor the gyratory spheres which reveal it. Nevertheless, the *unofficial* declaration that I have mentioned inspired many discussions of judicial-mathematical character. From some one of them the following conjecture was born: If the lottery is an intensification of chance, a periodical infusion of chaos in the cosmos, would it not be right for chance to intervene in all stages of the drawing and not in one alone? Is it not ridiculous for chance to dictate someone's death and have the circumstances of that death—secrecy, publicity, the fixed time of an hour or a century—not subject to chance? These just scruples finally caused a considerable reform, whose complexities (aggravated by centuries' practice) only a few specialists understand, but which I shall try to summarize, at least in a symbolic way.

Let us imagine a first drawing, which decrees the death of a man. For its fulfillment one proceeds to another drawing, which proposes (let us say) nine possible executors. Of these executors, four can initiate a third drawing which will tell the name of the executioner, two can replace the adverse order with a fortunate one (finding a treasure, let us say), another will intensify the death penalty (that is, will make it infamous or enrich it with tortures), others can refuse to fulfill it. This is the symbolic scheme. In reality *the number of drawings is infinite*. No decision is final, all branch into others. Ignorant people suppose that infinite drawings require an infinite time; actually it is sufficient for time to be infinitely subdivisible, as the famous parable of the contest with the tortoise teaches. This infinity harmonizes admirably with the sinuous numbers of Chance and with the Celestial Archetype of the Lottery, which the Platonists adore. Some warped echo of our rites seems to have resounded on the Tiber: Ellus Lampridius, in the *Life of Antoninus Heliogabalus*, tells us that this emperor wrote on shells the lots that were destined for his guests, so that one received ten pounds of gold and another ten flies, ten dormice, ten bears. It is permissible to recall that Heliogabalus was brought up in Asia Minor, among the priests of the eponymous god.

There are also impersonal drawings, with an indefinite purpose. One decrees that a sapphire of Taprobana be thrown into the waters of the Euphrates; another, that a bird be released rom the roof of a tower; another, that each century there be withdrawn (or added) a grain of sand from the innumerable ones on the beach. The consequences are, at times, terrible.

Under the beneficent influence of the Company, our customs are saturated with chance. The buyer of a dozen amphoras of Damascene wine will not be surprised if one of them contains a talisman or a snake. The scribe who writes a contract almost never fails to introduce some erroneous information. I myself, in this hasty declaration, have falsified some splendor, some atrocity. Perhaps, also, some mysterious monotony...Our historians, who are the most penetrating on the globe, have invented a method to correct chance. It is well known that the operations of this method are (in general) reliable, although, naturally, they are not divulged without some portion of deceit. Furthermore, there is nothing so contaminated with fiction as the history of the Company. A paleographic document, exhumed in a temple, can be the result of yesterday's lottery or of an age-old lottery. No book is published without some discrepancy in each one of the copies. Scribes take a secret oath to omit, to interpolate, to change. The indirect lie is also cultivated.

The Company, with divine modesty, avoids all publicity. Its agents, as is natural, are secret. The orders which it issues continually (perhaps incessantly) do not differ from those lavished by impostors. Moreover, who can brag about being a mere impostor? The drunkard who improvises an absurd order, the dreamer who awakens suddenly and strangles the woman who sleeps at his side, do they not execute, perhaps, a secret decision of the Company? That silent functioning, comparable to God's, gives rise to all sorts of conjectures. One abominably insinuates that the Company has not existed for centuries and that the sacred disorder of our lives is purely hereditary, traditional. Another judges it eternal and teaches that it will last until the last night, when the last god annihilates the world. Another declares that the Company is omnipotent, but that it only has influence in tiny things: in a bird's call, in the shadings of rust and of dust, in the half dreams of dawn. Another, in the words of masked heresiarchs, *that it has never existed and will not exist.* Another, no less vile, reasons that it is indifferent to affirm or deny the reality of the shadowy corporation, because Babylon is nothing else than an infinite game of chance.

2

Robert Nozick, "Distributive Justice," from *Anarchy, State, and Utopia*

Robert Nozick (b. 1938) is Arthur Kingsley Porter Professor of Philosophy at Harvard. He has written on a variety of philosophical topics ranging from the theory of knowledge to the meaning of life. As well as Anarchy, State, and Utopia *(1974), his works include the celebrated* Philosophical Explanations *(1981), which begins with the words, "I, too, seek an unreadable book: urgent thoughts to grapple with in agitation and excitement, revelations to be transformed by or to transform. . . ."*

The minimal state is the most extensive state that can be justified. Any state more extensive violates people's rights. Yet many persons have put forth reasons purporting to justify a more extensive state. It is impossible within the compass of this book to examine all the reasons that have been put forth. Therefore, I shall focus upon those generally acknowledged to be most weighty and influential, to see precisely wherein they fail. In this chapter we consider the claim that a more extensive state is justified, because necessary (or the best instrument) to achieve distributive justice; in the next chapter we shall take up diverse other claims.

The term "distributive justice" is not a neutral one. Hearing the term "distribution," most people presume that some thing or mechanism uses some principle or criterion to give out a supply of things. Into this process of distributing shares some error may have crept. So it is an open question, at least, whether *re*distribution should take place; whether we should do again what has already been done once, though poorly. However, we are not in the position of children who have been given portions of pie by someone who now makes last minute adjustments to rectify careless cutting. There is no *central* distribution, no person or group entitled to control all the resources, jointly deciding how they are to be doled out. What each person gets, he gets from others who give to him in exchange for something, or as a gift. In a free society, diverse persons control different resources, and new holdings arise out of the voluntary exchanges and actions of persons. There is no more a distributing or distribution of shares than there is a distributing of mates in a society in which persons choose whom they shall marry. The total result is the product of many individual decisions which the different individuals involved are entitled to make. Some uses of the term "distribution," it is true, do not imply a previous distributing appropriately judged by some criterion (for example, "probability distribution"); nevertheless, despite the title of this chapter, it would be best to use a terminology that clearly is neutral. We shall speak of people's holdings; a principle of justice in holdings describes (part of) what justice tells us (requires) about holdings. I shall state first what I take to be the correct view about justice in holdings, and then turn to the discussion of alternate views.[1]

The Entitlement Theory

The subject of justice in holdings consists of three major topics. The first is the *original acquisition of holdings*, the appropriation of unheld things. This includes the issues of how unheld things may come to be held, the process, or processes, by which unheld things may come to be held, the things that may come to be held by these processes, the extent of what comes to be held by a particular process, and so on. We shall refer to the complicated truth about this topic, which we shall not formulate here, as the principle of justice in acquisition. The second topic concerns the *transfer of holdings* from one person to another. By what processes may a person transfer holdings to another? How may a person acquire a holding from another who holds it? Under this topic come general descriptions of voluntary exchange, and gift and (on the other hand) fraud, as well as reference to particular conventional details fixed upon in a given society. The complicated truth about this subject (with placeholders for conventional details) we shall call the principle of justice in transfer. (And we shall suppose it also includes principles governing how a person may divest himself of a holding, passing it into an unheld state.)

---

1. The reader who has looked ahead and seen that the second part of this chapter discusses Rawls' theory mistakenly may think that every remark or argument in the first part against alternative theories of justice is meant to apply to, or anticipate, a criticism of Rawls' theory. This is not so; there are other theories also worth criticizing.

If the world were wholly just, the following inductive definition would exhaustively cover the subject of justice in holdings.

1. A person who acquires a holding in accordance with the principle of justice in acquisition is entitled to that holding.

2. A person who acquires a holding in accordance with the principle of justice in transfer, from someone else entitled to the holding, is entitled to the holding.

3. No one is entitled to a holding except by (repeated) applications of 1 and 2.

The complete principle of distributive justice would say simply that a distribution is just if everyone is entitled to the holdings they possess under the distribution.

A distribution is just if it arises from another just distribution by legitimate means. The legitimate means of moving from one distribution to another are specified by the principle of justice in transfer. The legitimate first "moves" are specified by the principle of justice in acquisition.* Whatever arises from a just situation by just steps is itself just. The means of change specified by the principle of justice in transfer preserve justice. As correct rules of inference are truth-preserving, and any conclusion deduced via repeated application of such rules from only true premises is itself true, so the means of transition from one situation to another specified by the principle of justice in transfer are justice-preserving, and any situation actually arising from repeated transitions in accordance with the principle from a just situation is itself just. The parallel between justice-preserving transformations and truth-preserving transformations illuminates where it fails as well as where it holds. That a conclusion could have been deduced by truth-preserving means from premises that are true suffices to show its truth. That from a just situation a situation *could* have arisen via justice-preserving means does *not* suffice to show its justice. The fact that a thief's victims voluntarily *could* have presented him with gifts does not entitle the thief to his ill-gotten gains. Justice in holdings is

---

* Applications of the principle of justice in acquisition may also occur as part of the move from one distribution to another. You may find an unheld thing now and appropriate it. Acquisitions also are to be understood as included when, to simplify, I speak only of transitions by transfers.

historical; it depends upon what actually has happened. We shall return to this point later.

Not all actual situations are generated in accordance with the two principles of justice in holdings: the principle of justice in acquisition and the principle of justice in transfer. Some people steal from others, or defraud them, or enslave them, seizing their product and preventing them from living as they choose, or forcibly exclude others from competing in exchanges. None of these are permissible modes of transition from one situation to another. And some persons acquire holdings by means not sanctioned by the principle of justice in acquisition. The existence of past injustice (previous violations of the first two principles of justice in holdings) raises the third major topic under justice in holdings: the rectification of injustice in holdings. If past injustice has shaped present holdings in various ways, some identifiable and some not, what now, if anything, ought to be done to rectify these injustices? What obligations do the performers of injustice have toward those whose position is worse than it would have been had the injustice not been done? Or, than it would have been had compensation been paid promptly? How, if at all, do things change if the beneficiaries and those made worse off are not the direct parties in the act of injustice, but, for example, their descendants? Is an injustice done to someone whose holding was itself based upon an unrectified injustice? How far back must one go in wiping clean the historical slate of injustices? What may victims of injustice permissibly do in order to rectify the injustices being done to them, including the many injustices done by persons acting through their government? I do not know of a thorough or theoretically sophisticated treatment of such issues.[2] Idealizing greatly, let us suppose theoretical investigation will produce a principle of rectification. This principle uses historical information about previous situations and injustices done in them (as defined by the first two principles of justice and rights against interference), and information about the actual course of events that flowed from these injustices, until the present, and it yields a description (or descriptions) of holdings in the society. The principle of rectification presumably will make use of its best estimate of subjunctive information about what would have occurred (or a probability distribution over what might have occurred, using the expected value) if the injustice had not taken place. If the actual description of

---

2. See, however, the useful book by Boris Bittker, *The Case for Black Reparations* (New York: Random House, 1973).

holdings turns out not to be one of the descriptions yielded by the principle, then one of the descriptions yielded must be realized.*

The general outlines of the theory of justice in holdings are that the holdings of a person are just if he is entitled to them by the principles of justice in acquisition and transfer, or by the principle of rectification of injustice (as specified by the first two principles). If each person's holdings are just, then the total set (distribution) of holdings is just. To turn these general outlines into a specific theory we would have to specify the details of each of the three principles of justice in holdings: the principle of acquisition of holdings, the principle of transfer of holdings, and the principle of rectification of violations of the first two principles. I shall not attempt that task here. (Locke's principle of justice in acquisition is discussed below.)

Historical Principles and End-Result Principles

The general outlines of the entitlement theory illuminate the nature and defects of other conceptions of distributive justice. The entitlement theory of justice in distribution is *historical*; whether a distribution is just depends upon how it came about. In contrast, *current time-slice principles* of justice hold that the justice of a distribution is determined by how things are distributed (who has what) as judged by some *structural* principle(s) of just distribution. A utilitarian who judges between any two distributions by seeing which has the greater sum of utility and, if the sums tie, applies some fixed equality criterion to choose the more equal distribution, would hold a current time-slice principle of justice. As would someone who had a fixed schedule of trade-offs between the sum of happiness and equality. According to a current time-slice principle, all that needs to be looked at, in judging the justice of a distribution, is who ends up with what; in comparing any two distributions one need look only at the matrix presenting the distributions. No further information need be fed into a principle of justice. It is a consequence of such principles of justice that any two structurally identical distributions are equally just.

---

* If the principle of rectification of violations of the first two principles yields more than one description of holdings, then some choice must be made as to which of these is to be realized. Perhaps the sort of considerations about distributive justice and equality that I argue against play a legitimate role in *this* subsidiary choice. Similarly, there may be room for such considerations in deciding which otherwise arbitrary features a statute will embody, when such features are unavoidable because other considerations do not specify a precise line; yet a line must be drawn.

(Two distributions are structurally identical if they present the same profile, but perhaps have different persons occupying the particular slots. My having ten and your having five, and my having five and your having ten are structurally identical distributions.) Welfare economics is the theory of current time-slice principles of justice. The subject is conceived as operating on matrices representing only current information about distribution. This, as well as some of the usual conditions (for example, the choice of distribution is invariant under relabeling of columns), guarantees that welfare economics will be a current time-slice theory, with all of its inadequacies.

Most persons do not accept current time-slice principles as constituting the whole story about distributive shares. They think it relevant in assessing the justice of a situation to consider not only the distribution it embodies, but also how that distribution came about. If some persons are in prison for murder or war crimes, we do not say that to assess the justice of the distribution in the society we must look only at what this person has, and that person has, and that person has, . . . at the current time. We think it relevant to ask whether someone did something so that he *deserved* to be punished, deserved to have a lower share. Most will agree to the relevance of further information with regard to punishments and penalties. Consider also desired things. One traditional socialist view is that workers are entitled to the product and full fruits of their labor; they have earned it; a distribution is unjust if it does not give the workers what they are entitled to. Such entitlements are based upon some past history. No socialist holding this view would find it comforting to be told that because the actual distribution A happens to coincide structurally with the one he desires D, A therefore is no less just than D; it differs only in that the "parasitic" owners of capital receive under A what the workers are entitled to under D, and the workers receive under A what the owners are entitled to under D, namely very little. This socialist rightly, in my view, holds onto the notions of earning, producing, entitlement, desert, and so forth, and he rejects current time-slice principles that look only to the structure of the resulting set of holdings. (The set of holdings resulting from what? Isn't it implausible that how holdings are produced and come to exist has no effect at all on who should hold what?) His mistake lies in his view of what entitlements arise out of what sorts of productive processes.

We construe the position we discuss too narrowly by speaking of *current* time-slice principles. Nothing is changed if structural principles operate upon a time sequence of current time-slice profiles and, for example, give someone more now to counterbalance the less he has had earlier. A utilitarian or an egalitarian or any mixture of the two over time will inherit the difficulties of his more myopic comrades. He is not helped by the fact that *some* of the information others consider relevant in assessing a distribution is reflected, unrecoverably, in past matrices. Henceforth, we shall refer to such unhistorical principles of distributive justice, including the current time-slice principles, as *end-result principles* or *end-state principles*.

In contrast to end-result principles of justice, *historical principles* of justice hold that past circumstances or actions of people can create differential entitlements or differential deserts to things. An injustice can be worked by moving from one distribution to another structurally identical one, for the second, in profile the same, may violate people's entitlements or deserts; it may not fit the actual history.

Patterning

The entitlement principles of justice in holdings that we have sketched are historical principles of justice. To better understand their precise character, we shall distinguish them from another subclass of the historical principles. Consider, as an example, the principle of distribution according to moral merit. This principle requires that total distributive shares vary directly with moral merit; no person should have a greater share than anyone whose moral merit is greater. (If moral merit could be not merely ordered but measured on an interval or ratio scale, stronger principles could be formulated.) Or consider the principle that results by substituting "usefulness to society" for "moral merit" in the previous principle. Or instead of "distribute according to moral merit," or "distribute according to usefulness to society," we might consider "distribute according to the weighted sum of moral merit, usefulness to society, and need," with the weights of the different dimensions equal. Let us call a principle of distribution *patterned* if it specifies that a distribution is to vary along with some natural dimension, weighted sum of natural dimensions, or lexicographic ordering of natural dimensions. And let us say a distribution is patterned if it accords with some patterned principle. (I speak of natural dimensions, admittedly without a general criterion for them, because for any set of holdings some artificial dimensions can be gimmicked up to vary along with the distribution of the set.) The principle of distribution in accordance with moral merit is a patterned historical principle, which specifies a patterned distribution. "Distribute according to I.Q." is a patterned principle that looks to information not contained in distributional matrices. It is not historical, however, in that it does not look to any past actions creating differential entitlements to evaluate a distribution; it requires only distributional matrices whose columns are labeled by I.Q. scores. The distribution in a society, however, may be composed of such simple patterned distributions, without itself being simply patterned. Different sectors may operate different patterns, or some combination of patterns may operate in different proportions across a society. A distribution composed in this manner, from a small number of patterned distributions, we also shall term "patterned." And we extend the use of "pattern" to include the overall designs put forth by combinations of end-state principles.

Almost every suggested principle of distributive justice is patterned: to each according to his moral merit, or needs, or marginal product, or how hard he tries, or the weighted sum of the foregoing, and so on. The principle of entitlement we have sketched is *not* patterned.* There is no one natural dimension or weighted sum or combination of a small number of natural dimensions that yields the distributions generated in accordance with the principle of entitlement. The set of holdings that results when some persons receive their marginal products, others win at gambling, others receive a share of their mate's income, others receive gifts from foundations, others receive interest on loans, others receive gifts from admirers, others receive returns on investment, others make for themselves much of what they have, others find things, and so on, will not be patterned. Heavy strands of patterns will run through it; significant portions of the variance in holdings will be accounted for by pattern-variables. If most people most of the time choose to transfer

---

* One might try to squeeze a patterned conception of distributive justice into the framework of the entitlement conception, by formulating a gimmicky obligatory "principle of transfer" that would lead to the pattern. For example, the principle that if one has more than the mean income one must transfer everything one holds above the mean to persons below the mean so as to bring them up to (but not over) the mean. We can formulate a criterion for a "principle of transfer" to rule out such obligatory transfers, or we can say that no correct principle of transfer, no principle of transfer in a free society will be like this. The former is probably the better course, though the latter also is true.

Alternatively, one might think to make the entitlement conception instantiate a pattern, by using matrix entries that express the relative strength of a person's entitlements as measured by some real-valued function. But even if the limitation to natural dimensions failed to exclude this function, the resulting edifice would *not* capture our system of entitlements to *particular* things.

some of their entitlements to others only in exchange for something from them, then a large part of what many people hold will vary with what they held that others wanted. More details are provided by the theory of marginal productivity. But gifts to relatives, charitable donations, bequests to children, and the like, are not best conceived, in the first instance, in this manner. Ignoring the strands of pattern, let us suppose for the moment that a distribution actually arrived at by the operation of the principle of entitlement is random with respect to any pattern. Though the resulting set of holdings will be unpatterned, it will not be incomprehensible, for it can be seen as arising from the operation of a small number of principles. These principles specify how an initial distribution may arise (the principle of acquisition of holdings) and how distributions may be transformed into others (the principle of transfer of holdings). The process whereby the set of holdings is generated will be intelligible, though the set of holdings itself that results from this process will be unpatterned.

The writings of F. A. Hayek focus less than is usually done upon what patterning distributive justice requires. Hayek argues that we cannot know enough about each person's situation to distribute to each according to his moral merit (but would justice demand we do so if we did have this knowledge?); and he goes on to say, "our objection is against all attempts to impress upon society a deliberately chosen pattern of distribution, whether it be an order of equality or of inequality."[3] However, Hayek concludes that in a free society there will be distribution in accordance with value rather than moral merit; that is, in accordance with the perceived value of a person's actions and services to others. Despite his rejection of a patterned conception of distributive justice, Hayek himself suggests a pattern he thinks justifiable: distribution in accordance with the perceived benefits given to others, leaving room for the complaint that a free society does not realize exactly this pattern. Stating this patterned strand of a free capitalist society more precisely, we get "To each according to how much he benefits others who have the resources for benefiting those who benefit them." This will seem arbitrary unless some acceptable initial set of holdings is specified, or unless it is held that the operation of the system over time washes out any significant effects from the initial set of holdings. As an example of the latter, if almost anyone would have bought a car from Henry Ford, the supposition that it was an arbitrary

3. F. A. Hayek, *The Constitution of Liberty* (Chicago: University of Chicago Press, 1960), p. 87.

matter who held the money then (and so bought) would not place Henry Ford's earnings under a cloud. In any event, *his* coming to hold is not arbitrary. Distribution according to benefits to others *is* a major patterned strand in a free capitalist society, as Hayek correctly points out, but it is only a strand and does not constitute the whole pattern of a system of entitlements (namely, inheritance, gifts for arbitrary reasons, charity, and so on) or a standard that one should insist a society fit. Will people tolerate for long a system yielding distributions that they believe are unpatterned?[4] No doubt people will not long accept a distribution they believe is *unjust*. People want their society to be and to look just. But must the look of justice reside in a resulting pattern rather than in the underlying generating principles? We are in no position to conclude that the inhabitants of a society embodying an entitlement conception of justice in holdings will find it unacceptable. Still, it must be granted that were people's reasons for transferring some of their holdings to others always irrational or arbitrary, we would find this disturbing. (Suppose people always determined what holdings they would transfer, and to whom, by using a random device.) We feel more comfortable upholding the justice of an entitlement system if most of the transfers under it are done for reasons. This does not mean necessarily that all deserve what holdings they receive. It means only that there is a purpose or point to someone's transferring a holding to one person rather than to another; that usually we can see what the transferrer thinks he's gaining, what cause he thinks he's serving, what goals he thinks he's helping to achieve, and so forth. Since in a capitalist society people often transfer holdings to others in accordance with how much they perceive these others benefiting them, the fabric constituted by the individual transactions and transfers is largely reasonable and intelligible.*

4. This question does not imply that they will tolerate any and every patterned distribution. In discussing Hayek's views, Irving Kristol has recently speculated that people will not long tolerate a system that yields distributions patterned in accordance with value rather than merit. ("'When Virtue Loses All Her Loveliness'—Some Reflections on Capitalism and 'The Free Society,'" *The Public Interest*, Fall 1970, pp. 3–15.) Kristol, following some remarks of Hayek's, equates the merit system with justice. Since some case can be made for the external standard of distribution in accordance with benefit to others, we ask about a weaker (and therefore more plausible) hypothesis.

* We certainly benefit because great economic incentives operate to get others to spend much time and energy to figure out how to serve us by providing things we will want to pay for. It is not mere paradox mongering to wonder whether capitalism should be criticized for most rewarding and hence encouraging, not

(Gifts to loved ones, bequests to children, charity to the needy also are nonarbitrary components of the fabric.) In stressing the large strand of distribution in accordance with benefit to others, Hayek shows the point of many transfers, and so shows that the system of transfer of entitlements is not just spinning its gears aimlessly. The system of entitlements is defensible when constituted by the individual aims of individual transactions. No overarching aim is needed, no distributional pattern is required.

To think that the task of a theory of distributive justice is to fill in the blank in "to each according to his _____" is to be predisposed to search for a pattern; and the separate treatment of "from each according to his _____" treats production and distribution as two separate and independent issues. On an entitlement view these are *not* two separate questions. Whoever makes something, having bought or contracted for all other held resources used in the process (transferring some of his holdings for these cooperating factors), is entitled to it. The situation is *not* one of something's getting made, and there being an open question of who is to get it. Things come into the world already attached to people having entitlements over them. From the point of view of the historical entitlement conception of justice in holdings, those who start afresh to complete "to each according to his _____" treat objects as if they appeared from nowhere, out of nothing. A complete theory of justice might cover this limit case as well; perhaps here is a use for the usual conceptions of distributive justice.[5]

So entrenched are maxims of the usual form that perhaps we should present the entitlement conception as a competitor. Ignoring acquisition and rectification, we might say:

> From each according to what he chooses to do, to each according to what he makes for himself (perhaps with the contracted aid of others) and what

---

individualists like Thoreau who go about their own lives, but people who are occupied with serving others and winning them as customers. But to defend capitalism one need not think businessmen are the finest human types. (I do not mean to join here the general maligning of businessmen, either.) Those who think the finest should acquire the most can try to convince their fellows to transfer resources in accordance with *that* principle.

5. Varying situations continuously from that limit situation to our own would force us to make explicit the underlying rationale of entitlements and to consider whether entitlement considerations lexicographically precede the considerations of the usual theories of distributive justice, so that the *slightest* strand of entitlement outweighs the considerations of the usual theories of distributive justice.

others choose to do for him and choose to give him of what they've been given previously (under this maxim) and haven't yet expended or transferred.

This, the discerning reader will have noticed, has its defects as a slogan. So as a summary and great simplification (and not as a maxim with any independent meaning) we have:

From each as they choose, to each as they are chosen.

How Liberty Upsets Patterns

It is not clear how those holding alternative conceptions of distributive justice can reject the entitlement conception of justice in holdings. For suppose a distribution favored by one of these non-entitlement conceptions is realized. Let us suppose it is your favorite one and let us call this distribution D_1; perhaps everyone has an equal share, perhaps shares vary in accordance with some dimension you treasure. Now suppose that Wilt Chamberlain is greatly in demand by basketball teams, being a great gate attraction. (Also suppose contracts run only for a year, with players being free agents.) He signs the following sort of contract with a team: In each home game, twenty-five cents from the price of each ticket of admission goes to him. (We ignore the question of whether he is "gouging" the owners, letting them look out for themselves.) The season starts, and people cheerfully attend his team's games; they buy their tickets, each time dropping a separate twenty-five cents of their admission price into a special box with Chamberlain's name on it. They are excited about seeing him play; it is worth the total admission price to them. Let us suppose that in one season one million persons attend his home games, and Wilt Chamberlain winds up with $250,000, a much larger sum than the average income and larger even than anyone else has. Is he entitled to this income? Is this new distribution D_2, unjust? If so, why? There is *no* question about whether each of the people was entitled to the control over the resources they held in D_1; because that was the distribution (your favorite) that (for the purposes of argument) we assumed was acceptable. Each of these persons *chose* to give twenty-five cents of their money to Chamberlain. They could have spent it on going to the movies, or on candy bars, or on copies of *Dissent* magazine, or of *Monthly Review*. But they all, at least one million of them, converged on giving it to Wilt Chamberlain in exchange for watching him play basketball. If D_1 was a just distribution, and people voluntarily moved from it to D_2, transferring parts of their shares they were given under D_1 (what was it for if not to do something with?), isn't D_2 also just? If the people were entitled to dispose of the resources to which they were entitled (under D_1), didn't this include their being entitled to give it to, or exchange it with, Wilt Chamberlain? Can anyone else complain on grounds of justice? Each other person already has his legitimate share under D_1. Under D_1, there is nothing that anyone has that anyone else has a claim of justice against. After someone transfers something to Wilt Chamberlain, third parties *still* have their legitimate shares; *their* shares are not changed. By what process could such a transfer among two persons give rise to a legitimate claim of distributive justice on a portion of what was transferred, by a third party who had no claim of justice on any holding of the others *before* the transfer?* To cut off objections irrelevant here, we might imagine the exchanges occurring in a socialist society, after hours. After playing whatever basketball he does in his daily work, or doing whatever other daily work he does, Wilt Chamberlain decides to put in *overtime* to earn additional money. (First his work quota is set; he works time over that.) Or imagine it is a skilled juggler people like to see, who puts on shows after hours.

Why might someone work overtime in a society in which it is assumed their needs are satisfied? Perhaps because they care about things other than needs. I like to write in books that I read, and to have easy access to books for browsing at odd hours. It would be very pleasant and convenient to have the resources of Widener Library in my back yard. No society, I assume, will provide such resources close to each person who would

* Might not a transfer have instrumental effects on a third party, changing his feasible options? (But what if the two parties to the transfer independently had used their holdings in this fashion?) I discuss this question below, but note here that this question concedes the point for distributions of ultimate intrinsic noninstrumental goods (pure utility experiences, so to speak) that are transferable. It also might be objected that the transfer might make a third party more envious because it worsens his position relative to someone else. I find it incomprehensible how this can be thought to involve a claim of justice. On envy, see Chapter 8.

Here and elsewhere in this chapter, a theory which incorporates elements of pure procedural justice might find what I say acceptable, *if* kept in its proper place; that is, if background institutions exist to ensure the satisfaction of certain conditions on distributive shares. But if these institutions are not themselves the sum or invisible-hand result of people's voluntary (nonaggressive) actions, the constraints they impose require justification. At no point does *our* argument assume any background institutions more extensive than those of the minimal nightwatchman state, a state limited to protecting persons against murder, assault, theft, fraud, and so forth.

like them as part of his regular allotment (under D_1). Thus, persons either must do without some extra things that they want, or be allowed to do something extra to get some of these things. On what basis could the inequalities that would eventuate be forbidden? Notice also that small factories would spring up in a socialist society, unless forbidden. I melt down some of my personal possessions (under D_1) and build a machine out of the material. I offer you, and others, a philosophy lecture once a week in exchange for your cranking the handle on my machine, whose products I exchange for yet other things, and so on. (The raw materials used by the machine are given to me by others who possess them under D_1, in exchange for hearing lectures.) Each person might participate to gain things over and above their allotment under D_1. Some persons even might want to leave their job in socialist industry and work full time in this private sector. I shall say something more about these issues in the next chapter. Here I wish merely to note how private property even in means of production would occur in a socialist society that did not forbid people to use as they wished some of the resources they are given under the socialist distribution D_1.[6] The socialist society would have to forbid capitalist acts between consenting adults.

The general point illustrated by the Wilt Chamberlain example and the

---

6. See the selection from John Henry MacKay's novel, *The Anarchists*, reprinted in Leonard Krimmerman and Lewis Perry, eds., *Patterns of Anarchy* (New York: Doubleday Anchor Books, 1966), in which an individualist anarchist presses upon a communist anarchist the following question: "Would you, in the system of society which you call 'free Communism' prevent individuals from exchanging their labor among themselves by means of their own medium of exchange? And further: Would you prevent them from occupying land for the purpose of personal use?" The novel continues: "[the] question was not to be escaped. If he answered 'Yes!' he admitted that society had the right of control over the individual and threw overboard the autonomy of the individual which he had always zealously defended; if on the other hand, he answered 'No!' he admitted the right of private property which he had just denied so emphatically. . . . Then he answered 'In Anarchy any number of men must have the right of forming a voluntary association, and so realizing their ideas in practice. Nor can I understand how any one could justly be driven from the land and house which he uses and occupies . . . every serious man must declare himself: for Socialism, and thereby for force and against liberty, or for Anarchism, and thereby for liberty and against force.'" In contrast, we find Noam Chomsky writing, "Any consistent anarchist must oppose private ownership of the means of production," "the consistent anarchist then . . . will be a socialist . . . of a particular sort." Introduction to Daniel Guerin, *Anarchism: From Theory to Practice* (New York: Monthly Review Press, 1970), pages xiii, xv.

example of the entrepreneur in a socialist society is that no end-state principle or distributional patterned principle of justice can be continuously realized without continuous interference with people's lives. Any favored pattern would be transformed into one unfavored by the principle, by people choosing to act in various ways; for example, by people exchanging goods and services with other people, or giving things to other people, things the transferrers are entitled to under the favored distributional pattern. To maintain a pattern one must either continually interfere to stop people from transferring resources as they wish to, or continually (or periodically) interfere to take from some persons resources that others for some reason chose to transfer to them. (But if some time limit is to be set on how long people may keep resources others voluntarily transfer to them, why let them keep these resources for *any* period of time? Why not have immediate confiscation?) It might be objected that all persons voluntarily will choose to refrain from actions which would upset the pattern. This presupposes unrealistically (1) that all will most want to maintain the pattern (are those who don't, to be "reeducated" or forced to undergo "self-criticism"?), (2) that each can gather enough information about his own actions and the ongoing activities of others to discover which of his actions will upset the pattern, and (3) that diverse and far-flung persons can coordinate their actions to dovetail into the pattern. Compare the manner in which the market is neutral among persons' desires, as it reflects and transmits widely scattered information via prices, and coordinates persons' activities.

It puts things perhaps a bit too strongly to say that every patterned (or end-state) principle is liable to be thwarted by the voluntary actions of the individual parties transferring some of their shares they receive under the principle. For perhaps some *very* weak patterns are not so thwarted. Any distributional pattern with any egalitarian component is overturnable by the voluntary actions of individual persons over time; as is every patterned condition with sufficient content so as actually to have been proposed as presenting the central core of distributive justice. Still, given the possibility that some weak conditions or patterns may not be unstable in this way, it would be better to formulate an explicit description of the kind of interesting and contentful patterns under discussion, and to prove a theorem about their instability. Since the weaker the patterning, the more likely it is that the entitlement system itself satisfies it, a plausible conjecture is that any patterning either is unstable or is satisfied by the entitlement system.

3

John Rawls,
"Principles of Justice,"
from *A Theory of Justice*

John Rawls (b. 1921) is James Bryant Conant University Professor at Harvard University. In his principal work, A Theory of Justice *(1971), he wrote, "Each person possesses an inviolability founded on justice that not even the welfare of society as a whole can override. . . . Therefore in a just society . . . the rights se-cured by justice are not subject to political bargaining or to the calculus of social interests" (pp. 3–4).*

The Main Idea of the Theory of Justice

My aim is to present a conception of justice which generalizes and carries to a higher level of abstraction the familiar theory of the social contract as found, say, in Locke, Rousseau, and Kant.[1] In order to do this we are not to think of the original contract as one to enter a particular society or to set up a particular form of government. Rather, the guiding idea is that the principles of justice for the basic structure of society are the object of the original agreement. They are the principles that free and rational persons concerned to further their own interests would accept in an initial position of equality defining the fundamental terms of their association. These principles are to regulate all further agreements; they specify the

1. As the text suggests, I shall regard Locke's *Second Treatise of Government*, Rousseau's *The Social Contract*, and Kant's ethical works beginning with *The Foundations of the Metaphysics of Morals* as definitive of the contract tradition. For all of its greatness, Hobbes' *Leviathan* raises special problems. A general historical survey is provided by J. W. Gough, *The Social Contract*, 2nd ed. (Oxford, The Clarendon Press, 1957), and Otto Gierke, *Natural Law and the Theory of Society*, trans. with an introduction by Ernest Barker (Cambridge, The University Press, 1934). A presentation of the contract view as primarily an ethical theory is to be found in G. R. Grice, *The Grounds of Moral Judgment* (Cambridge, The University Press, 1967).

kinds of social cooperation that can be entered into and the forms of government that can be established. This way of regarding the principles of justice I shall call justice as fairness.

Thus we are to imagine that those who engage in social cooperation choose together, in one joint act, the principles which are to assign basic rights and duties and to determine the division of social benefits. Men are to decide in advance how they are to regulate their claims against one another and what is to be the foundation charter of their society. Just as each person must decide by rational reflection what constitutes his good, that is, the system of ends which it is rational for him to pursue, so a group of persons must decide once and for all what is to count among them as just and unjust. The choice which rational men would make in this hypothetical situation of equal liberty, assuming for the present that this choice problem has a solution, determines the principles of justice.

In justice as fairness the original position of equality corresponds to the state of nature in the traditional theory of the social contract. This original position is not, of course, thought of as an actual historical state of affairs, much less as a primitive condition of culture. It is understood as a purely hypothetical situation characterized so as to lead to a certain conception of justice.[2] Among the essential features of this situation is that no one knows his place in society, his class position or social status, nor does any one know his fortune in the distribution of natural assets and abilities, his intelligence, strength, and the like. I shall even assume that the parties do not know their conceptions of the good or their special psychological propensities. The principles of justice are chosen behind a veil of ignorance. This ensures that no one is advantaged or disadvantaged in the choice of principles by the outcome of natural chance or the contingency of social circumstances. Since all are similarly situated and no one is able to design principles to favor his particular condition, the principles of justice are the result of a fair agreement or bargain. For given the circumstances of the original position, the symmetry of everyone's relations to each other, this initial situation is fair between individuals as moral

2. Kant is clear that the original agreement is hypothetical. See *The Metaphysics of Morals*, pt. I (*Rechtslehre*), especially §§47, 52; and pt. II of the essay "Concerning the Common Saying: This May Be True in Theory but It Does Not Apply in Practice," in *Kant's Political Writings*, ed. Hans Reiss and trans. by H. B. Nisbet (Cambridge, The University Press, 1970), pp. 73–87. See George Vlachos, *La Pensée politique de Kant* (Paris, Presses Universitaires de France, 1962), pp. 326–335, and J. G. Murphy, *Kant: The Philosophy of Right* (London, Macmillan, 1970), pp. 109–112, 133–136, for a further discussion.

persons, that is, as rational beings with their own ends and capable, I shall assume, of a sense of justice. The original position is, one might say, the appropriate initial status quo, and thus the fundamental agreements reached in it are fair. This explains the propriety of the name "justice as fairness": it conveys the idea that the principles of justice are agreed to in an initial situation that is fair. The name does not mean that the concepts of justice and fairness are the same, any more than the phrase "poetry as metaphor" means that the concepts of poetry and metaphor are the same.

Justice as fairness begins, as I have said, with one of the most general of all choices, which persons might make together, namely, with the choice of the first principles of a conception of justice which is to regulate all subsequent criticism and reform of institutions. Then, having chosen a conception of justice, we can suppose that they are to choose a constitution and a legislature to enact laws, and so on, all in accordance with the principles of justice initially agreed upon. Our social situation is just if it is such that by this sequence of hypothetical agreements we would have contracted into the general system of rules which defines it. Moreover, assuming that the original position does determine a set of principles (that is, that a particular conception of justice would be chosen), it will then be true that whenever social institutions satisfy these principles those engaged in them can say to one another that they are cooperating on terms to which they would agree if they were free and equal persons whose relations with respect to one another were fair. They could all view their arrangements as meeting the stipulations which they would acknowledge in an initial situation that embodies widely accepted and reasonable constraints on the choice of principles. The general recognition of this fact would provide the basis for a public acceptance of the corresponding principles of justice. No society can, of course, be a scheme of cooperation which men enter voluntarily in a literal sense; each person finds himself placed at birth in some particular position in some particular society, and the nature of this position materially affects his life prospects. Yet a society satisfying the principles of justice as fairness comes as close as a society can to being a voluntary scheme, for it meets the principles which free and equal persons would assent to under circumstances that are fair. In this sense its members are autonomous and the obligations they recognize self-imposed.

One feature of justice as fairness is to think of the parties in the initial situation as rational and mutually disinterested. This does not mean that the parties are egoists, that is, individuals with only certain kinds of interests, say in wealth, prestige, and domination. But they are conceived as not taking an interest in one another's interests. They are to presume that even their spiritual aims may be opposed, in the way that the aims of those of different regions may be opposed. Moreover, the concept of rationality must be interpreted as far as possible in the narrow sense, standard in economic theory, of taking the most effective means to given ends. I shall modify this concept to some extent, as explained later (§25), but one must try to avoid introducing into it any controversial ethical elements. The initial situation must be characterized by stipulations that are widely accepted.

In working out the conception of justice as fairness one main task clearly is to determine which principles of justice would be chosen in the original position. To do this we must describe this situation in some detail and formulate with care the problem of choice which it presents. . . . It may be observed, however, that once the principles of justice are thought of as arising from an original agreement in a situation of equality, it is an open question whether the principle of utility would be acknowledged. Offhand it hardly seems likely that persons who view themselves as equals, entitled to press their claims upon one another, would agree to a principle which may require lesser life prospects for some simply for the sake of a greater sum of advantages enjoyed by others. Since each desires to protect his interests, his capacity to advance his conception of the good, no one has a reason to acquiesce in an enduring loss for himself in order to bring about a greater net balance of satisfaction. In the absence of strong and lasting benevolent impulses, a rational man would not accept a basic structure merely because it maximized the algebraic sum of advantages irrespective of its permanent effects on his own basic rights and interests. Thus it seems that the principle of utility is incompatible with the conception of social cooperation among equals for mutual advantage. It appears to be inconsistent with the idea of reciprocity implicit in the notion of a well-ordered society. Or, at any rate, so I shall argue.

I shall maintain instead that the persons in the initial situation would choose two rather different principles: the first requires equality in the assignment of basic rights and duties, while the second holds that social and economic inequalities, for example inequalities of wealth and authority, are just only if they result in compensating benefits for everyone, and in particular for the least advantaged members of society. These principles rule out justifying institutions on the grounds that the hardships of some are offset by a greater good in the aggregate. It may be expedient but it is not just that some should have less in order that others may prosper. But there is no injustice in the greater benefits earned by a few provided that the situation of persons not so fortunate is thereby improved. The intuitive idea is that since everyone's well-being depends upon a scheme of cooperation without which no one could have a satisfactory life, the division of advantages should be such as to draw forth the willing cooperation of everyone taking part in it, including those less well situated. Yet this can be expected only if reasonable terms are proposed. The two principles mentioned seem to be a fair agreement on the basis of which those better endowed, or more fortunate in their social position, neither of which we can be said to deserve, could expect the willing cooperation of others when some workable scheme is a necessary condition of the welfare of all.[3] Once we decide to look for a conception of justice that nullifies the accidents of natural endowment and the contingencies of social circumstance as counters in quest for political and economic advantage, we are led to these principles. They express the result of leaving aside those aspects of the social world that seem arbitrary from a moral point of view.

The problem of the choice of principles, however, is extremely difficult. I do not expect the answer I shall suggest to be convincing to everyone. It is, therefore, worth noting from the outset that justice as fairness, like other contract views, consists of two parts: (1) an interpretation of the initial situation and of the problem of choice posed there, and (2) a set of principles which, it is argued, would be agreed to. One may accept the first part of the theory (or some variant thereof), but not the other, and conversely. The concept of the initial contractual situation may seem reasonable although the particular principles proposed are rejected. To be sure, I want to maintain that the most appropriate conception of this situation does lead to principles of justice contrary to utilitarianism and perfectionism, and therefore that the contract doctrine provides an alternative to these views. Still, one may dispute this contention even though one grants that the contractarian method is a useful way of studying ethical theories and of setting forth their underlying assumptions.

Justice as fairness is an example of what I have called a contract theory. Now there may be an objection to the term "contract" and related expressions, but I think it will serve reasonably well. Many words have misleading connotations which at first are likely to confuse. The terms "utility" and "utilitarianism" are surely no exception. They too have unfortunate suggestions which hostile critics have been willing to exploit; yet they are clear enough for those prepared to study utilitarian doctrine. The same

3. For the formulation of this intuitive idea I am indebted to Allan Gibbard.

should be true of the term "contract" applied to moral theories. As I have mentioned, to understand it one has to keep in mind that it implies a certain level of abstraction. In particular, the content of the relevant agreement is not to enter a given society or to adopt a given form of government, but to accept certain moral principles. Moreover, the undertakings referred to are purely hypothetical: a contract view holds that certain principles would be accepted in a well-defined initial situation.

The merit of the contract terminology is that it conveys the idea that principles of justice may be conceived as principles that would be chosen by rational persons, and that in this way conceptions of justice may be explained and justified. The theory of justice is a part, perhaps the most significant part, of the theory of rational choice. Furthermore, principles of justice deal with conflicting claims upon the advantages won by social cooperation; they apply to the relations among several persons or groups. The word "contract" suggests this plurality as well as the condition that the appropriate division of advantages must be in accordance with principles acceptable to all parties. The condition of publicity for principles of justice is also connoted by the contract phraseology. Thus, if these principles are the outcome of an agreement, citizens have a knowledge of the principles that others follow. It is characteristic of contract theories to stress the public nature of political principles. Finally there is the long tradition of the contract doctrine. Expressing the tie with this line of thought helps to define ideas and accords with natural piety. There are then several advantages in the use of the term "contract." With due precautions taken, it should not be misleading.

A final remark. Justice as fairness is not a complete contract theory. For it is clear that the contractarian idea can be extended to the choice of more or less an entire ethical system, that is, to a system including principles for all the virtues and not only for justice. Now for the most part I shall consider only principles of justice and others closely related to them; I make no attempt to discuss the virtues in a systematic way. Obviously if justice as fairness succeeds reasonably well, a next step would be to study the more general view suggested by the name "rightness as fairness." But even this wider theory fails to embrace all moral relationships, since it would seem to include only our relations with other persons and to leave out of account how we are to conduct ourselves toward animals and the rest of nature. I do not contend that the contract notion offers a way to approach these questions which are certainly of the first importance; and I shall have to put them aside. We must recognize the limited scope of justice as fairness and of the general type of view that it exemplifies. How far its conclusions must be revised once these other matters are understood cannot be decided in advance.

The Original Position and Justification

I have said that the original position is the appropriate initial status quo which insures that the fundamental agreements reached in it are fair. This fact yields the name "justice as fairness." It is clear, then, that I want to say that one conception of justice is more reasonable than another, or justifiable with respect to it, if rational persons in the initial situation would choose its principles over those of the other for the role of justice. Conceptions of justice are to be ranked by their acceptability to persons so circumstanced. Understood in this way the question of justification is settled by working out a problem of deliberation: we have to ascertain which principles it would be rational to adopt given the contractual situation. This connects the theory of justice with the theory of rational choice.

If this view of the problem of justification is to succeed, we must, of course, describe in some detail the nature of this choice problem. A problem of rational decision has a definite answer only if we know the beliefs and interests of the parties, their relations with respect to one another, the alternatives between which they are to choose, the procedure whereby they make up their minds, and so on. As the circumstances are presented in different ways, correspondingly different principles are accepted. The concept of the original position, as I shall refer to it, is that of the most philosophically favored interpretation of this initial choice situation for the purposes of a theory of justice.

But how are we to decide what is the most favored interpretation? I assume, for one thing, that there is a broad measure of agreement that principles of justice should be chosen under certain conditions. To justify a particular description of the initial situation one shows that it incorporates these commonly shared presumptions. One argues from widely accepted but weak premises to more specific conclusions. Each of the presumptions should by itself be natural and plausible; some of them may seem innocuous or even trivial. The aim of the contract approach is to establish that taken together they impose significant bounds on acceptable principles of justice. The ideal outcome would be that these conditions determine a unique set of principles; but I shall be satisfied if they suffice to rank the main traditional conceptions of social justice.

One should not be misled, then, by the somewhat unusual conditions which characterize the original position. The idea here is simply to make vivid to ourselves the restrictions that it seems reasonable to impose on arguments for principles of justice, and therefore on these principles themselves. Thus it seems reasonable and generally acceptable that no one should be advantaged or disadvantaged by natural fortune or social circumstances in the choice of principles. It also seems widely agreed that it should be impossible to tailor principles to the circumstances of one's own case. We should insure further that particular inclinations and aspirations, and persons' conceptions of their good do not affect the principles adopted. The aim is to rule out those principles that it would be rational to propose for acceptance, however little the chance of success, only if one knew certain things that are irrelevant from the standpoint of justice. For example, if a man knew that he was wealthy, he might find it rational to advance the principle that various taxes for welfare measures be counted unjust; if he knew that he was poor, he would most likely propose the contrary principle. To represent the desired restrictions one imagines a situation in which everyone is deprived of this sort of information. One excludes the knowledge of those contingencies which sets men at odds and allows them to be guided by their prejudices. In this manner the veil of ignorance is arrived at in a natural way. This concept should cause no difficulty if we keep in mind the constraints on arguments that it is meant to express. At any time we can enter the original position, so to speak, simply by following a certain procedure, namely, by arguing for principles of justice in accordance with these restrictions.

It seems reasonable to suppose that the parties in the original position are equal. That is, all have the same rights in the procedure for choosing principles; each can make proposals, submit reasons for their acceptance, and so on. Obviously the purpose of these conditions is to represent equality between human beings as moral persons, as creatures having a conception of their good and capable of a sense of justice. The basis of equality is taken to be similarity in these two respects. Systems of ends are not ranked in value; and each man is presumed to have the requisite ability to understand and to act upon whatever principles are adopted. Together with the veil of ignorance, these conditions define the principles of justice as those which rational persons concerned to advance their interests would consent to as equals when none are known to be advantaged or disadvantaged by social and natural contingencies.

There is, however, another side to justifying a particular description of the original position. This is to see if the principles which would be chosen match our considered convictions of justice or extend them in an acceptable way. We can note whether applying these principles would lead us to make the same judgments about the basic structure of society which we now make intuitively and in which we have the greatest confidence; or whether, in cases where our present judgments are in doubt and given with hesitation, these principles offer a resolution which we can affirm on reflection. There are questions which we feel sure must be answered in a certain way. For example, we are confident that religious intolerance and racial discrimination are unjust. We think that we have examined these things with care and have reached what we believe is an impartial judgment not likely to be distorted by an excessive attention to our own interests. These convictions are provisional fixed points which we presume any conception of justice must fit. But we have much less assurance as to what is the correct distribution of wealth and authority. Here we may be looking for a way to remove our doubts. We can check an interpretation of the initial situation, then, by the capacity of its principles to accommodate our firmest convictions and to provide guidance where guidance is needed.

In searching for the most favored description of this situation we work from both ends. We begin by describing it so that it represents generally shared and preferably weak conditions. We then see if these conditions are strong enough to yield a significant set of principles. If not, we look for further premises equally reasonable. But if so, and these principles match our considered convictions of justice, then so far well and good. But presumably there will be discrepancies. In this case we have a choice. We can either modify the account of the initial situation or we can revise our existing judgments, for even the judgments we take provisionally as fixed points are liable to revision. By going back and forth, sometimes altering the conditions of the contractual circumstances, at others withdrawing our judgments and conforming them to principle, I assume that eventually we shall find a description of the initial situation that both expresses reasonable conditions and yields principles which match our considered judgments duly pruned and adjusted. This state of affairs I refer to as reflective equilibrium.[4] It is an equilibrium because at last our principles and judgments coincide; and it is reflective since we know to what principles our judgments conform and the premises of their derivation. At the mo-

4. The process of mutual adjustment of principles and considered judgments is not peculiar to moral philosophy. See Nelson Goodman, *Fact, Fiction, and Forecast* (Cambridge, Mass., Harvard University Press, 1955), pp. 65–68, for parallel remarks concerning the justification of the principles of deductive and inductive inference.

ment everything is in order. But this equilibrium is not necessarily stable. It is liable to be upset by further examination of the conditions which should be imposed on the contractual situation and by particular cases which may lead us to revise our judgments. Yet for the time being we have done what we can to render coherent and to justify our convictions of social justice. We have reached a conception of the original position.

I shall not, of course, actually work through this process. Still, we may think of the interpretation of the original position that I shall present as the result of such a hypothetical course of reflection. It represents the attempt to accommodate within one scheme both reasonable philosophical conditions on principles as well as our considered judgments of justice. In arriving at the favored interpretation of the initial situation there is no point at which an appeal is made to self-evidence in the traditional sense either of general conceptions or particular convictions. I do not claim for the principles of justice proposed that they are necessary truths or derivable from such truths. A conception of justice cannot be deduced from self-evident premises or conditions on principles; instead, its justification is a matter of the mutual support of many considerations, of everything fitting together into one coherent view.

A final comment. We shall want to say that certain principles of justice are justified because they would be agreed to in an initial situation of equality. I have emphasized that this original position is purely hypothetical. It is natural to ask why, if this agreement is never actually entered into, we should take any interest in these principles, moral or otherwise. The answer is that the conditions embodied in the description of the original position are ones that we do in fact accept. Or if we do not, then perhaps we can be persuaded to do so by philosophical reflection. Each aspect of the contractual situation can be given supporting grounds. Thus what we shall do is to collect together into one conception a number of conditions on principles that we are ready upon due consideration to recognize as reasonable. These constraints express what we are prepared to regard as limits on fair terms of social cooperation. One way to look at the idea of the original position, therefore, is to see it as an expository device which sums up the meaning of these conditions and helps us to extract their consequences. On the other hand, this conception is also an intuitive notion that suggests its own elaboration, so that led on by it we are drawn to define more clearly the standpoint from which we can best interpret moral relationships. We need a conception that enables us to envision our objective from afar: the intuitive notion of the original position is to do this for us.

Two Principles of Justice

I shall now state in a provisional form the two principles of justice that I believe would be chosen in the original position. In this section I wish to make only the most general comments, and therefore the first formulation of these principles is tentative. As we go on I shall run through several formulations and approximate step by step the final statement to be given much later. I believe that doing this allows the exposition to proceed in a natural way.

The first statement of the two principles reads as follows.

> First: each person is to have an equal right to the most extensive basic liberty compatible with a similar liberty for others.
>
> Second: social and economic inequalities are to be arranged so that they are both (a) reasonably expected to be to everyone's advantage, and (b) attached to positions and offices open to all.

By way of general comment, these principles primarily apply, as I have said, to the basic structure of society. They are to govern the assignment of rights and duties and to regulate the distribution of social and economic advantages. As their formulation suggests, these principles presuppose that the social structure can be divided into two more or less distinct parts, the first principle applying to the one, the second to the other. They distinguish between those aspects of the social system that define and secure the equal liberties of citizenship and those that specify and establish social and economic inequalities. The basic liberties of citizens are, roughly speaking, political liberty (the right to vote and to be eligible for public office) together with freedom of speech and assembly; liberty of conscience and freedom of thought; freedom of the person along with the right to hold (personal) property; and freedom from arbitrary arrest and seizure as defined by the concept of the rule of law. These liberties are all required to be equal by the first principle, since citizens of a just society are to have the same basic rights.

The second principle applies, in the first approximation, to the distribution of income and wealth and to the design of organizations that make use of differences in authority and responsibility, or chains of command. While the distribution of wealth and income need not be equal, it must be to everyone's advantage, and at the same time, positions of authority and offices of command must be accessible to all. One applies the second principle by holding positions open, and then, subject to this constraint, arranges social and economic inequalities so that everyone benefits.

These principles are to be arranged in a serial order with the first principle prior to the second. This ordering means that a departure from the institutions of equal liberty required by the first principle cannot be justified by, or compensated for, by greater social and economic advantages. The distribution of wealth and income, and the hierarchies of authority, must be consistent with both the liberties of equal citizenship and equality of opportunity.

It is clear that these principles are rather specific in their content, and their acceptance rests on certain assumptions that I must eventually try to explain and justify. A theory of justice depends upon a theory of society in ways that will become evident as we proceed. For the present, it should be observed that the two principles (and this holds for all formulations) are a special case of a more general conception of justice that can be expressed as follows.

> All social values—liberty and opportunity, income and wealth, and the bases of self-respect—are to be distributed equally unless an unequal distribution of any, or all, of these values is to everyone's advantage.

Injustice, then, is simply inequalities that are not to the benefit of all. Of course, this conception is extremely vague and requires interpretation.

As a first step, suppose that the basic structure of society distributes certain primary goods, that is, things that every rational man is presumed to want. These goods normally have a use whatever a person's rational plan of life. For simplicity, assume that the chief primary goods at the disposition of society are rights and liberties, powers and opportunities, income and wealth. . . . These are the social primary goods. Other primary goods such as health and vigor, intelligence and imagination, are natural goods; although their possession is influenced by the basic structure, they are not so directly under its control. Imagine, then, a hypothetical initial arrangement in which all the social primary goods are equally distributed: everyone has similar rights and duties, and income and wealth are evenly shared. This state of affairs provides a benchmark for judging improvements. If certain inequalities of wealth and organizational powers would make everyone better off than in this hypothetical starting situation, then they accord with the general conception.

Now it is possible, at least theoretically, that by giving up some of their fundamental liberties men are sufficiently compensated by the resulting social and economic gains. The general conception of justice imposes no restrictions on what sort of inequalities are permissible; it only requires that everyone's position be improved. We need not suppose anything so drastic as consenting to a condition of slavery. Imagine instead that men forgo certain political rights when the economic returns are significant and their capacity to influence the course of policy by the exercise of these rights would be marginal in any case. It is this kind of exchange which the two principles as stated rule out; being arranged in serial order they do not permit exchanges between basic liberties and economic and social gains. The serial ordering of principles expresses an underlying preference among primary social goods. When this preference is rational so likewise is the choice of these principles in this order.

In developing justice as fairness I shall, for the most part, leave aside the general conception of justice and examine instead the special case of the two principles in serial order. The advantage of this procedure is that from the first the matter of priorities is recognized and an effort made to find principles to deal with it. One is led to attend throughout to the conditions under which the acknowledgment of the absolute weight of liberty with respect to social and economic advantages, as defined by the lexical order of the two principles, would be reasonable. Offhand, this ranking appears extreme and too special a case to be of much interest; but there is more justification for it than would appear at first sight. Or at any rate, so I shall maintain. Furthermore, the distinction between fundamental rights and liberties and economic and social benefits marks a difference among primary social goods that one should try to exploit. It suggests an important division in the social system. Of course, the distinctions drawn and the ordering proposed are bound to be at best only approximations. There are surely circumstances in which they fail. But it is essential to depict clearly the main lines of a reasonable conception of justice; and under many conditions anyway, the two principles in serial order may serve well enough. When necessary we can fall back on the more general conception.

The fact that the two principles apply to institutions has certain consequences. Several points illustrate this. First of all, the rights and liberties referred to by these principles are those which are defined by the public rules of the basic structure. Whether men are free is determined by the rights and duties established by the major institutions of society. Liberty is a certain pattern of social forms. The first principle simply requires that certain sorts of rules, those defining basic liberties, apply to everyone equally and that they allow the most extensive liberty compatible with a like liberty for all. The only reason for circumscribing the rights defining liberty and making men's freedom less extensive than it might otherwise be is that these equal rights as institutionally defined would interfere with one another.

Another thing to bear in mind is that when principles mention persons, or require that everyone gain from an inequality, the reference is to representative persons holding the various social positions, or offices, or whatever, established by the basic structure. Thus in applying the second principle I assume that it is possible to assign an expectation of well-being to representative individuals holding these positions. This expectation indicates their life prospects as viewed from their social station. In general, the expectations of representative persons depend upon the distribution of rights and duties throughout the basic structure. When this changes, expectations change. I assume, then, that expectations are connected: by raising the prospects of the representative man in one position we presumably increase or decrease the prospects of representative men in other positions. Since it applies to institutional forms, the second principle (or rather the first part of it) refers to the expectations of representative individuals. As I shall discuss below, neither principle applies to distributions of particular goods to particular individuals who may be identified by their proper names. The situation where someone is considering how to allocate certain commodities to needy persons who are known to him is not within the scope of the principles. They are meant to regulate basic institutional arrangements. We must not assume that there is much similarity from the standpoint of justice between an administrative allotment of goods to specific persons and the appropriate design of society. Our common sense intuitions for the former may be a poor guide to the latter.

Now the second principle insists that each person benefit from permissible inequalities in the basic structure. This means that it must be reasonable for each relevant representative man defined by this structure, when he views it as a going concern, to prefer his prospects with the inequality to his prospects without it. One is not allowed to justify differences in income or organizational powers on the ground that the disadvantages of those in one position are outweighed by the greater advantages of those in another. Much less can infringements of liberty be counterbalanced in this way. Applied to the basic structure, the principle of utility would have us maximize the sum of expectations of representative men (weighted by the number of persons they represent, on the classical view); and this would permit us to compensate for the losses of some by the gains of others. Instead, the two principles require that everyone benefit from economic and social inequalities. It is obvious, however, that there are indefinitely many ways in which all may be advantaged when the initial arrangement of equality is taken as a benchmark. How then are we to choose among these possibilities? The principles must be specified so that they yield a determinate conclusion. I now turn to this problem.

4

Plato,
"Justice,"
from the *Republic*

*Plato (c. 428 B.C.– 348 B.C.) was one of the two large figures in classical or
Greek philosophy. Plato's own teacher, Socrates, who published nothing, was put
to death in 399 B.C. Socrates is the main character in Plato's dialogues. In the
Republic, Socrates uses refutation and counterexample to destroy inadequate
accounts of justice. Plato's own positive view is that "justice in the soul" is a harmony between the different parts of the soul and also that justice in society is a
harmony between its different parts. According to the modern British political
philosopher D. D. Raphael, "It also gives expression to the idea of a spirit of con-
scientiousness in all forms of moral action. From this point of view, it approaches
the Judeo–Christian ideas about the authority of conscience and the value of the
individual soul, though without the equalitarianism that was implicit in those
ideas. They were the notions which eventually brought into full consciousness the
aspect of justice that is concerned with the rights of the individual."*

From Book I

While we were speaking, Thrasymachus had tried many times to take over
the discussion but was restrained by those sitting near him, who wanted to
hear our arguments to the end. When we paused after what I'd just said,
however, he couldn't keep quiet any longer. He coiled himself up like a wild
beast about to spring, and he hurled himself at us as if to tear us to pieces.

Polemarchus and I were frightened as he roared into our midst: What
nonsense have you two been talking, Socrates? Why do you act like idiots
by giving way to one another? If you truly want to know what justice is,
don't just ask questions and then refute the answers simply to satisfy your
competitiveness or love of honor. You know very well that it is easier to
ask questions than answer them. Give an answer yourself, and tell us what
you say the just is. And don't tell me that it's the right, the beneficial, the

From Plato, *Republic*, translated by George Grube, revised by C.D.C. Reeve,
1992, Hackett Publishing Company, Inc.
The footnotes are those of Grube and Reeve.

profitable, the gainful, or the advantageous, but tell me clearly and exactly what you mean; for I won't accept such nonsense from you.

His words startled me, and, looking at him, I was afraid. And I think that if I hadn't seen him before he stared at me, I'd have been dumbstruck. But as it was, I happened to look at him just as our discussion began to exasperate him, so I was able to answer, and, trembling a little, I said: Don't be too hard on us, Thrasymachus, for if Polemarchus and I made an error in our investigation, you should know that we did so unwillingly. If we were searching for gold, we'd never willingly give way to each other, if by doing so we'd destroy our chance of finding it. So don't think that in searching for justice, a thing more valuable than even a large quantity of gold, we'd mindlessly give way to one another or be less than completely serious about finding it. You surely mustn't think that, but rather—as I do—that we're incapable of finding it. Hence it's surely far more appropriate for us to be pitied by you clever people than to be given rough treatment.

When he heard that, he gave a loud, sarcastic laugh. By Heracles, he said, that's just Socrates' usual irony.[1] I knew, and I said so to these people earlier, that you'd be unwilling to answer and that, if someone questioned *you*, you'd be ironical and do anything rather than give an answer.

That's because you're a clever fellow, Thrasymachus. You knew very well that if you ask someone how much twelve is, and, as you ask, you warn him by saying "Don't tell me, man, that twelve is twice six, or three times four, or six times two, or four times three, for I won't accept such nonsense," then you'll see clearly, I think, that no one could answer a question framed like that. And if he said to you: "What are you saying, Thrasymachus, am I not to give any of the answers you mention, not even if twelve happens to be one of those things? I'm amazed. Do you want me to say something other than the truth? Or do you mean something else?" What answer would you give him?

Well, so you think the two cases are alike?

Why shouldn't they be alike? But even if they aren't alike, yet seem so to the person you asked, do you think him any less likely to give the answer that seems right to him, whether we forbid him to or not?

Is that what you're going to do, give one of the forbidden answers?

I wouldn't be surprised—provided that it's the one that seems right to

---

1. [The Greek word *eirōneia*, unlike its usual translation "irony," is correctly applied only to someone who intends to deceive. Thus Thrasymachus is not simply accusing Socrates of saying one thing while meaning another; he is accusing him of trying to deceive those present. See G. Vlastos, "Socratic Irony," *Classical Quarterly* 37 (1987): 79–96.]

me after I've investigated the matter.

What if I show you a different answer about justice than all these—and a better one? What would you deserve then?

What else than the appropriate penalty for one who doesn't know, namely, to learn from the one who does know? Therefore, that's what I deserve.

You amuse me, but in addition to learning, you must pay a fine.

I will as soon as I have some money.

He has some already, said Glaucon. If it's a matter of money, speak, Thrasymachus, for we'll all contribute for Socrates.

I know, he said, so that Socrates can carry on as usual. He gives no answer himself, and then, when someone else does give one, he takes up the argument and refutes it.

How can someone give an answer, I said, when he doesn't know it and doesn't claim to know it, and when an eminent man forbids him to express the opinion he has? It's much more appropriate for you to answer, since you say you know and can tell us. So do it as a favor to me, and don't begrudge your teaching to Glaucon and the others.

While I was saying this, Glaucon and the others begged him to speak. It was obvious that Thrasymachus thought he had a fine answer and that he wanted to earn their admiration by giving it, but he pretended that he wanted to indulge his love of victory by forcing me to answer. However, he agreed in the end, and then said: There you have Socrates' wisdom; he himself isn't willing to teach, but he goes around learning from others and isn't even grateful to them.

When you say that I learn from others you are right, Thrasymachus, but when you say that I'm not grateful, that isn't true. I show what gratitude I can, but since I have no money, I can give only praise. But just how enthusiastically I give it when someone seems to me to speak well, you'll know as soon as you've answered, for I think that you will speak well.

Listen, then. I say that justice is nothing other than the advantage of the stronger. Well, why don't you praise me? But then you'd do anything to avoid having to do that.

I must first understand you, for I don't yet know what you mean. The advantage of the stronger, you say, is just. What do you mean, Thrasymachus? Surely you don't mean something like this: Polydamus, the pancratist,[2] is stronger than we are; it is to his advantage to eat beef to

---

2. [*Pancration* was a mixture of boxing and wrestling combined with kicking and strangling. Biting and gouging were forbidden, but pretty well everything else, including breaking and dislocating limbs, was permitted.]

build up his physical strength; therefore, this food is also advantageous and just for us who are weaker than he is?

You disgust me, Socrates. Your trick is to take hold of the argument at the point where you can do it the most harm.

Not at all, but tell us more clearly what you mean.

Don't you know that some cities are ruled by a tyranny, some by a democracy, and some by an aristocracy?

Of course.

And in each city this element is stronger, namely, the ruler?

Certainly.

And each makes laws to its own advantage. Democracy makes democratic laws, tyranny makes tyrannical laws, and so on with the others. And they declare what they have made—what is to their own advantage—to be just for their subjects, and they punish anyone who goes against this as lawless and unjust. This, then, is what I say justice is, the same in all cities, the advantage of the established rule. Since the established rule is surely stronger, anyone who reasons correctly will conclude that the just is the same everywhere, namely, the advantage of the stronger.

Now I see what you mean. Whether it's true or not, I'll try to find out. But you yourself have answered that the just is the advantageous, Thrasymachus, whereas you forbade that answer to me. True, you've added "of the stronger" to it.

And I suppose you think that's an insignificant addition.

It isn't clear yet whether it's significant. But it is clear that we must investigate to see whether or not it's true. I agree that the just is some kind of advantage. But you add that it's *of the stronger*. I don't know about that. We'll have to look into it.

Go ahead and look.

We will. Tell me, don't you also say that it is just to obey the rulers?

I do.

And are the rulers in all cities infallible, or are they liable to error?

No doubt they are liable to error.

When they undertake to make laws, therefore, they make some correctly, others incorrectly?

I suppose so.

And a law is correct if it prescribes what is to the rulers' own advantage and incorrect if it prescribes what is to their disadvantage? Is that what you mean?

It is.

And whatever laws they make must be obeyed by their subjects, and this is justice?

Of course.

Then, according to your account, it is just to do not only what is to the advantage of the stronger, but also the opposite, what is not to their advantage.

What are you saying?

The same as you. But let's examine it more fully. Haven't we agreed that, in giving orders to their subjects, the rulers are sometimes in error as to what is best for themselves, and yet that it is just for their subjects to do whatever their rulers order? Haven't we agreed to that much?

I think so.

Then you must also think that you have agreed that it is just to do what is disadvantageous to the rulers and those who are stronger, whenever they unintentionally order what is bad for themselves. But you also say that it is just for the others to obey the orders they give. You're terribly clever, Thrasymachus, but doesn't it necessarily follow that it is just to do the opposite of what you said, since the weaker are then ordered to do what is disadvantageous to the stronger?

By god, Socrates, said Polemarchus, that's quite clear.

If you are to be his witness anyway, said Cleitophon, interrupting.

Who needs a witness? Polemarchus replied. Thrasymachus himself agrees that the rulers sometimes order what is bad for themselves and that it is just for the others to do it.

That, Polemarchus, is because Thrasymachus maintained that it is just to obey the orders of the rulers.

He also maintained, Cleitophon, that the advantage of the stronger is just. And having maintained both principles he went on to agree that the stronger sometimes gives orders to those who are weaker than he is—in other words, to his subjects—that are disadvantageous to the stronger himself. From these agreements it follows that what is to the advantage of the stronger is no more just than what is not to his advantage.

But, Cleitophon responded, he said that the advantage of the stronger is what the stronger believes to be his advantage. This is what the weaker must do, and this is what he maintained the just to be.

That isn't what he said, Polemarchus replied.

It makes no difference, Polemarchus, I said. If Thrasymachus wants to put it that way now, let's accept it. Tell me, Thrasymachus, is this what you wanted to say the just is, namely, what the stronger believes to be to his advantage, whether it is in fact to his advantage or not? Is that what we are to say you mean?

Not at all. Do you think I'd call someone who is in error stronger at the very moment he errs?

I did think that was what you meant when you agreed that the rulers aren't infallible but are liable to error.

That's because you are a false witness in arguments, Socrates. When someone makes an error in the treatment of patients, do you call him a doctor in regard to that very error? Or when someone makes an error in accounting, do you call him an accountant in regard to that very error in calculation? I think that we express ourselves in words that, taken literally, do say that a doctor is in error, or an accountant, or a grammarian. But each of these, insofar as he is what we call him, never errs, so that, according to the precise account (and you are a stickler for precise accounts), no craftsman ever errs. It's when his knowledge fails him that he makes an error, and in regard to that error he is no craftsman. No craftsman, expert, or ruler makes an error at the moment when he is ruling, even though everyone will say that a physician or a ruler makes errors. It's in this loose way that you must also take the answer I gave earlier. But the most precise answer is this. A ruler, insofar as he is ruler, never makes errors and unerringly decrees what is best for himself, and this his subject must do. Thus, as I said from the first, it is just to do what is to the advantage of the stronger.

All right, Thrasymachus, so you think I'm a false witness?

You certainly are.

And you think that I asked the questions I did in order to harm you in the argument?

I know it very well, but it won't do you any good. You'll never be able to trick me, so you can't harm me that way, and without trickery you'll never be able to overpower me in argument.

I wouldn't so much as try, Thrasymachus. But in order to prevent this sort of thing from happening again, define clearly whether it is the ruler and stronger in the ordinary sense or in the precise sense whose advantage you said it is just for the weaker to promote as the advantage of the stronger.

I mean the ruler in the most precise sense. Now practice your harmdoing and false witnessing on that if you can—I ask no concessions from you—but you certainly won't be able to.

Do you think that I'm crazy enough to try to shave a lion or to bear false witness against Thrasymachus?

You certainly tried just now, though you were a loser at that too.

Enough of this. Tell me: Is a doctor in the precise sense, whom you mentioned before, a money-maker or someone who treats the sick? Tell me about the one who is really a doctor.

He's the one who treats the sick.

What about a ship's captain? Is a captain in the precise sense a ruler of sailors or a sailor?

A ruler of sailors.

We shouldn't, I think, take into account the fact that he sails in a ship, and he shouldn't be called a sailor for that reason, for it isn't because of his sailing that he is called a ship's captain, but because of his craft and his rule over sailors?

That's true.

And is there something advantageous to each of these, that is, to bodies and to sailors?

Certainly.

And aren't the respective crafts by nature set over them to seek and provide what is to their advantage?

They are.

And is there any advantage for each of the crafts themselves except to be as complete or perfect as possible?

What are you asking?

This: If you asked me whether our bodies are sufficient in themselves, or whether they need something else, I'd answer: "They certainly have needs. And because of this, because our bodies are deficient rather than self-sufficient, the craft of medicine has now been discovered. The craft of medicine was developed to provide what is advantageous for a body." Do you think that I'm right in saying this or not?

You are right.

Now, is medicine deficient? Does a craft need some further virtue, as the eyes are in need of sight, and the ears of hearing, so that another craft is needed to seek and provide what is advantageous to them?[3] Does a craft itself have some similar deficiency, so that each craft needs another, to seek out what is to its advantage? And does the craft that does the seeking need still another, and so on without end? Or does each seek out what is to its own advantage by itself? Or does it need neither itself nor another craft to seek out what is advantageous to it, because of its own deficiencies? Or is it that there is no deficiency or error in any craft? That it isn't

3. [Sight is the virtue or excellence of the eyes (see 335b n. 12). Without it, the eyes cannot achieve what is advantageous to them, namely sight. So eyes need some further virtue to seek and provide what is advantageous to them. But Socrates assumes throughout Book I that virtues are crafts (see 332d). Hence he can conclude that the eyes need a further craft to achieve what is advantageous to them.]

appropriate for any craft to seek what is to the advantage of anything except that of which it is the craft? And that, since it is itself correct, it is without either fault or impurity, as long as it is wholly and precisely the craft that it is? Consider this with the preciseness of language you mentioned. Is it so or not?

It appears to be so.

Medicine doesn't seek its own advantage, then, but that of the body?

Yes.

And horse-breeding doesn't seek its own advantage, but that of horses? Indeed, no other craft seeks its own advantage—for it has no further needs—but the advantage of that of which it is the craft?

Apparently so.

Now, surely, Thrasymachus, the crafts rule over and are stronger than the things of which they are the crafts?

Very reluctantly, he conceded this as well.

No kind of knowledge seeks or orders what is advantageous to itself, then, but what is advantageous to the weaker, which is subject to it.

He tried to fight this conclusion, but he conceded it in the end. And after he had, I said: Surely, then, no doctor, insofar as he is a doctor, seeks or orders what is advantageous to himself, but what is advantageous to his patient? We agreed that a doctor in the precise sense is a ruler of bodies, not a money-maker. Wasn't that agreed?

Yes.

So a ship's captain in the precise sense is a ruler of sailors, not a sailor?

That's what we agreed.

Doesn't it follow that a ship's captain or ruler won't seek and order what is advantageous to himself, but what is advantageous to a sailor?

He reluctantly agreed.

So, then, Thrasymachus, no one in any position of rule, insofar as he is a ruler, seeks or orders what is advantageous to himself, but what is advantageous to his subjects; the ones of whom he is himself the craftsman. It is to his subjects and what is advantageous and proper to them that he looks, and everything he says and does he says and does for them.

When we reached this point in the argument, and it was clear to all that his account of justice had turned into its opposite, instead of answering, Thrasymachus said: Tell me, Socrates, do you still have a wet nurse?

What's this? Hadn't you better answer *my* questions rather than asking *me* such things?

Because she's letting you run around with a snotty nose, and doesn't wipe it when she needs to! Why, for all she cares, you don't even know about sheep and shepherds.

Just what is it I don't know?

You think that shepherds and cowherds seek the good of their sheep and cattle, and fatten them and take care of them, looking into something other than their master's good and their own. Moreover, you believe that rulers in cities—true rulers, that is—think about their subjects differently than one does about sheep, and that night and day they think of something besides their own advantage. You are so far from understanding about justice and what's just, about injustice and what's unjust, that you don't realize that justice is really the good of another, the advantage of the stronger and the ruler, and harmful to the one who obeys and serves. Injustice is the opposite, it rules the truly simple and just, and those it rules do what is to the advantage of the other and stronger, and they make the one they serve happy, but themselves not at all. You must look at it as follows, my most simple Socrates: A just man always get less than an unjust one. First, in their contracts with one another, you'll never find, when the partnership ends, that a just partner has got more than an unjust one, but less. Second, in matters relating to the city, when taxes are to be paid, a just man pays more on the same property, an unjust one less, but when the city is giving out refunds, a just man gets nothing, while an unjust one makes a large profit. Finally, when each of them holds a ruling position in some public office, a just person, even if he isn't penalized in other ways, finds that his private affairs deteriorate because he has to neglect them, that he gains no advantage from the public purse because of his justice, and that he's hated by his relatives and acquaintances when he's unwilling to do them an unjust favor. The opposite is true of an unjust man in every respect. Therefore, I repeat what I said before: A person of great power outdoes everyone else.[4] Consider him if you want to figure out how much more advantageous it is for the individual to be just rather than unjust. You'll understand this most easily if you turn your thoughts to the most complete injustice, the one that makes the doer of injustice happiest and the sufferers of it, who are unwilling to do injustice, most wretched. This is tyranny, which through stealth or force appropriates the property of others, whether sacred or profane, public or private, not little by little, but all at once. If someone commits only one part of injustice and is

---

4. [Outdoing (*pleonektein*) is an important notion in the remainder of the *Republic*. It is connected to *pleonexia*, which is what one succumbs to when one always wants to outdo everyone else by getting and having more and more. *Pleonexia* is, or is the cause of, injustice (359c), since always wanting to outdo others leads one to try to get what belongs to them, what isn't *one's own*. It is contrasted with *doing or having one's own*, which is, or is the cause of, justice (434a, 441e).]

caught, he's punished and greatly reproached—such partly unjust people are called temple-robbers,[5] kidnappers, housebreakers, robbers, and thieves when they commit these crimes. But when someone, in addition to appropriating their possessions, kidnaps and enslaves the citizens as well, instead of these shameful names he is called happy and blessed, not only by the citizens themselves, but by all who learn that he has done the whole of injustice. Those who reproach injustice do so because they are afraid not of doing it but of suffering it. So, Socrates, injustice, if it is on a large enough scale, is stronger, freer, and more masterly than justice. And, as I said from the first, justice is what is advantageous to the stronger, while injustice is to one's own profit and advantage.

Having emptied this great flood of words into our ears all at once like a bath attendant, Thrasymachus intended to leave. But those present didn't let him and made him stay to give an account of what he had said. I too begged him to stay, and I said to him: After hurling such a speech at us, Thrasymachus, do you intend to leave before adequately instructing us or finding out whether you are right or not? Or do you think it a small matter to determine which whole way of life would make living most worthwhile for each of us?

Is *that* what I seem to you to think? Thrasymachus said.

Either that, or else you care nothing for us and aren't worried about whether we'll live better or worse lives because of our ignorance of what you say you know. So show some willingness to teach it to us. It wouldn't be a bad investment for you to be the benefactor of a group as large as ours. For my own part, I'll tell you that I am not persuaded. I don't believe that injustice is more profitable than justice, not even if you give it full scope and put no obstacles in its way. Suppose that there *is* an unjust person, and suppose he *does* have the power to do injustice, whether by trickery or open warfare; nonetheless, he doesn't persuade me that injustice is more profitable than justice. Perhaps someone here, besides myself, feels the same as I do. So come now, and persuade us that we are wrong to esteem justice more highly than injustice in planning our lives.

And how am I to persuade you, if you aren't persuaded by what I said just now? What more can I do? Am I to take my argument and pour it into your very soul?

God forbid! Don't do that! But, first, stick to what you've said, and then, if you change your position, do it openly and don't deceive us. You

5. [The temples acted as public treasuries, so that a temple robber is the equivalent of a present-day bank robber.]

see, Thrasymachus, that having defined the true doctor—to continue examining the things you said before—you didn't consider it necessary later
to keep a precise guard on the true shepherd. You think that, insofar as
he's a shepherd, he fattens sheep, not looking to what is best for the sheep
but to a banquet, like a guest about to be entertained at a feast, or to a future sale, like a money-maker rather than a shepherd. Shepherding is concerned only to provide what is best for the things it is set over, and it is
itself adequately provided with all it needs to be at its best when it doesn't
fall short in any way of being the craft of shepherding. That's why I
thought it necessary for us to agree before that every kind of rule, insofar
as it rules, doesn't seek anything other than what is best for the things it
rules and cares for, and this is true both of public and private kinds of rule.
But do you think that those who rule cities, the true rulers, rule willingly?

I don't think it, by god, I know it.

But, Thrasymachus, don't you realize that in other kinds of rule no one
wants to rule for its own sake, but they ask for pay, thinking that their
ruling will benefit not themselves but their subjects? Tell me, doesn't every craft differ from every other in having a different function? Please
don't answer contrary to what you believe, so that we can come to some
definite conclusion.

Yes, that's what differentiates them.

And each craft benefits us in its own peculiar way, different from the
others. For example, medicine gives us health, navigation gives us safety
while sailing, and so on with the others?

Certainly.

And wage-earning gives us wages, for this is its function? Or would you
call medicine the same as navigation? Indeed, if you want to define matters precisely, as you proposed, even if someone who is a ship's captain
becomes healthy because sailing is advantageous to his health, you
wouldn't for that reason call his craft medicine?

Certainly not.

Nor would you call wage-earning medicine, even if someone becomes
healthy while earning wages?

Certainly not.

Nor would you call medicine wage-earning, even if someone earns pay
while healing?

No.

We are agreed, then, that each craft brings its own peculiar benefit?

It does.

Then whatever benefit all craftsmen receive in common must clearly result from their joint practice of some additional craft that benefits each of them?

So it seems.

And we say that the additional craft in question, which benefits the craftsmen by earning them wages, is the craft of wage-earning?

He reluctantly agreed.

Then this benefit, receiving wages, doesn't result from their own craft, but rather, if we're to examine these precisely, medicine provides health, and wage-earning provides wages; house-building provides a house, and wage-earning, which accompanies it, provides a wage; and so on with the other crafts. Each of them does its own work and benefits the things it is set over. So, if wages aren't added, is there any benefit that the craftsman gets from his craft?

Apparently none.

But he still provides a benefit when he works for nothing?

Yes, I think he does.

Then, it is clear now, Thrasymachus, that no craft or rule provides for its own advantage, but, as we've been saying for some time, it provides and orders for its subject and aims at its advantage, that of the weaker, not of the stronger. That's why I said just now, Thrasymachus, that no one willingly chooses to rule and to take other people's troubles in hand and straighten them out, but each asks for wages; for anyone who intends to practice his craft well never does or orders what is best for himself—at least not when he orders as his craft prescribes—but what is best for his subject. It is because of this, it seems, that wages must be provided to a person if he's to be willing to rule, whether in the form of money or honor or a penalty if he refuses.

What do you mean, Socrates? said Glaucon. I know the first two kinds of wages, but I don't understand what penalty you mean or how you can call it a wage.

Then you don't understand the best people's kind of wages, the kind that moves the most decent to rule, when they are willing to rule at all. Don't you know that the love of honor and the love of money are despised, and rightly so?

I do.

Therefore good people won't be willing to rule for the sake of either money or honor. They don't want to be paid wages openly for ruling and get called hired hands, nor to take them in secret from their rule and be called thieves. And they won't rule for the sake of honor, because they aren't ambitious honor-lovers. So, if they're to be willing to rule, some

compulsion or punishment must be brought to bear on them—perhaps
that's why it is thought shameful to seek to rule before one is compelled
to. Now, the greatest punishment, if one isn't willing to rule, is to be ruled
by someone worse than oneself. And I think that it's fear of this that makes
decent people rule when they do. They approach ruling not as something
good or something to be enjoyed, but as something necessary, since it
can't be entrusted to anyone better than—or even as good as—themselves. In a city of good men, if it came into being, the citizens would fight
in order *not to rule*, just as they do now in order to rule. There it would be
quite clear that anyone who is really a true ruler doesn't by nature seek
his own advantage but that of his subjects. And everyone, knowing
this, would rather be benefited by others than take the trouble to benefit
them. So I can't at all agree with Thrasymachus that justice is the advantage of the stronger—but we'll look further into that another time. What
Thrasymachus is now saying—that the life of an unjust person is better
than that of a just one—seems to be of far greater importance. Which life
would you choose, Glaucon? And which of our views do you consider
truer?

I certainly think that the life of a just person is more profitable.

Did you hear all of the good things Thrasymachus listed a moment ago
for the unjust life?

I heard, but I wasn't persuaded.

Then, do you want us to persuade him, if we're able to find a way, that
what he says isn't true?

Of course I do.

If we oppose him with a parallel speech about the blessings of the just
life, and then he replies, and then we do, we'd have to count and measure
the good things mentioned on each side, and we'd need a jury to decide
the case. But if, on the other hand, we investigate the question, as we've
been doing, by seeking agreement with each other, we ourselves can be
both jury and advocates at once.

Certainly.

Which approach do you prefer? I asked.

The second.

Come, then, Thrasymachus, I said, answer us from the beginning. You
say that complete injustice is more profitable than complete justice?

I certainly do say that, and I've told you why.

Well, then, what do you say about this? Do you call one of the two a
virtue and the other a vice?

Of course.

That is to say, you call justice a virtue and injustice a vice?

That's hardly likely, since I say that injustice is profitable and justice isn't.

Then, what exactly do you say?

The opposite.

That justice is a vice?

No, just very high-minded simplicity.

Then do you call being unjust being low-minded?

No, I call it good judgment.

You consider unjust people, then, Thrasymachus, to be clever and good?

Yes, those who are completely unjust, who can bring cities and whole communities under their power. Perhaps, you think I meant pickpockets? Not that such crimes aren't also profitable, if they're not found out, but they aren't worth mentioning by comparison to what I'm talking about.

I'm not unaware of what you want to say. But I wonder about this: Do you really include injustice with virtue and wisdom, and justice with their opposites?

I certainly do.

That's harder, and it isn't easy now to know what to say. If you had declared that injustice is more profitable, but agreed that it is a vice or shameful, as some others do, we could have discussed the matter on the basis of conventional beliefs. But now, obviously, you'll say that injustice is fine and strong and apply it to all the attributes we used to apply to justice, since you dare to include it with virtue and wisdom.

You've divined my views exactly.

Nonetheless, we mustn't shrink from pursuing the argument and looking into this, just as long as I take you to be saying what you really think. And I believe that you aren't joking now, Thrasymachus, but are saying what you believe to be the truth.

What difference does it make to you, whether *I* believe it or not? It's *my account* you're supposed to be refuting.

It makes no difference. But try to answer this further question: Do you think that a just person wants to outdo[6] someone else who's just?

Not at all, for he wouldn't then be as polite and innocent as he is.

Or to outdo someone who does a just action?

No, he doesn't even want to do that.

And does he claim that he deserves to outdo an unjust person and believe that it is just for him to do so, or doesn't he believe that?

6. [*Pleon echein.*]

He'd want to outdo him, and he'd claim to deserve to do so, but he wouldn't be able.

That's not what I asked, but whether a just person wants to outdo an unjust person but not a just one, thinking that this is what he deserves?

He does.

What about an unjust person? Does he claim that he deserves to outdo a just person or someone who does a just action?

Of course he does; he thinks he deserves to outdo everyone.

Then will an unjust person also outdo an *unjust* person or someone who does an *unjust* action, and will he strive to get the most he can for himself from everyone?

He will.

Then, let's put it this way: A just person doesn't outdo someone like himself but someone unlike himself, whereas an unjust person outdoes both like and unlike.

Very well put.

An unjust person is clever and good, and a just one is neither?

That's well put, too.

It follows, then, that an unjust person is like clever and good people, while the other isn't?

Of course that's so. How could he fail to be like them when he has their qualities, while the other isn't like them?

Fine. Then each of them has the qualities of the people he's like?

Of course.

All right, Thrasymachus. Do you call one person musical and another nonmusical?

I do.

Which if them is clever in music, and which isn't?

The musical one is clever, of course, and the other isn't.

And the things he's clever in, he's good in, and the things he isn't clever in, he's bad in?

Yes.

Isn't the same true of a doctor?

It is.

Do you think that a musician, in tuning his lyre and in tightening and loosening the strings, wants to outdo another musician, claiming that this is what he deserves?[7]

I do not.

---

7. [Socrates' point may seem obscure, but what he has in mind is explained at 350a. All expert musicians try to get the same thing, perfect harmony, so they

But he does want to outdo a nonmusician?

Necessarily.

What about a doctor? Does he, when prescribing food and drink, want to outdo another doctor or someone who does the action that medicine prescribes?

Certainly not.

But he does want to outdo a nondoctor?

Yes.

In any branch of knowledge or ignorance, do you think that a knowledgeable person would intentionally try to outdo another knowledgeable people or say something better or different than they do, rather than doing or saying the very same thing as those like him?

Well, perhaps it must be as you say.

And what about an ignorant person? Doesn't he want to outdo both a knowledgeable person and an ignorant one?

Probably.

A knowledgeable person is clever?

I agree.

And a clever one is good?

I agree.

Therefore, a good and clever person doesn't want to outdo those like himself but those who are unlike him and his opposite.

So it seems.

But a bad and ignorant person wants to outdo both his like and his opposite.

Apparently.

Now, Thrasymachus, we found that an unjust person tries to outdo those like him and those unlike him? Didn't you say that?

I did.

And that a just person won't outdo his like but his unlike?

Yes.

Then, a just person is like a clever and good one, and an unjust is like an ignorant and bad one.

It looks that way.

---

tighten and loosen their strings to exactly the same degree, namely, the one that will produce the right pitch. In the same way, all doctors who are masters of medicine prescribe the same diet for people with the same diseases, namely, the one that will best restore them to health.]

Moreover, we agreed that each has the qualities of the one he resembles.

Yes, we did.

Then, a just person has turned out to be good and clever, and an unjust one ignorant and bad.

Thrasymachus agreed to all this, not easily as I'm telling it, but reluctantly, with toil, trouble, and—since it was summer—a quantity of sweat that was a wonder to behold. And then I saw something I'd never seen before—Thrasymachus blushing. But, in any case, after we'd agreed that justice is virtue and wisdom and that injustice is vice and ignorance, I said: All right, let's take that as established. But we also said that injustice is powerful, or don't you remember that, Thrasymachus?

I remember, but I'm not satisfied with what you're now saying. I could make a speech about it, but, if I did, I know that you'd accuse me of engaging in oratory. So either allow me to speak, or, if you want to ask questions, go ahead, and I'll say, "All right," and nod yes and no, as one does to old wives' tales.

Don't do that, contrary to your own opinion.

I'll answer so as to please you, since you won't let me make a speech. What else do you want?

Nothing, by god. But if that's what you're going to do, go ahead and do it. I'll ask my questions.

Ask ahead.

I'll ask what I asked before, so that we may proceed with our argument about justice and injustice in an orderly fashion, for surely it was claimed that injustice is stronger and more powerful than justice. But, now, if justice is indeed wisdom and virtue, it will easily be shown to be stronger than injustice, since injustice is ignorance (no one could now be ignorant of that). However, I don't want to state the matter so unconditionally, Thrasymachus, but to look into it in some such way as this. Would you say that it is unjust for a city to try to enslave other cities unjustly and to hold them in subjection when it has enslaved many of them?

Of course, that's what the best city will especially do, the one that is most completely unjust.

I understand that's your position, but the point I want to examine is this: Will the city that becomes stronger than another achieve this power without justice, or will it need the help of justice?

If what you said a moment ago stands, and justice is cleverness or wisdom, it will need the help of justice, but if things are as I stated, it will need the help of injustice.

I'm impressed, Thrasymachus, that you don't merely nod yes or no but give very fine answers.

That's because I'm trying to please you.

You're doing well at it, too. So please me some more by answering this question: Do you think that a city, an army, a band of robbers or thieves, or any other tribe with a common unjust purpose would be able to achieve it if they were unjust to each other?

No, indeed.

What if they weren't unjust to one another? Would they achieve more?

Certainly.

Injustice, Thrasymachus, causes civil war, hatred, and fighting among themselves, while justice brings friendship and a sense of common purpose. Isn't that so?

Let it be so, in order not to disagree with you.

You're still doing well on that front. So tell me this: If the effect of injustice is to produce hatred wherever it occurs, then, whenever it arises, whether among free men or slaves, won't it cause them to hate one another, engage in civil war, and prevent them from achieving any common purpose?

Certainly.

What if it arises between two people? Won't they be at odds, hate each other, and be enemies to one another and to just people?

They will.

Does injustice lose its power to cause dissension when it arises within a single individual, or will it preserve it intact?

Let it preserve it intact.

Apparently, then, injustice has the power, first, to make whatever it arises in—whether it is a city, a family, an army, or anything else—incapable of achieving anything as a unit, because of the civil wars and differences it creates, and, second, it makes that unit an enemy to itself and to what is in every way its opposite, namely, justice. Isn't that so?

Certainly.

And even in a single individual, it has by its nature the very same effect. First, it makes him incapable of achieving anything, because he is in a state of civil war and not of one mind; second, it makes him his own enemy, as well as the enemy of just people. Hasn't it that effect?

Yes.

And the gods too are just?

Let it be so.

So an unjust person is also an enemy of the gods, Thrasymachus, while a just person is their friend?

Enjoy your banquet of words! Have no fear, I won't oppose you. That would make these people hate me.

Come, then, complete the banquet for me by continuing to answer as you've been doing. We have shown that just people are cleverer and more capable of doing things, while unjust ones aren't even able to act together, for when we speak of a powerful achievement by unjust men acting together, what we say isn't altogether true. They would never have been able to keep their hands off each other if they were completely unjust. But clearly there must have been some sort of justice in them that at least prevented them from doing injustice among themselves at the same time as they were doing it to others. And it was this that enabled them to achieve what they did. When they started doing unjust things, they were only halfway corrupted by their injustice (for those who are all bad and completely unjust are completely incapable of accomplishing anything). These are the things I understand to hold, not the ones you first maintained. We must now examine, as we proposed before, whether just people also live better and are happier than unjust ones. I think it's clear already that this is so, but we must look into it further, since the argument concerns no ordinary topic but the way we ought to live.

Go ahead and look.

I will. Tell me, do you think there is such a thing as the function of a horse?

I do.

And would you define the function of a horse or of anything else as that which one can do only with it or best with it?

I don't understand.

Let me put it this way: Is it possible to see with anything other than eyes?

Certainly not.

Or to hear with anything other than ears?

No.

Then, we are right to say that seeing and hearing are the functions of eyes and ears?

Of course.

What about this? Could you use a dagger or a carving knife or lots of other things in pruning a vine?

Of course.

But wouldn't you do a finer job with a pruning knife designed for the purpose than with anything else?

You would.

Then shall we take pruning to be its function?

Yes.

Now, I think you'll understand what I was asking earlier when I asked whether the function of each thing is what it alone can do or what it does better than anything else.

I understand, and I think that this is the function of each.

All right. Does each thing to which a particular function is assigned also have a virtue? Let's go over the same ground again. We say that eyes have some function?

They do.

So there is also a virtue of eyes?

There is.

And ears have a function?

Yes.

So there is also a virtue of ears?

There is.

And all other things are the same, aren't they?

They are.

And could eyes perform their function well if they lacked their peculiar virtue and had the vice instead?

How could they, for don't you mean if they had blindness instead of sight?

Whatever their virtue is, for I'm not now asking about that but about whether anything that has a function performs it well by means of its own peculiar virtue and badly by means of its vice?

That's true, it does.

So ears, too, deprived of their own virtue, perform their function badly?

That's right.

And the same could be said about everything else?

So it seems.

Come, then, and let's consider this: Is there some function of a soul that you couldn't perform with anything else, for example, taking care of things, ruling, deliberating, and the like? Is there anything other than a soul to which you could rightly assign these, and say that they are its peculiar function?

No, none of them.

What of living? Isn't that a function of a soul?

It certainly is.

And don't we also say that there is a virtue of a soul?
We do.
Then, will a soul ever perform its function well, Thrasymachus, if it is deprived of its own peculiar virtue, or is that impossible?
It's impossible.
Doesn't it follow, then, that a bad soul rules and takes care of things badly and that a good soul does all these things well?
It does.
Now, we agreed that justice is a soul's virtue, and injustice its vice?
We did.
Then, it follows that a just soul and a just man will live well, and an unjust one badly.
Apparently so, according to your argument.
And surely anyone who lives well is blessed and happy, and anyone who doesn't is the opposite.
Of course.
Therefore, a just person is happy, and an unjust one wretched.
So be it.
It profits no one to be wretched but to be happy.
Of course.
And so, Thrasymachus, injustice is never more profitable than justice.
Let that be your banquet, Socrates, at the feast of Bendis.
Given by you, Thrasymachus, after you became gentle and ceased to give me rough treatment. Yet I haven't had a fine banquet. But that's my fault not yours. I seem to have behaved like a glutton, snatching at every dish that passes and tasting it before properly savoring its predecessor. Before finding the answer to our first inquiry about what justice is, I let that go and turned to investigate whether it is a kind of vice and ignorance or a kind of wisdom and virtue. Then an argument came up about injustice being more profitable than justice, and I couldn't refrain from abandoning the previous one and following up on that. Hence the result of the discussion, as far as I'm concerned, is that I know nothing, for when I don't know what justice is, I'll hardly know whether it is a kind of virtue or not, or whether a person who has it is happy or unhappy.

From Book IV

Then, Glaucon, we must station ourselves like hunters surrounding a wood and focus our understanding, so that justice doesn't escape us and vanish into obscurity, for obviously it's around here somewhere. So look and try eagerly to catch sight of it, and if you happen to see it before I do, you can tell me about it.

I wish I could, but you'll make better use of me if you take me to be a follower who can see things when you point them out to him.

Follow, then, and join me in a prayer.

I'll do that, just so long as you lead.

I certainly will, though the place seems to be impenetrable and full of shadows. It is certainly dark and hard to search though. But all the same, we must go on.

Indeed we must.

And then I caught sight of something. Ah ha! Glaucon, it looks as though there's a track here, so it seems that our quarry won't altogether escape us.

That's good news.

Either that, or we've just been stupid.

In what way?

Because what we are looking for seems to have been rolling around at our feet from the very beginning, and we didn't see it, which was ridiculous of us. Just as people sometimes search for the very thing they are holding in their hands, so we didn't look in the right direction but gazed off into the distance, and that's probably why we didn't notice it.

What do you mean?

I mean that, though we've been talking and hearing about it for a long time, I think we didn't understand what we were saying or that, in a way, we were talking about justice.

That's a long prelude for someone who wants to hear the answer.

Then listen and see whether there's anything in what I say. Justice, I think, is exactly what we said must be established throughout the city when we were founding it—either that or some form of it. We stated, and often repeated, if you remember, that everyone must practice one of the occupations in the city for which he is naturally best suited.

Yes, we did keep saying that.

Moreover, we've heard many people say and have often said ourselves that justice is doing one's own work and not meddling with what isn't one's own.

Yes, we have.

Then, it turns out that this doing one's own work—provided that it comes to be in a certain way—is justice. And do you know what I take as evidence of this?

No, tell me.

I think that this is what was left over in the city when moderation, courage, and wisdom have been found. It is the power that makes it possible for them to grow in the city and that preserves them when they've grown for as long as it remains there itself. And of course we said that justice would be what was left over when we had found the other three.

Yes, that must be so.

And surely, if we had to decide which of the four will make the city good by its presence, it would be a hard decision. Is it the agreement in belief between the rulers and the ruled? Or the preservation among the soldiers of the law-inspired belief about what is to be feared and what isn't? Or the wisdom and guardianship of the rulers? Or is it, above all, the fact that every child, woman, slave, freeman, craftsman, ruler, and ruled each does his own work and doesn't meddle with what is other people's?

How could this fail to be a hard decision?

It seems, then, that the power that consists in everyone's doing his own work rivals wisdom, moderation, and courage in its contribution to the virtue of the city.

It certainly does.

And wouldn't you call this rival to the others in its contribution to the city's virtue justice?

Absolutely.

Look at it this way if you want to be convinced. Won't you order your rulers to act as judges in the city's courts?

Of course.

And won't their sole aim in delivering judgments be that no citizen should have what belongs to another or be deprived of what is his own?

They'll have no aim but that.

Because that is just?

Yes.

Therefore, from this point of view, also, the having and doing of one's own would be accepted as justice.

That's right.

Consider, then, and see whether you agree with me about this. If a carpenter attempts to do the work of a cobbler, or a cobbler that of a carpenter, or they exchange their tools or honors with one another, or if the same person tries to do both jobs, and all other such exchanges are made, do you think that does any great harm to the city?

Not much.

But I suppose that when someone, who is by nature a craftsman or some other kind of money-maker, is puffed up by wealth, or by having a majority of votes, or by his own strength, or by some other such thing, and attempts to enter the class of soldiers, or one of the unworthy soldiers tries to enter that of the judges and guardians, and these exchange their tools and honors, or when the same person tries to do all these things at once, then I think you'll agree that these exchanges and this sort of meddling bring the city to ruin.

Absolutely.

Meddling and exchange between these three classes, then, is the greatest harm that can happen to the city and would rightly be called the worst thing someone could do to it.

Exactly.

And wouldn't you say that the worst thing that someone could do to his city is injustice?

Of course.

Then, that exchange and meddling is injustice. Or to put it the other way around: For the money-making, auxiliary, and guardian classes each to do its own work in the city, is the opposite. That's justice, isn't it, and makes the city just?

I agree. Justice is that and nothing else.

Let's not take that as secure just yet, but if we find that the same form, when it comes to be in each individual person, is accepted as justice there as well, we can assent to it. What else can we say? But if that isn't what we find, we must look for something else to be justice. For the moment, however, let's complete the present inquiry. We thought that, if we first tried to observe justice in some larger thing that possessed it, this would make it easier to observe in a single individual. We agreed that this larger thing is a city, and so we established the best city we could, knowing well that justice would be in one that was good. So, let's apply what has come to light in the city to an individual, and if it is accepted there, all will be well. But if something different is found in the individual, then we must go back and test that on the city. And if we do this, and compare them side by side, we might well make justice light up as if we were rubbing firesticks together. And, when it has come to light, we can get a secure grip on it for ourselves.

You're following the road we set, and we must do as you say.

Well, then, are things called by the same name, whether they are bigger or smaller than one another, like or unlike with respect to that to which that name applies?

Alike.

Then a just man won't differ at all from a just city in respect to the form of justice; rather he'll be like the city.

He will.

But a city was thought to be just when each of the three natural classes within it did its own work, and it was thought to be moderate, courageous, and wise because of certain other conditions and states of theirs.

That's true.

Then, if an individual has these same three parts in his soul, we will expect him to be correctly called by the same names as the city if he has the same conditions in them.

Necessarily so.

Then once again we've come upon an easy question, namely, does the soul have these three parts in it or not?

It doesn't look easy to me. Perhaps, Socrates, there's some truth in the old saying that everything fine is difficult.

Apparently so. But you should know, Glaucon, that in my opinion, we will never get a precise answer using our present methods of argument— although there is another longer and fuller road that does lead to such an answer. But perhaps we can get an answer that's up to the standard of our previous statements and inquiries.

Isn't that satisfactory? It would be enough for me at present.

In that case, it will be fully enough for me too.

Then don't weary, but go on with the inquiry.

Well, then, we are surely compelled to agree that each of us has within himself the same parts and characteristics as the city? Where else would they come from? It would be ridiculous for anyone to think that spiritedness didn't come to be in cities from such individuals as the Thracians, Scythians, and others who live to the north of us who are held to possess spirit, or that the same isn't true of the love of learning, which is mostly associated with our part of the world, or the love of money, which one might say is conspicuously displayed by the Phoenicians and Egyptians.

It would.

That's the way it is, anyway, and it isn't hard to understand.

Certainly not.

But this *is* hard. Do we do these things with the same part of ourselves, or do we do them with three different parts? Do we learn with one part, get angry with another, and with some third part desire the pleasures of food, drink, sex, and the others that are closely akin to them? Or, when we set out after something, do we act with the whole of our soul, in each case? This is what's hard to determine in a way that's up to the standards of our argument.

I think so too.

Well, then, let's try to determine in that way whether these parts are the same or different.

How?

It is obvious that the same thing will not be willing to do or undergo opposites in the same part of itself, in relation to the same thing, at the same time. So, if we ever find this happening in the soul, we'll know that we aren't dealing with one thing but many.

All right.

Then consider what I'm about to say.

Say on.

Is it possible for the same thing to stand still and move at the same time in the same part of itself?

Not at all.

Let's make our agreement more precise in order to avoid disputes later on. If someone said that a person who is standing still but moving his hands and head is moving and standing still at the same time, we wouldn't consider, I think, that he ought to put it like that. What he ought to say is that one part of the person is standing still and another part is moving. Isn't that so?

It is.

And if our interlocutor became even more amusing and was sophisticated enough to say that whole spinning tops stand still and move at the same time when the peg is fixed in the same place and they revolve, and that the same is true of anything else moving in a circular motion on the same spot, we wouldn't agree, because it isn't with respect to the same parts of themselves that such things both stand still and move. We'd say that they have an axis and a circumference and that with respect to the axis they stand still, since they don't wobble to either side, while with respect to the circumference they move in a circle. But if they do wobble to the left or right, front or back, while they are spinning, we'd say that they aren't standing still in any way.

And we'd be right.

No such statement will disturb us, then, or make us believe that the same thing can be, do, or undergo opposites, at the same time, in the same respect, and in relation to the same thing.

They won't make me believe it, at least.

Nevertheless, in order to avoid going through all these objections one by one and taking a long time to prove them all untrue, let's assume that our hypothesis is correct and carry on. But we agree that if it should ever be shown to be incorrect, all the consequences we've drawn from it will also be invalidated.

We should agree to that.

Then wouldn't you consider all the following, whether they are doings or undergoings, as pairs of opposites: Assent and dissent, wanting to have something and rejecting it, taking something and pushing it away?

Yes, they are opposites.

What about these? Wouldn't you include thirst, hunger, the appetites as a whole, and wishing and willing somewhere in the class we mentioned? Wouldn't you say that the soul of someone who has an appetite for a thing wants what he has an appetite for and takes to himself what it is his will to have, and that insofar as he wishes something to be given to him, his soul, since it desires this to come about, nods assent to it as if in answer to a question?

I would.

What about not willing, not wishing, and not having an appetite? Aren't these among the very opposites—cases in which the soul pushes and drives things away?

Of course.

Then won't we say that there is a class of things called appetites and that the clearest examples are hunger and thirst?

We will.

One of these is for food and the other for drink?

Yes.

Now, insofar as it is thirst, is it an appetite in the soul for more than that for which we say that it is the appetite? For example, is thirst thirst for hot drink or cold, or much drink or little, or, in a word, for drink of a certain sort? Or isn't it rather that, where heat is present as well as thirst, it causes the appetite to be for something cold as well, and where cold for something hot, and where there is much thirst because of the presence of muchness, it will cause the desire to be for much, and where little for little? But thirst itself will never be for anything other than what it is in its nature to be for, namely, drink itself, and hunger for food.

That's the way it is, each appetite itself is only for its natural object, while the appetite for something of a certain sort depends on additions.

Therefore, let no one catch us unprepared or disturb us by claiming that no one has an appetite for drink but rather good drink, nor food but good food, so that if thirst is an appetite, it will be an appetite for good drink or whatever, and similarly with the others.[1]

All the same, the person who says that has a point.

But it seems to me that, in the case of all things that are related to something, those that are of a particular sort are related to a particular sort of thing, while those that are merely themselves are related to a thing that is merely itself.

I don't understand.

Don't you understand that the greater is such as to be greater than something?

Of course.

Than the less?

Yes.

And the much greater than the much less, isn't that so?

Yes.

And the once greater to the once less? And the going-to-be greater than the going-to-be less?

Certainly.

And isn't the same true of the more and the fewer, the double and the half, heavier and lighter, faster and slower, the hot and the cold, and all other such things?

Of course.

And what about the various kinds of knowledge? Doesn't the same apply? Knowledge itself is knowledge of what can be learned itself (or whatever it is that knowledge is of), while a particular sort of knowledge is of a particular sort of thing. For example, when knowledge of building houses came to be, didn't it differ from the other kinds of knowledge, and so was called knowledge of building?

Of course.

And wasn't that because it was a different sort of knowledge from all the others?

Yes.

And wasn't it because it was of a particular sort of thing that it itself became a particular sort of knowledge? And isn't this true of all crafts and kinds of knowledge?

It is.

Well, then, this is what I was trying to say—if you understand it now—when I said that of all things that are related to something, those that are

1. [Plato is here laying the foundations for his rejection of the principle, espoused by Socrates in many earlier dialogues, that weakness of will is impossible.]

merely themselves are related to things that are merely themselves, while those that are of a particular sort are related to things of a particular sort. However, I don't mean that the sorts in question have to be the same for them both. For example, knowledge of health or disease isn't healthy or diseased, and knowledge of good and bad doesn't itself become good or bad. I mean that, when knowledge became, not knowledge of the thing itself that knowledge is of, but knowledge of something of a particular sort, the result was that it itself became a particular sort of knowledge, and this caused it to be no longer called knowledge without qualification, but—with the addition of the relevant sort—medical knowledge or whatever.

I understand, and I think that that's the way it is.

Then as for thirst, wouldn't you include it among things that are related to something? Surely thirst is related to . . .

I know it's related to drink.

Therefore a particular sort of thirst is for a particular sort of drink. But thirst itself isn't for much or little, good or bad, or, in a word, for drink of a particular sort. Rather, thirst itself is in its nature only for drink itself.

Absolutely.

Hence the soul of the thirsty person, insofar as he's thirsty, doesn't wish anything else but to drink, and it wants this and is impelled towards it.

Clearly.

Therefore, if something draws it back when it is thirsting, wouldn't that be something different in it from whatever thirsts and drives it like a beast to drink? It can't be, we say, that the same thing, with the same part of itself, in relation to the same, at the same time, does opposite things.

No, it can't.

In the same way, I suppose, it's wrong to say of the archer that his hands at the same time push the bow away and draw it towards him. We ought to say that one hand pushes it away and the other draws it towards him.

Absolutely.

Now, would we assert that sometimes there are thirsty people who don't wish to drink?

Certainly, it happens often to many different people.

What, then, should one say about them? Isn't it that there is something in their soul, bidding them to drink, and something different, forbidding them to do so, that overrules the thing that bids?

I think so.

Doesn't that which forbids in such cases come into play—if it comes into play at all—as a result of rational calculation, while what drives and drags them to drink is a result of feelings and diseases?

Apparently.

Hence it isn't unreasonable for us to claim that they are two, and different from one another. We'll call the part of the soul with which it calculates the rational part and the part with which it lusts, hungers, thirsts, and gets excited by other appetites the irrational appetitive part, companion of certain indulgences and pleasures.

Yes. Indeed, that's a reasonable thing to think.

Then, let these two parts be distinguished in the soul. Now, is the spirited part by which we get angry a third part or is it of the same nature as either of the other two?

Perhaps it's like the appetitive part.

But I've heard something relevant to this, and I believe it. Leontius, the son of Aglaion, was going up from the Piraeus along the outside of the North Wall when he saw some corpses lying at the executioner's feet. He had an appetite to look at them but at the same time he was disgusted and turned away. For a time he struggled with himself and covered his face, but, finally, overpowered by the appetite, he pushed his eyes wide open and rushed towards the corpses, saying, "Look for yourselves, you evil wretches, take your fill of the beautiful sight!"[2]

I've heard that story myself.

It certainly proves that anger sometimes makes war against the appetites, as one thing against another.

Besides, don't we often notice in other cases that when appetite forces someone contrary to rational calculation, he reproaches himself and gets angry with that in him that's doing the forcing, so that of the two factions that are fighting a civil war, so to speak, spirit allies itself with reason? But I don't think you can say that you've ever seen spirit, either in yourself or anyone else, ally itself with an appetite to do what reason has decided must not be done.

No, by god, I haven't.

What happens when a person thinks that he has done something unjust? Isn't it true that the nobler he is, the less he resents it if he suffers hunger, cold, or the like at the hands of someone whom he believes to be inflicting this on him justly, and won't his spirit, as I say, refuse to be aroused?

2. [Leontius' desire to look at the corpses is sexual in nature, for a fragment of contemporary comedy tells us that Leontius was known for his love of boys as pale as corpses.]

That's true.

But what happens if, instead, he believes that someone has been unjust to him? Isn't the spirit within him boiling and angry, fighting for what he believes to be just? Won't it endure hunger, cold, and the like and keep on till it is victorious, not ceasing from noble actions until it either wins, dies, or calms down, called to heel by the reason within him, like a dog by a shepherd?

Spirit is certainly like that. And, of course, we made the auxiliaries in our city like dogs obedient to the rulers, who are themselves like shepherds of a city.

You well understand what I'm trying to say. But also reflect on this further point.

What?

The position of the spirited part seems to be the opposite of what we thought before. Then we thought of it as something appetitive, but now we say that it is far from being that, for in the civil war in the soul it aligns itself far more with the rational part.

Absolutely.

Then is it also different from the rational part, or is it some form of it, so that there are two parts in the soul—the rational and the appetitive—instead of three? Or rather, just as there were three classes in the city that held it together, the money-making, the auxiliary, and the deliberative, is the spirited part a third thing in the soul that is by nature the helper of the rational part, provided that it hasn't been corrupted by a bad upbringing?

It must be a third.

Yes, provided that we can show it is different from the rational part, as we saw earlier it was from the appetitive one.

It isn't difficult to show that it is different. Even in small children, one can see that they are full of spirit right from birth, while as far as rational calculation is concerned, some never seem to get a share of it, while the majority do so quite late.

That's really well put. And in animals too one can see that what you say is true. Besides, our earlier quotation from Homer bears it out, where he says,

He struck his chest and spoke to his heart.

For here Homer clearly represents the part that has calculated about better and worse as different from the part that is angry without calculation.

That's exactly right.

Well, then, we've now made our difficult way through a sea of argument. We are pretty much agreed that the same number and the same kinds of classes as are in the city are also in the soul of each individual.

That's true.

Therefore, it necessarily follows that the individual is wise in the same way and in the same part of himself as the city.

That's right.

And isn't the individual courageous in the same way and in the same part of himself as the city? And isn't everything else that has to do with virtue the same in both?

Necessarily.

Moreover, Glaucon, I suppose we'll say that a man is just in the same way as a city.

That too is entirely necessary.

And we surely haven't forgotten that the city was just because each of the three classes in it was doing its own work.

I don't think we could forget that.

Then we must also remember that each one of us in whom each part is doing its own work will himself be just and do his own.

Of course, we must.

Therefore, isn't it appropriate for the rational part to rule, since it is really wise and exercises foresight on behalf of the whole soul, and for the spirited part to obey it and be its ally?

It certainly is.

And isn't it, as we were saying, a mixture of music and poetry, on the one hand, and physical training, on the other, that makes the two parts harmonious, stretching and nurturing the rational part with fine words and learning, relaxing the other part through soothing stories, and making it gentle by means of harmony and rhythm?

That's precisely it.

And these two, having been nurtured in this way, and having truly learned their own roles and been educated in them, will govern the appetitive part, which is the largest part in each person's soul and is by nature most insatiable for money. They'll watch over it to see that it isn't filled with the so-called pleasures of the body and that it doesn't become so big and strong that it no longer does its own work but attempts to enslave and rule over the classes it isn't fitted to rule, thereby overturning everyone's whole life.

That's right.

Then, wouldn't these two parts also do the finest job of guarding the whole soul and body against external enemies—reason by planning, spirit by fighting, following its leader, and carrying out the leader's decisions through its courage?

Yes, that's true.

And it is because of the spirited part, I suppose, that we call a single individual courageous, namely, when it preserves through pains and pleasures the declarations of reason about what is to be feared and what isn't.

That's right.

And we'll call them wise because of that small part of himself that rules in him and makes those declarations and has within it the knowledge of what is advantageous for each part and for the whole soul, which is the community of all three parts.

Absolutely.

And isn't he moderate because of the friendly and harmonious relations between these same parts, namely, when the ruler and the ruled believe in common that the rational part should rule and don't engage in civil war against it?

Moderation is surely nothing other than that, both in the city and in the individual.

And, of course, a person will be just because of what we've so often mentioned, and in that way.

Necessarily.

Well, then, is the justice in us at all indistinct? Does it seem to be something different from what we found in the city?

It doesn't seem so to me.

If there are still any doubts in our soul about this, we could dispel them altogether by appealing to ordinary cases.

Which ones?

For example, if we had to come to an agreement about whether someone similar in nature and training to our city had embezzled a deposit of gold or silver that he had accepted, who do you think would consider him to have done it rather than someone who isn't like him?

No one.

And would he have anything to do with temple robbers, thefts, betrayals of friends in private life or of cities in public life?

No, nothing.

And he'd be in no way untrustworthy in keeping an oath or other agreement.

How could he be?

And adultery, disrespect for parents, and neglect of the gods would be more in keeping with every other kind of character than his.

With every one.

And isn't the cause of all this that every part within him does its own work, whether it's ruling or being ruled?

Yes, that and nothing else.

Then, are you still looking for justice to be something other than this power, the one that produces men and cities of the sort we've described?

No, I certainly am not.

Then the dream we had has been completely fulfilled—our suspicion that, with the help of some god, we had hit upon the origin and pattern of justice right at the beginning in founding our city.

Absolutely.

Indeed, Glaucon, the principle that it is right for someone who is by nature a cobbler to practice cobblery and nothing else, for the carpenter to practice carpentry, and the same for the others is a sort of image of justice—that's why it's beneficial.

Apparently.

And in truth justice is, it seems, something of this sort. However, it isn't concerned with someone's doing his own externally, but with what is inside him, with what is truly himself and his own. One who is just does not allow any part of himself to do the work of another part or allow the various classes within him to meddle with each other. He regulates well what is really his own and rules himself. He puts himself in order, is his own friend, and harmonizes the three parts of himself like three limiting notes in a musical scale—high, low, and middle. He binds together those parts and any others there may be in between, and from having been many things he becomes entirely one, moderate and harmonious. Only then does he act. And when he does anything, whether acquiring wealth, taking care of his body, engaging in politics, or in private contracts—in all of these, he believes that the action is just and fine that preserves this inner harmony and helps achieve it, and calls it so, and regards as wisdom the knowledge that oversees such actions. And he believes that the action that destroys this harmony is unjust, and calls it so, and regards the belief that oversees it as ignorance.

That's absolutely true, Socrates.

Well, then, if we claim to have found the just man, the just city, and what the justice is that is in them, I don't suppose that we'll seem to be telling a complete falsehood.

No, we certainly won't.

Shall we claim it, then?

We shall.

So be it. Now, I suppose we must look for injustice.

Clearly.

Surely, it must be a kind of civil war between the three parts, a meddling and doing of another's work, a rebellion by some part against the whole soul in order to rule it inappropriately. The rebellious part is by nature suited to be a slave, while the other part is not a slave but belongs to the ruling class. We'll say something like that, I suppose, and that the turmoil and straying of these parts are injustice, licentiousness, cowardice, ignorance, and, in a word, the whole of vice.

That's what they are.

So, if justice and injustice are really clear enough to us, then acting justly, acting unjustly, and doing injustice are also clear.

How so?

Because just and unjust actions are no different for the soul than healthy and unhealthy things are for the body.

In what way?

Healthy things produce health, unhealthy ones disease.

Yes.

And don't just actions produce justice in the soul and unjust ones injustice?

Necessarily.

To produce health is to establish the components of the body in a natural relation of control and being controlled, one by another, while to produce disease is to establish a relation of ruling and being ruled contrary to nature.

That's right.

Then, isn't to produce justice to establish the parts of the soul in a natural relation of control, one by another, while to produce injustice is to establish a relation of ruling and being ruled contrary to nature?

Precisely.

Virtue seems, then, to be a kind of health, fine condition, and well-being of the soul, while vice is disease, shameful condition, and weakness.

That's true.

And don't fine ways of living lead one to the possession of virtue, shameful ones to vice?

Necessarily.

So it now remains, it seems, to enquire whether it is more profitable to act justly, live in a fine way, and be just, whether one is known to be so or not, or to act unjustly and be unjust, provided that one doesn't pay the penalty and become better as a result of punishment.

But, Socrates, this inquiry looks ridiculous to me now that justice and injustice have been shown to be as we have described. Even if one has every kind of food and drink, lots of money, and every sort of power to rule, life is thought to be not worth living when the body's nature is ruined. So even if someone can do whatever he wishes, except what will free him from vice and injustice and make him acquire justice and virtue, how can it be worth living when his soul—the very thing by which he lives—is ruined and in turmoil?

Yes, it is ridiculous. Nevertheless, now that we've come far enough to be able to see most clearly that this is so, we mustn't give up.

That's absolutely the last thing we must do.

Then come here, so that you can see how many forms of vice there are, anyhow that I consider worthy of examination.

I'm following you, just tell me.

Well, from the vantage point we've reached in our argument, it seems to me that there is one form of virtue and an unlimited number of forms of vice, four of which are worth mentioning.

How do you mean?

It seems likely that there are as many types of soul as there are specific types of political constitution.

How many is that?

Five forms of constitution and five of souls.

What are they?

One is the constitution we've been describing. And it has two names. If one outstanding man emerges among the rulers, it's called a kingship; if more than one, it's called an aristocracy.

That's true.

Therefore, I say that this is one form of constitution. Whether one man emerges or many, none of the significant laws of the city would be changed, if they followed the upbringing and education we described.

Probably not.

5

Aristotle,
"Justice,"
from the *Nicomachean Ethics*

The philosopher Aristotle (422 B.C.–384 B.C.) is celebrated as the originator of the study of physics, biology, and formal logic. Instead of constructing an imaginary perfect society as Plato had done, he gathered empirical information on 158 constitutions of Greek city-states in much the same way as he gathered information about different organisms. His works in political philosophy include the Nicomachean Ethics *and the* Politics.

The Definition of Justice

The questions we must examine about justice and injustice are these: What sorts of actions are they concerned with? What sort of mean is justice? What are the extremes between which justice is intermediate? Let us examine them by the same type of investigation that we used in the topics discussed before.

We see that the state everyone means in speaking of justice is the state that makes us doers of just actions, that makes us do justice and wish what is just. In the same way they mean by injustice the state that makes us do injustice and wish what is unjust. Let us also, then, [follow the common beliefs and] begin by assuming this in outline.

For what is true of sciences and capacities is not true of states. For while one and the same capacity or science seems to have contrary activities, a state that is a contrary has no contrary activities. Health, e.g., only makes us do healthy actions, not their contraries; for we say we are walking in a healthy way if [and only if] we are walking in the way a healthy person would.

Often one of a pair of contrary states is recognized from the other con-

From Aristotle, *Nicomachean Ethics*, translated by Terence Irwin, 1985, Hackett Publishing Company, Inc.

The footnotes are those of Irwin.

The contents of the square brackets in the text are alternate renderings, clarifications, or resolutions of ambiguities.

trary; and often the states are recognized from their subjects. For if, e.g., the good state is evident, the bad state becomes evident too; and moreover the good state becomes evident from the things that have it, and the things from the state. For if, e.g., the good state is thickness of flesh, then the bad state will necessarily be thinness of flesh, and the thing that produces the good state will be what produces thickness of flesh.

It follows, usually, that if one of a pair of contraries is spoken of in more ways than one, so is the other; if, e.g., what is just is spoken of in more ways than one, so is what is unjust.

Now it would seem that justice and injustice are both spoken of in more ways than one, but since the different ways are closely related, their homonymy is unnoticed, and is less clear than it is with distant homonyms where the distance in appearance is wide (e.g., the bone below an animal's neck and what we lock doors with are called keys homonymously).

Let us, then, find the number of ways an unjust person is spoken of. Both the lawless person and the greedy and unfair person seem to be unjust; and so, clearly, both the lawful and the fair person will be just. Hence what is just will be both what is lawful and what is fair, and what is unjust will be both what is lawless and what is unfair.

Since the unjust person is greedy, he will be concerned with goods— not with all goods, but only with those involved in good and bad fortune, goods which are, [considered] unconditionally, always good, but for this or that person not always good. Though human beings pray for these and pursue them, they are wrong; the right thing is to pray that what is good unconditionally will also be good for us, but to choose [only] what is good for us.

Now the unjust person [who chooses these goods] does not choose more in every case; in the case of what is bad unconditionally he actually chooses less. But since what is less bad also seems to be good in a way, and greed aims at more of what is good, he seems to be greedy. In fact he is unfair; for unfairness includes [all these actions], and is a common feature [of his choice of the greater good and of the lesser evil].

General Justice

Since, as we saw, the lawless person is unjustified and the lawful person is just, it clearly follows that whatever is lawful is in some way just; for the provisions of legislative science are lawful, and we say that each of them is just. Now in every matter they deal with the laws aim either at the common benefit of all, or at the benefit of those in control, whose control rests on virtue or on some other such basis. And so in one way what we call just is whatever produces and maintains happiness and its parts for a political community.

Now the law instructs us to do the actions of a brave person—not to leave the battle-line, e.g., or to flee, or to throw away our weapons; of a temperate person—not to commit adultery or wanton aggression; of a mild person—not to strike or revile another; and similarly requires actions that express the other virtues, and prohibits those that express the vices. The correctly established law does this correctly, and the less carefully framed one does this worse.

This type of justice, then, is complete virtue, not complete virtue unconditionally, but complete virtue in relation to another. And this is why justice often seems to be supreme among the virtues, and 'neither the evening star nor the morning star is so marvellous',[1] and the proverb says 'And in justice all virtue is summed up.'[2]

Moreover, justice is complete virtue to the highest degree because it is the complete exercise of complete virtue. And it is the complete exercise because the person who has justice is able to exercise virtue in relation to another, not only in what concerns himself; for many are able to exercise virtue in their own concerns but unable in what relates to another.

And hence Bias[3] seems to have been correct in saying that ruling will reveal the mean, since a ruler is automatically related to another, and in a community. And for the same reason justice is the only virtue that seems to be another person's good, because it is related to another; for it does what benefits another, either the ruler or the fellow-member of the community.

The worst person, therefore, is the one who exercises his vice towards himself and his friends, as well [as towards others]. And the best person is not the one who exercises virtue [only] towards himself, but the one who [also] exercises it in relation to another, since this is a difficult task.

This type of justice, then, is the whole, not a part, of virtue, and the injustice contrary to it is the whole, not a part, of vice.

At the same time our discussion makes clear the difference between

1. [The quotation is thought to be from Euripides' lost play *Melanippe*.]

2. [The quotation derives from the work of Theognis, a sixth-century B.C. poet from Megara.]

3. [Bias of Priene was a sixth-century B.C. Ionian statesman, one of the Seven Wise Men of Greece, who distinguished themselves in public affairs. His most famous saying was, "Most men are bad."]

virtue and this type of justice. For virtue is the same as justice, but what it is to be virtue is not the same as what it is to be justice. Rather, in so far as virtue is related to another, it is justice, and in so far as it is a certain sort of state unconditionally it is virtue.

Special Justice Contrasted With General

But we are looking for the type of justice, since we say there is one, that consists in a part of virtue, and correspondingly for the type of injustice that is a part [of vice].

Here is evidence that there is this type of justice and injustice:

First, if someone's activities express the other vices—if, e.g., cowardice made him throw away his shield, or irritability made him revile someone, or ungenerosity made him fail to help someone with money—what he does is unjust, but not greedy. But when one acts from greed, in many cases his action expresses none of these vices—certainly not all of them; but it still expresses some type of wickedness, since we blame him, and [in particular] it expresses injustice. Hence there is another type of injustice that is a part of the whole, and a way for a thing to be unjust that is a part of the whole that is contrary to law.

Moreover, if A commits adultery for profit and makes a profit, while B commits adultery because of his appetite, and spends money on it to his own loss, B seems intemperate rather than greedy, while A seems unjust, not intemperate. Clearly, then, this is because A acts to make a profit.

Further, we can refer every other unjust action to some vice—to intemperance if he committed adultery, to cowardice if he deserted his comrade in the battle-line, to anger if he struck someone. But if he made an [unjust] profit, we can refer it to no other vice except injustice.

Hence evidently (a) there is another type of injustice, special injustice, besides the whole of injustice; and (b) it is synonymous with the whole, since the definition is in the same genus. For (b) both have their area of competence in relation to another. But (a) special injustice is concerned with honour or wealth or safety, or whatever single name will include all these, and aims at the pleasure that results from making a profit; but the concern of injustice as a whole is whatever concerns the excellent person.

Clearly, then, there is more than one type of justice, and there is another type besides [the type that is] the whole of virtue; but we must still grasp what it is, and what sort of thing it is.

What is unjust is divided into what is lawless and what is unfair, and what is just into what is lawful and what is fair. The [general] injustice previously described, then, is concerned with what is lawless. But what is unfair is not the same as what is lawless, but related to it as part to whole, since whatever is unfair is lawless, but not everything lawless is unfair. Hence also the type of injustice and the way for a thing to be unjust [that expresses unfairness] are not the same as the type [that expresses lawlessness], but differ as parts from wholes. For this injustice [as unfairness] is a part of the whole of injustice, and similarly justice [as fairness] is a part of the whole of justice.

Hence we must describe special [as well as general] justice and injustice, and equally this way for a thing to be just or unjust.

Let us, then, set to one side the type of justice and injustice that corresponds to the whole of virtue, justice being the exercise of the whole of virtue, and injustice of the whole of vice, in relation to another.

And it is evident how we must distinguish the way for a thing to be just or unjust that expresses this type of justice and injustice; for the majority of lawful actions, we might say, are the actions resulting from virtue as a whole. For the law instructs us to express each virtue, and forbids us to express each vice, in how we live. Moreover, the actions producing the whole of virtue are the lawful actions that the laws prescribe for education promoting the common good.

We must wait till later, however, to determine whether the education that makes an individual an unconditionally good man is a task for political science or for another science; for, presumably, being a good man is not the same as being every sort of good citizen.

Special justice, however, and the corresponding way for something to be just [must be divided].

One species is found in the distribution of honours or wealth or anything else that can be divided among members of a community who share in a political system; for here it is possible for one member to have a share equal or unequal to another's.

Another species concerns rectification in transactions. This species has two parts, since one sort of transaction is voluntary, and one involuntary. Voluntary transactions include selling, buying, lending, pledging, renting, depositing, hiring out—these are called voluntary because the origin of these transactions is voluntary. Some involuntary ones are secret, e.g. theft, adultery, poisoning, pimping, slave-deception, murder by treachery, false witness; others are forcible, e.g. assault, imprisonment, murder, plunder, mutilation, slander, insult.

Justice in Distribution

Since the unjust person is unfair, and what is unjust is unfair, there is clearly an intermediate between the unfair [extremes], and this is what is fair; for in any action where too much and too little are possible, the fair [amount] is also possible. And so if what is unjust is unfair, what is just is fair (*ison*), as seems true to everyone even without argument.

And since what is equal (*ison*) [and fair] is intermediate, what is just is some sort of intermediate. And since what is equal involves at least two things [equal to each other], it follows that what is just must be intermediate and equal, and related to some people. In so far as it is intermediate, it must be between too much and too little; in so far as it is equal, it involves two things; and in so far as it is just, it is just for some people. Hence what is just requires four things at least; the people for whom it is just are two, and the [equal] things that are involved are two.

Equality for the people involved will be the same as for the things involved, since [in a just arrangement] the relation between the people will be the same as the relation between the things involved. For if the people involved are not equal, they will not [justly] receive equal shares; indeed, whenever equals receive unequal shares, or unequals equal shares, in a distribution, that is the source of quarrels and accusations.

This is also clear from considering what fits a person's worth. For everyone agrees that what is just in distribution must fit some sort of worth, but what they call worth is not the same; supporters of democracy say it is free citizenship, some supporters of oligarchy say it is wealth, others good birth, while supporters of aristocracy say it is virtue.

Hence what is just [since it requires equal shares for equal people] is in some way proportionate. For proportion is special to number as a whole, not only to numbers consisting of [abstract] units, since it is equality of ratios and requires at least four terms.

Now divided proportion clearly requires four terms. But so does continuous proportion, since here we use one term as two, and mention it twice. When, e.g., line A is to line B as B is to C, B is mentioned twice; and so if B is introduced twice, the terms in the proportion will be four.

What is just will also require at least four terms, with the same ratio [between the pairs], since the people [A and B] and the items [C and D] involved are divided in the same way. Term C, then, is to term D as A is to B, and, taking them alternately, B is to D as A is to C. Hence there will also be the same relation of whole [A and C] to whole [B and D]; this is the relation in which the distribution pairs them, and it pairs them justly if this is how they are combined.

Hence the combination of term A with C and of B with D is what is just in distribution, and this way of being just is intermediate, while what is unjust is contrary to what is proportionate. For what is proportionate is intermediate, and what is just is proportionate.

This is the sort of proportion that mathematicians call geometrical, since in geometrical proportion the relation of whole to whole is the same as the relation of each [part] to each [part]. But this proportion [involved in justice] is not continuous, since there is no single term for both the person and the item.

What is just, then, is what is proportionate, and what is unjust is what is counterproportionate. Hence [in an unjust action] one term becomes more and the other less; and this is indeed how it turns out in practice, since the one doing injustice has more of the good, and the victim less. With an evil the ratio is reversed, since the lesser evil, compared to the greater, counts as a good; for the lesser evil is more choiceworthy than the greater, what is choiceworthy is good, and what is more choiceworthy is a greater good.

This, then, is the first species of what is just.

Justice in Rectification

The other way of being just is the rectificatory, found in transactions both voluntary and involuntary; and this way of being just belongs to a different species from the first.

For what is just in distribution of common assets will always fit the proportion mentioned above, since distribution from common funds will also fit the ratio to one another of different people's deposits. Similarly, the way of being unjust that is opposed to this way of being just is what is counter-proportionate. On the other hand, what is just in transactions is certainly equal in a way, and what is unjust is unequal; but still it fits numerical proportion, not the [geometrical] proportion of the other species.

For here it does not matter if a decent person has taken from a base person, or a base person from a decent person, or if a decent or a base person has committed adultery. Rather, the law looks only at differences in the harm [inflicted], and treats the people involved as equals, when one does injustice while the other suffers it, and one has done the harm while the other has suffered it. Hence the judge tries to restore this unjust situation to equality, since it is unequal.

For [not only both when one steals from another but also] and when one is wounded and the other wounds him, or one kills and the other is killed, the action and the suffering are unequally divided [with profit for the offender and loss for the victim]; and the judge tries to restore the [profit and] loss to a position of equality, by subtraction from [the offender's] profit. For in such cases, stating it without qualification, we speak of profit for, e.g., the attacker who wounded his victim, even if that is not the proper word for some cases, and of loss for the victim who suffers the wound. At any rate, when what was suffered has been measured, one part is called the [victim's] loss, and the other the [offender's] profit.

In fact, however, these names 'loss' and 'profit' are derived from voluntary exchange. For having more than one's own share is called making a profit, and having less than what one had at the beginning is called suffering a loss, e.g. in buying and selling and in other transactions permitted by law. And when people get neither more nor less, but precisely what belongs to them, they say they have their own share, and make neither a loss nor a profit.

Hence what is equal is intermediate between more and less; profit and loss are more and less in contrary ways, since more good and less evil is profit, and the contrary is loss; and the intermediate area between [profit and loss], we have found, is what is equal, which we say is just. Hence what is just in rectification is what is intermediate between loss and profit.

Hence parties to a dispute resort to a judge, and an appeal to a judge is an appeal to what is just; for the judge is intended to be a sort of living embodiment of what is just. Moreover, they seek the judge as an intermediary, and in some cities they actually call judges mediators, assuming that if they are awarded an intermediate amount, the award will be just. If, then, the judge is an intermediary, what is just is in some way intermediate.

The judge restores equality, as though a line [AB] had been cut into unequal parts [AC and CB], and he removed from the larger part [AC] the amount [DC] by which it exceeds the half [AD] of the line [AB], and added this amount [DC] to the smaller part [CB]. And when the whole [AB] has been halved [into AD and DB], then they say that each person has what is properly his own, when he has got an equal share. This is also why it is called just (*dikaion*), because it is a bisection (*dicha*), as though we said bisected (*dichaion*), and the judge (*dikastes*) is a bisector (*dichastes*).

What is equal [in this case] is intermediate, by numerical proportion, between the larger [AC] and the smaller line [CB]. For when [the same amount] is subtracted from one of two equal things and added to the other, then the one part exceeds the other by the two parts; for if a part had been subtracted from the one, but not added to the other, the larger part would have exceeded the smaller by just one part. Hence the larger part exceeds the intermediate by one part, and the intermediate from which [a part] was subtracted [exceeds the smaller] by one part.

In this way, then, we will recognize what we must subtract from the one who has more and add to the one who has less [to restore equality]; for to the one who has less we must add the amount by which the intermediate exceeds what he has, and from the greatest amount [which the one who has more has] we must subtract the amount by which it exceeds the intermediate. Let lines AA', BB' and CC' be equal; let AE be subtracted from AA' and CD be added to CC', so that the whole line DCC' will exceed the line EA' by the parts CD and CF [where CF equals AE]; it follows that DCC' exceeds BB' by CD.

Hence what is just is intermediate between a certain kind of loss and gain, since it is having the equal amount both before and after [the transaction].

Justice in Exchange

It seems to some people, however, that reciprocity is also unconditionally just. This was the Pythagoreans' view, since their definition stated unconditionally that what is just is reciprocity with another.

The truth is that reciprocity suits neither distributive nor rectificatory justice, though people take even Rhadamanthys' [primitive] conception of justice to describe rectificatory justice: 'If he suffered what he did, upright justice would be done.'[4]

For in many cases reciprocity conflicts [with rectificatory justice]. If, e.g., a ruling official [exercising his office] wounded someone else, he must not be wounded in retaliation, but if someone wounded a ruling official, he must not only be wounded but also receive corrective treatment. Moreover, the voluntary or involuntary character of the action makes a great difference.

In associations for exchange, however, this way of being just, reciprocity that is proportionate rather than equal, holds people together; for a city is maintained by proportionate reciprocity. For people seek to return

4. [According to Greek mythology, Rhadamanthys, a son of Zeus and Europa, was renowned during his life as a just lawgiver and afterwards was appointed one of the three judges of the dead. The quotation has been attributed to Hesiod.]

either evil for evil, since otherwise [their condition] seems to be slavery, or good for good, since otherwise there is no exchange; and they are maintained [in an association] by exchange.

Indeed, that is why they make a temple of the Graces prominent, so that there will be a return of benefits received. For this is what is special to grace; when someone has been gracious to us, we must do a service for him in return, and also ourselves take the lead in being gracious again.

It is diagonal combination that produces proportionate exchange. Let A be a builder, B a shoemaker, C a house, D a shoe. The builder must receive the shoemaker's product from him, and give him the builder's own product in return. If, then, first of all, proportionate equality is found, and, next, reciprocity is also achieved, then the proportionate return will be reached. Otherwise it is not equal, and the exchange will not be maintained, since the product of one may well be superior to the product of the other. These products, then, must be equalized.

This is true of the other crafts also; for they would have been destroyed unless the producer produced the same thing, of the same quantity and quality as the thing affected underwent.

For no association [for exchange] is formed from two doctors. It is formed from a doctor and a farmer, and, in general, from people who are different and unequal and who must be equalized.

This is why all items for exchange must be comparable in some way. Currency came along to do exactly this, and in a way it becomes an intermediate, since it measures everything, and so measures excess and deficiency—how many shoes are equal to a house.

Hence, as builder is to shoemaker, so must the number of shoes be to a house; for if this does not happen, there will be no exchange and no association, and the proportionate equality will not be reached unless they are equal in some way. Everything, then, must be measured by some one measure, as we said before.

In reality, this measure is need, which holds everything together; for if people required nothing, or needed things to different extents, there would be either no exchange or not the same exchange. And currency has become a sort of pledge of need, by convention; in fact it has its name (*nomisma*) because it is not by nature, but by the current law (*nomos*), and it is within our power to alter it and to make it useless.

Reciprocity will be secured, then, when things are equalized, so that the shoemaker's product is to the farmer's as the farmer is to the shoemaker. However, they must be introduced into the figure of proportion not when they have already exchanged and one extreme has both excesses, but when they still have their own; in that way they will be equals and associates, because this sort of equality can be found in them. Let A be a farmer, C food, B a shoemaker and D his product that has been equalized; if this sort of reciprocity were not possible, there would be no association.

Now clearly need holds [an association] together as a single unit, since people with no need of each other, both of them or either one, do not exchange, as they exchange whenever another requires what one has oneself, e.g. wine, when they allow the export of corn. This, then, must be equalized.

If an item is not required at the moment, currency serves to guarantee us a future exchange, guaranteeing that the item will be there for us if we require it; for it must be there for us to take if we pay. Now the same thing happens to currency [as to other goods], and it does not always count for the same; still, it tends to be more stable. Hence everything must have a price; for in that way there will always be exchange, and then there will be association.

Currency, then, by making things commensurate as a measure does, equalizes them; for there would be no association without exchange, no exchange without equality, no equality without commensurability. And so, though things so different cannot become commensurate in reality, they can become commensurate enough in relation to our needs. Hence there must be some single unit fixed [as current] by a stipulation. This is why it is called currency; for this makes everything commensurate, since everything is measured by currency.

Let A, for instance, be a house, B ten minae, C a bed. A is half of B if a house is worth five minae or equal to them; and C, the bed, is a tenth of B. It is clear, then, how many beds are equal to one house—five. This is clearly how exchange was before there was currency; for it does not matter whether a house is exchanged for five beds or for the currency for which five beds are exchanged.

Political Justice

We have previously described, then, the relation of reciprocity to what is just. We must now notice that we are looking not only for what is just unconditionally, but also for what is just in a political association. This is found among associates in a life aiming at self-sufficiency, who are free and either proportionately or numerically equal.

Hence those who lack these features have nothing politically just in their relations, though they have something just in so far as it is similar [to what is politically just].

For what is just is found among those who have law in their relations. Where there is law, there is injustice, since the judicial process is judgement that distinguishes what is just from what is unjust. Where there is injustice there is also doing injustice, though where there is doing injustice there need not also be injustice. And doing injustice is awarding to oneself too many of the things that, [considered] unconditionally, are good, and too few of the things that, [considered] unconditionally, are bad.

This is why we allow only reason, not a human being, to be ruler; for a human being awards himself too many goods and becomes a tyrant, but a ruler is a guardian of what is just and hence of what is equal [and so must not award himself too many goods].

If a ruler is just, he seems to profit nothing by it. For since he does not award himself more of what, [considered] unconditionally, is good if it is not proportionate to him, he seems to labour for another's benefit; that is why justice is said, as we also remarked before, to be another person's good. Hence some payment [for ruling] should be given; this is honour and privilege, and the people who are unsatisfied by these are the ones who become tyrants.

What is just for a master and a father is similar to this, not the same. For there is no unconditional injustice in relation to what is one's own; one's own possession, or one's child until it is old enough and separated, is as though it were a part of oneself, and no one decides to harm himself. Hence there is no injustice in relation to them, and so nothing politically unjust or just either. For we found that what is politically just must conform to law, and apply to those who are naturally suited for law, hence to those who have equality in ruling and being ruled. [Approximation to this equality] explains why relations with a wife more than with children or possessions allow something to count as just—for that is what is just in households; still, this too is different from what is politically just.

One part of what is politically just is natural, and the other part legal. What is natural is what has the same validity everywhere alike, independent of its seeming so or not. What is legal is what originally makes no difference [whether it is done] one way or another, but makes a difference whenever people have laid down the rule—e.g. that a mina is the price of a ransom, or that a goat rather than two sheep should be sacrificed; and also laws passed for particular cases, e.g. that sacrifices should be offered to Brasidas,[5] and enactments by decree.

Now it seems to some people that everything just is merely legal, since what is natural is unchangeable and equally valid everywhere—fire, e.g. burns both here and in Persia—while they see that what is just changes [from city to city].

This is not so, though in a way it is so. With us, though presumably not at all with the gods, there is such a thing as what is natural, but still all is changeable; despite the change there is such a thing as what is natural and what is not.

What sort of thing that [is changeable and hence] admits of being otherwise is natural, and what sort is not natural, but legal and conventional, if both natural and legal are changeable? It is clear in other cases also, and the same distinction [between the natural and the unchangeable] will apply; for the right hand, e.g., is naturally superior, even though it is possible for everyone to become ambidextrous.

The sorts of things that are just by convention and expediency are like measures. For measures for wine and for corn are not of equal size everywhere, but in wholesale markets they are bigger, and in retail smaller. Similarly, the things that are just by human [enactment] and not by nature differ from place to place, since political systems also differ; still, only one system is by nature the best everywhere.

The Relation of Justice to Just Action

We have now said what it is that is unjust and just. And now that we have defined them, it is clear that doing justice is intermediate between doing injustice and suffering injustice, since doing injustice is having too much and suffering injustice is having too little.

Justice is a mean, not as the other virtues are, but because it concerns an intermediate condition, while injustice concerns the extremes. Justice is the virtue that the just person is said to express in the just actions expressing his decision, distributing good things and bad, both between himself and others and between others. He does not award too much of what is choiceworthy to himself and too little to his neighbour (and the reverse with what is harmful), but awards what is proportionately equal; and he does the same in distributing between others.

Injustice, on the other hand, is related [in the same way] to what is

5. [Brasidas, a leading fifth-century B.C. Spartan general, died in battle with the Athenians and was worshipped as a hero.]

unjust. What is unjust is disproportionate excess and deficiency in what is beneficial or harmful; hence injustice is excess and deficiency because it concerns excess and deficiency. The unjust person awards himself an excess of what is beneficial, [considered] unconditionally, and a deficiency of what is harmful, and speaking as a whole, he acts similarly [in distributions between] others, but deviates from proportion in either direction. In an unjust action getting too little good is suffering injustice, and getting too much is doing injustice.

So much, then, for the nature of justice and the nature of injustice, and similarly for what is just and unjust in general.

Since it is possible to do injustice without thereby being unjust, what sort of injustice must someone do to be unjust by having one of the different types of injustice, e.g. as a thief or adulterer or brigand?

But perhaps it is not the type of action that makes the difference [between merely doing injustice and being unjust]. For someone might lie with a woman and know who she is, but the origin might be feeling rather than decision; in that case he is not unjust, though he does injustice—e.g. not a thief, though he stole, not an adulterer though he committed adultery, and so on in the other cases.

Each [type of] just and lawful [action] is related as a universal to the particulars [that embody it]; for the [particular] actions that are done are many, but each [type] is one, since it is universal.

An act of injustice is different from what is unjust, and an act of justice from what is just. For what is unjust is unjust by nature or enactment; and when this has been done, it is an act of injustice, but until then it is only unjust.

The same applies to an act of justice [in contrast to what is just]. Here, however, the general [type of action contrary to an act of injustice] is more usually called a just act, and what is called an act of justice is the [specific type of just act] that rectifies an act of injustice.

Later we must examine each of these actions, to see what sorts of species, and how many, they have, and what they are concerned with.

The Relation of Voluntary Action
to Just Action and to Justice

Given this account of just and unjust actions, someone does injustice or does justice whenever he does them willingly, and does neither justice nor injustice whenever he does them unwillingly, except coincidentally, since the actions he does are coincidentally just or unjust.

Further, an act of injustice and a just act are defined by what is voluntary and what is involuntary. For when the action is voluntary, the agent is blamed, and thereby also it is an act of injustice. Hence something will be injust without thereby being an act of injustice, if it is not also voluntary.

And as I said before, I say that an action is voluntary under these conditions:

(1) It is up to the agent.

(2) He does it in knowledge, and [hence] not in ignorance of the person, instrument and goal, e.g. whom he is striking, with what, and for what goal.

(3) He [does] each of these neither coincidentally nor by force; if, e.g., someone seized your hand and struck another [with it] you [would not have struck the other] willingly, since it was not up to you.

However [the question about knowledge is more complicated. For] it is possible that the victim is your father, and you know he is a human being or a bystander, but do not know he is your father. The same distinction must be made for the goal and for the action as a whole.

Actions are involuntary, then, if they are done in ignorance; or not done in ignorance, but not up to the agent; or done by force. For we also do or undergo many of our natural [actions and processes], e.g. growing old and dying, in knowledge; but none of them is either voluntary or involuntary.

Both unjust and just actions may also be coincidental in the same way. For if someone returned a deposit unwillingly and because of fear, we should say that he neither does anything just nor does justice, except coincidentally. And similarly if someone is under compulsion and unwilling when he fails to return the deposit, we should say that he coincidentally does injustice and does something unjust.

In some of our voluntary actions we act on a previous decision, and in some we act without any; we act on a previous decision when we act on previous deliberation, and without any when we act without previous deliberation.

Among the three ways of inflicting harms in an association, actions done with ignorance are errors if someone does neither the action he supposed, nor to the person, nor with the instrument, nor for the result he supposed. For he thought, e.g., that he was not hitting, or not hitting this person, or not for this result; but coincidentally the result that was achieved was not what he thought (e.g. [he hit him] to graze, not to wound), or the victim or the instrument was not the one he thought.

If the infliction of harm violates reasonable expectation, the action is a misfortune. If it does not violate reasonable expectation, but is done without vice, it is an error. For someone is in error if the origin of the cause is in him, and unfortunate when it is outside.

If he does it in knowledge, but without previous deliberation, it is an act of injustice—e.g. actions caused by emotion and other feelings that are natural or necessary for human beings. For when someone inflicts these harms and commits these errors, he does injustice and these are acts of injustice; but he is not thereby unjust or wicked, since it is not vice that causes him to inflict the harm.

But when his decision is the cause, he is unjust and vicious. Hence it is a sound judgment that actions caused by emotion do not result from forethought [and hence do not result from decision], since the origin is not the agent who acted on the emotion, but the person who provoked him to anger.

Moreover [in these cases] the dispute is not about whether [the action caused by anger] happened or not, but about whether it was just, since anger is a response to apparent injustice.

For they do not dispute about whether it happened or not, as they do in commercial transactions, where one party or the other must be vicious, unless forgetfulness is the cause of the dispute. Rather [in cases of anger] they agree about the fact and dispute about which action was just; but [in commercial transactions] the [cheater] who has plotted against his victim knows very well [that what he is doing is unjust]. Hence [in cases of anger the agent] thinks he is suffering injustice, while [in transactions the cheater] does not think so.

And if [the cheater's] decision causes him to inflict the harm, he does injustice, and in doing *this* sort of act of injustice the agent is unjust, if it violates proportion or equality. In the same way, a person is just if his decision causes him to do justice; but he [merely] does justice if he merely does it voluntarily.

Some involuntary actions are to be pardoned, and some are not. For when someone's error is not only committed in ignorance, but also caused by ignorance, it is to be pardoned. But when it is committed in ignorance, but is caused by some feeling that is neither natural nor human, and not by ignorance, it is not to be pardoned.

Puzzles About Justice and Injustice

If we have adequately defined suffering injustice and doing injustice, some puzzles might be raised.

First of all, are those bizarre words of Euripides correct, where he writes, "'I killed my mother—a short tale to tell.' 'Were both of you willing or both unwilling?''"?[6] For is it really possible to suffer injustice willingly, or is it always involuntary, as doing injustice is always voluntary? And is it always one way or the other, or is it sometimes voluntary and sometimes involuntary?

The same question arises about receiving justice. Since doing justice is always voluntary [as doing injustice is], it is reasonable for the same opposition to apply in both cases, so that both receiving justice and suffering injustice will be either alike voluntary or alike involuntary. Now it seems absurd in the case of receiving justice as well [as in the case of suffering injustice] for it to be always voluntary, since some people receive justice, but not willingly.

We might also raise the following puzzle: Does everyone who has received something unjust suffer injustice, or is it the same with receiving as it is with doing? For certainly it is possible, in the case both of doing and of receiving, to have a share in just things coincidentally; and clearly the same is true of unjust things, since doing something unjust is not the same as doing injustice, and suffering something unjust is not the same as suffering injustice. The same is true of doing justice and receiving it; for it is impossible to suffer injustice if no one does injustice and impossible to receive justice if no one does justice.

Now if doing injustice is simply harming someone willingly (and doing something willingly is doing it with knowledge of the victim, the instrument and the way) with no further conditions; and if the incontinent person harms himself willingly; then he suffers injustice willingly. Hence someone can do injustice to himself; and one of our puzzles was just this, whether someone can do injustice to himself.

Moreover, someone's incontinence might cause him to be willingly harmed by another who is willing, so that it would be possible to suffer injustice willingly.

Perhaps, however, our definition [of doing injustice] was incorrect, and we should add to 'harming with knowledge of the victim, the instrument

6. [The quotation is thought to be from Euripides' lost play *Alcmaeon*.]

and the way', the condition 'against the wish of the victim'. If so, then someone is harmed and suffers something unjust willingly, but no one suffers injustice willingly. For no one wishes it, not even the incontinent, but he acts against his wish; for no one wishes for what he does not think is excellent, and what the incontinent does is not what he thinks it is right [and hence excellent] to do.

And if someone gives away what is his own, as Homer says Glaucus gave to Diomede 'gold for bronze, a hundred cows' worth for nine cows' worth',[7] he does not suffer injustice. For it is up to him to give them, whereas suffering injustice is not up to him, but requires someone to do him injustice.

Clearly, then, suffering injustice is not voluntary.

Two further questions that we decided to discuss still remain: If A distributes to B more than B deserves, is it A, the distributor, or B, who has more, who does injustice? And is it possible to do injustice to oneself?

For if the first alternative is possible, and A rather than B does injustice, then if A knowingly and willingly distributes more to B than to himself, A does injustice to himself. And indeed this is what a moderate person seems to do; for the decent person tends to take less than his share.

Perhaps, however, it is not true without qualification that he takes less. For perhaps he is greedy for some other good, e.g. for reputation or for what is unconditionally fine.

Moreover, our definition of doing injustice allows us to solve the puzzle. For since he suffers nothing against his own wish, he does not suffer injustice, at least not from his distribution, but, at most, is merely harmed.

But it is evidently the distributor who does injustice, and the one who has more does not always do it. For the one who receives an unjust share does not do injustice, but rather the one who willingly does what is unjust, i.e. the one who originates the action; and he is the distributor, not the recipient. Besides, doing is spoken of in many ways, and there is a way in which soulless things, or hands, or servants at someone else's order, kill; the recipient, then, does not do injustice, but does something that is unjust.

Further, if the distributor judged in ignorance, he does not do injustice in violation of what is legally just, and his judgment is not unjust; in a way, though, it is unjust, since what is legally just is different from what is primarily just.

7. [The quotation is from the *Iliad*.]

If, however, he judged unjustly, and did it knowingly, then he himself as well [as the recipient] is greedy—to win gratitude or exact a penalty. So someone who had judged unjustly for these reasons has also got more, exactly as though he got a share of the [profits of] the act of injustice. For if he gave judgment about some land, e.g., on this condition [that he would share the profits], and what he got was not land, but money.

Since human beings think that doing injustice is up to them, they think that being just is also easy, when in fact it is not. For while lying with a neighbour's wife, wounding a neighbour, bribing, are all easy and up to us, being in a certain state when we do them is not easy, and not up to us.

Similarly, people think it takes no wisdom to know the things that are just and unjust, because it is not hard to comprehend what the laws speak of. But these are not the things that are just, except coincidentally. Knowing how actions must be done, and how distributions must be made, if they are to be just, takes more work than it takes to know about healthy things. And even in the case of healthy things, knowing about honey, wine, hellebore, burning and cutting is easy, but knowing how these must be distributed to produce health, and to whom, and when, takes all the work that it takes to be a doctor.

For the same reason they think that doing injustice is no less proper to the just than to the unjust person, because the just person is no less, and even more, able to do each of the actions. For he is able to lie with a woman, and to wound someone; and the brave person, similarly, is able to throw away his shield, and to turn and run this way or that.

In fact, however, doing acts of cowardice or injustice is not doing these actions, except coincidentally; it is being in a certain state when we do them. Similarly, practising medicine or healing is not cutting or not cutting, giving drugs or not giving them, but doing all these things in a certain way.

What is just is found among those who have a share in things that [considered] unconditionally are good, who can have an excess or a deficiency of them. Some (as, presumably, the gods) can have no excess of them; others, the incurably evil, benefit from none of them, but are harmed by them all; others again benefit from these goods up to a point; and this is why what is just is something human.

The next task is to discuss how decency is related to justice and how what is decent is related to what is just.

For on examination they appear as neither unconditionally the same nor as states of different kinds. Sometimes we praise what is decent and the decent person, so that even when we praise someone for other things we transfer the term 'decent' and use it instead of 'good', making it clear that what is more decent is better.

And yet, sometimes, when we reason about the matter, it appears absurd for what is decent to be something beyond what is just, and still praiseworthy. For [apparently] either what is just is not excellent or what is decent is not excellent, if it is something other than what is just, or else, if they are both excellent, they are the same.

These, then, are roughly the claims that raise the puzzle about what is decent; but in fact they are all correct in a way, and none is contrary to any other. For what is decent is better than any way of being just, but it is still just, and not better than what is just by being a different genus. Hence the same thing is just and decent, and while both are excellent, what is decent is superior.

The puzzle arises because what is decent is just, but is not what is legally just, but a rectification of it. The reason is that all law is universal, but in some areas no universal rule can be correct; and so where a universal rule has to be made, but cannot be correct, the law chooses the [universal rule] that is usually [correct], well aware of the error being made. And the law is no less correct on this account; for the source of the error is not the law or the legislator, but the nature of the object itself, since this is what the subject-matter of actions is bound to be like.

Hence whenever the law makes a universal rule, but in this particular case what happens violates the [intended scope of] the universal rule, here the legislator falls short, and has made an error by making an unconditional rule. Then it is correct to rectify the deficiency; this is what the legislator would have said himself if he had been present there, and what he would have prescribed, had he known, in his legislation.

Hence what is decent is just, and better than a certain way of being just—not better than what is unconditionally just, but better than the error resulting from the omission of any condition [in the rule]. And this is the nature of what is decent—rectification of law in so far as the universality of law makes it deficient.

This is also the reason why not everything is guided by law. For on some matters legislation is impossible, and so a decree is needed. For the standard applied to what is indefinite is itself indefinite, as the lead standard is in Lesbian building,[8] where it is not fixed, but adapts itself to the shape of the stone; likewise, a decree is adapted to fit its objects.

---

8. [The reference is to residents of Lesbos, an island off the coast of Asia Minor, where Aristotle once resided.]

It is clear from this what is decent, and clear that it is just, and better than a certain way of being just. It is also evident from this who the decent person is; for he is the one who decides for and does such actions, not an exact stickler for justice in the bad way, but taking less than he might even though he has the law on his side. This is the decent person, and his state is decency; it is a sort of justice, and not some state different from it.

Is it possible to do injustice to oneself or not? The answer is evident from what has been said.

First of all, some just actions are the legal prescriptions expressing each virtue; e.g., we are legally forbidden to kill ourselves. Moreover, if someone illegally and willingly inflicts harm on another, not returning harm for harm, he does injustice (a person acting willingly is one who knows the victim and the instrument). Now if someone murders himself because of anger, he does this willingly, in violation of correct reason, when the law forbids it; hence he does injustice. But injustice to whom? Surely to the city, not to himself, since he suffers it willingly, and no one willingly suffers injustice. That is why the city both penalizes him and inflicts further dishonour on him for destroying himself, on the assumption that he is doing injustice to the city.

Now consider the type of injustice doing which makes the agent only unjust, not base generally. Clearly this type of unjust action is different from the first type. For one type of unjust person is wicked in the same [special] way as the coward is, not by having total wickedness; hence his acts of injustice do not express total wickedness either.

Here also one cannot do injustice to oneself. For if one could, the same person could lose and get the same thing at the same time. But this is impossible; on the contrary, what is just or unjust must always involve more than one person.

Moreover, doing injustice is voluntary, and results from a decision, and strikes first, since a victim who retaliates does not seem to do injustice; but if someone does injustice to himself, he does and suffers the same thing at the same time.

Further, on this view, it would be possible to suffer injustice willingly.

Besides, no one does injustice without doing one of the particular acts of injustice. But no one commits adultery with his own wife, or burgles his own house, or steals his own possessions.

And in general the puzzle about doing injustice to oneself is also solved by the distinction about voluntarily suffering injustice.

Besides, it is evident that both doing and suffering injustice are bad, since one is having more, one having less, than the intermediate amount, in the same way as with what is healthy in medicine and what is fit in gymnastics [both more and less than the intermediate amount are bad]. But doing injustice is worse; for it is blameworthy, involving vice that is either complete and unconditional or close to it (since not all voluntary doing of injustice is combined with [the state of] injustice). Suffering injustice, however, involves no vice or injustice.

In itself, then, suffering injustice is less bad; and though it might still be coincidentally a greater evil, that is no concern of a craft. Rather, the craft says that pleurisy is a worse illness than a stumble, even though a stumble might sometimes coincidentally turn out worse, e.g. if someone stumbled and by coincidence was captured by the enemy or killed because he fell.

It is possible for there to be a justice, by similarity and transference, not of a person to himself, but of certain parts of a person—not every kind of justice, but the kind that belongs to masters or households. For in these discussions the part of the soul that has reason is distinguished from the non-rational part. People look at these and it seems to them that there is injustice to oneself, because in these parts it is possible to suffer something against one's own desire. Hence it is possible for those parts to be just to each other, as it is for ruler and ruled.

So much, then, for our definitions of justice and the other virtues of character.

6

Thomas Aquinas,
"Of Justice,"
from the *Summa Theologica*

Thomas Aquinas (1225–1274), the author of the Summa Theologica, *the great medieval synthesis of reason and faith, was canonized by the Catholic Church in 1323. In 1879, he was posthumously named the official philosopher of the Catholic Church. Although he followed Aristotle in his political philosophy, his view was that the nature of Aristotle's political man was not removed but perfected by the grace of God:* gratia non tollit naturam, sed perfecit.

(In Twelve Articles)

We must now consider justice. Under this head there are twelve points of inquiry: (1) What is justice? (2) Whether justice is always toward another? (3) Whether it is a virtue? (4) Whether it is in the will as its subject? (5) Whether it is a general virtue? (6) Whether, as a general virtue, it is essentially the same as every virtue? (7) Whether there is a particular justice? (8) Whether particular justice has a matter of its own? (9) Whether it is about passions or about operations only? (10) Whether the mean of justice is the real mean? (11) Whether the act of justice is to render to everyone his own? (12) Whether justice is the chief of the moral virtues?

First Article

Whether Justice Is Fittingly Defined as Being the Perpetual and Constant Will to Render to Each One His Right?

We proceed thus to the First Article:

Objection 1. It would seem that lawyers have unfittingly defined justice as being "the perpetual and constant will to render to each one his

From Aquinas, *Summa Theologica*, translated by Fathers of the Dominican Province, Burns, Oates and Washburn.

right."[1] For, according to the Philosopher, justice is a habit which makes a man "capable of doing what is just, and of being just in action and in intention."[2] Now "will" denotes a power or also an act. Therefore, justice is unfittingly defined as being a will.

Obj. 2. Further, rectitude of the will is not the will; else if the will were its own rectitude, it would follow that no will is unrighteous. Yet, according to Anselm, justice is rectitude.[3] Therefore justice is not the will.

Obj. 3. Further, no will is perpetual save God's. If therefore justice is a perpetual will, in God alone will there be justice.

Obj. 4. Further, whatever is perpetual is constant, since it is unchangeable. Therefore it is needless, in defining justice, to say that it is both "perpetual" and "constant."

Obj. 5. Further, it belongs to the sovereign to give each one his right. Therefore, if justice gives each one his right, it follows that it is in none but the sovereign, which is absurd.

Obj. 6. Further, Augustine says that "justice is love serving God alone."[4] Therefore it does not render to each one his right.

I answer that, The aforesaid definition of justice is fitting if understood aright. For since every virtue is a habit which is the principle of a good act, a virtue must needs be defined by means of the good act bearing on the matter proper to that virtue. Now the proper matter of justice consists of those things that belong to our intercourse with other men, as shall be shown further on (A. 2). Hence the act of justice in relation to its proper matter and object is indicated in the words, "Rendering to each one his right," since, as Isidore says, "a man is said to be just because he respects the rights (*ius*) of others."[5]

Now in order that an act bearing upon any matter whatever be virtuous, it requires to be voluntary, stable, and firm, because the Philosopher says that in order for an act to be virtuous it needs first of all to be done "knowingly," secondly to be done "by choice" and "for a due end," thirdly to be done "immovably."[6] Now the first of these is included in the second, since "what is done through ignorance is involuntary."[7] Hence the definition of justice mentions first the "will," in order to show that

1. D. F.: *Digest* i. 1. 10.
2. *Eth.* v. 1.
3. *De verit.* xii.
4. *De mor. Eccl.* xv.
5. *Etym.* x.
6. *Eth.* ii. 4.
7. *Ibid.*, iii. 10.

the act of justice must be voluntary; and mention is made afterwards of its "constancy" and "perpetuity" in order to indicate the firmness of the act.

Accordingly this is a complete definition of justice, save that the act is mentioned instead of the habit which takes its species from that act, because habit implies relation to act. And if anyone would reduce it to the proper form of a definition, he might say that *justice is a habit whereby a man renders to each one his due by a constant and perpetual will*; and this is about the same definition as that given by the Philosopher, who says that "justice is a habit whereby a man is said to be capable of doing just actions in accordance with his choice."[8]

Reply Obj. 1: Will here denotes the act, not the power, and it is customary among writers to define habits by their acts: thus Augustine says that "faith is to believe what one sees not."[9]

Reply Obj. 2. Justice is the same as rectitude, not essentially but causally; for it is a habit which rectifies the deed and the will.

Reply Obj. 3. The will may be called perpetual in two ways. First, on the part of the will's act which endures forever, and thus God's will alone is perpetual. Secondly, on the part of the subject, because, to wit, a man wills to do a certain thing always, and this is a necessary condition of justice. For it does not satisfy the conditions of justice that one wish to observe justice in some particular matter for the time being, because one could scarcely find a man willing to act unjustly in every case; and it is requisite that one should have the will to observe justice at all times and in all cases.

Reply Obj. 4. Since "perpetual" does not imply perpetuity of the act of the will, it is not superfluous to add "constant"; for while the "perpetual will" denotes the purpose of observing justice always, "constant" signifies a firm perseverance in this purpose.

Reply Obj. 5. A judge renders to each one what belongs to him by way of command and direction, because a judge is the "personification of justice," and "the sovereign is its guardian."[10] On the other hand, the subjects render to each one what belongs to him by way of execution.

Reply Obj. 6. Just as love of God includes love of our neighbor, as stated above,[11] so, too, the service of God includes rendering to each one his due.

8. *Ibid.*, v. 5.
9. *Tract. in Ioan.* xl.
10. *Eth.* v. 4.
11. *S.* II–II, Q. 25, A. 1.

Second Article

Whether Justice Is Always Toward Another?

We proceed thus to the Second Article:

Objection 1. It would seem that justice is not always toward another. For the Apostle says that "the justice of God is by faith of Jesus Christ."[12] Now faith does not concern the dealings of one man with another. Neither therefore does justice.

Obj. 2. Further, according to Augustine, "it belongs to justice that man should direct to the service of God his authority over the things that are subject to him."[13] Now the sensitive appetite is subject to man, according to Genesis iv. 7, where it is written: "The lust thereof," viz., of sin, "shall be under thee, and thou shalt have dominion over it." Therefore it belongs to justice to have dominion over one's own appetite, so that justice is toward oneself.

Obj. 3. Further, the justice of God is eternal. But nothing else is coeternal with God. Therefore justice is not essentially toward another.

Obj. 4. Further, man's dealings with himself need to be rectified no less than his dealings with another. Now man's dealings are rectified by justice; according to Proverbs xi. 5, "The justice of the upright shall make his way prosperous." Therefore justice is about our dealings not only with others, but also with ourselves.

On the contrary, Cicero says that "the object of justice is to keep men together in society and mutual intercourse."[14] Now this implies relationship of one man to another. Therefore, justice is concerned only about our dealings with others.

I answer that, As stated above (Q. 57, A. 1), since justice by its name implies equality, it denotes essentially relation to another, for a thing is equal, not to itself, but to another. And forasmuch as it belongs to justice to rectify human acts, as stated above (Q. 57, A. 1; I–II, Q. 93, A. 1), this otherness which justice demands must needs be between beings capable of action. Now actions belong to supposits* and wholes and, properly speaking, not to parts and forms or powers, for we do not say properly that the hand strikes, but a man with his hand, nor that heat makes a thing hot, but fire by heat, although such expressions may be employed meta-

12. Rom. iii. 22.

13. *De mor. Eccl.* xv.

14. *De offic.* i. 7.

* [or subjects, persons.—J.W.]

phorically. Hence, justice, properly speaking, demands a distinction of supposits and consequently is only in one man toward another. Nevertheless in one and the same man we may speak metaphorically of his various principles of action, such as the reason, the irascible, and the concupiscible, as though they were so many agents; so that metaphorically in one and the same man there is said to be justice in so far as the reason commands the irascible and concupiscible and these obey reason, and in general in so far as to each part of man is ascribed what is becoming to it. Hence the Philosopher calls this "metaphorical justice."[15]

Reply Obj. 1. The justice which faith works in us is that whereby the ungodly is justified; it consists in the due co-ordination of the parts of the soul, as stated above (I–II, Q. 93, A. 1) where we were treating of the justification of the ungodly.[16] Now this belongs to metaphorical justice, which may be found even in a man who lives all by himself.

This suffices for the *Reply* to the *Second Objection.*

Reply Obj. 3. God's justice is from eternity in respect of the eternal will and purpose (and it is chiefly in this that justice consists), although it is not eternal as regards its effect, since nothing is coeternal with God.

Reply Obj. 4. Man's dealings with himself are sufficiently rectified by the rectification of the passions by the other moral virtues. But his dealings with others need a special rectification, not only in relation to the agent, but also in relation to the person to whom they are directed. Hence about such dealings there is a special virtue, and this is justice.

Third Article

Whether Justice Is a Virtue?

We proceed thus to the Third Article:

Objection 1. It would seem that justice is not a virtue. For it is written: "When you shall have done all these things that are commanded you, say: 'We are unprofitable servants; we have done that which we ought to do.'"[17] Now it is not unprofitable to do a virtuous deed, for Ambrose says: "We look to a profit that is estimated not by pecuniary gain but by the acquisition of godliness."[18] Therefore to do what one ought to do is not a virtuous deed. And yet it is an act of justice. Therefore justice is not a virtue.

15. *Eth.* v. 2.
16. *S.* I–II, Q. 113, A. 1.
17. Luke xvii. 10.
18. *De offic. min.* ii. 6.

Obj. 2. Further, that which is done of necessity is not meritorious. But to render to a man what belongs to him, as justice requires, is of necessity. Therefore it is not meritorious. Yet it is by virtuous actions that we gain merit. Therefore justice is not a virtue.

Obj. 3. Further, every moral virtue is about matters of action. Now those things which are wrought externally are not things concerning behavior but concerning handicraft, according to the Philosopher.[19] Therefore since it belongs to justice to produce externally a deed that is just in itself, it seems that justice is not a moral virtue.

On the contrary, Gregory says that "the entire structure of good works is built on four virtues,"[20] viz., temperance, prudence, fortitude and justice.

I answer that, A human virtue is one "which renders a human act and man himself good,"[21] and this can be applied to justice. For a man's act is made good through attaining the rule of reason, which is the rule whereby human acts are regulated. Hence, since justice regulates human operations, it is evident that it renders man's operations good; and, as Cicero declares, good men are so called chiefly from their justice, wherefore, as he says again, "the luster of virtue appears above all in justice."[22]

Reply Obj. 1. When a man does what he ought, he brings no gain to the person to whom he does what he ought, but only abstains from doing him a harm. He does, however, profit himself, in so far as he does what he ought spontaneously and readily, and this is to act virtuously. Hence it is written that divine wisdom "teacheth temperance, and prudence, and justice, and fortitude, which are such things as men (i.e. *virtuous men*) can have nothing more profitable in life."[23]

Reply Obj. 2. Necessity is twofold. One arises from *constraint*, and this removes merit, since it runs counter to the will. The other arises from the obligation of a *command* or from the necessity of obtaining an end when, to wit, a man is unable to achieve the end of virtue without doing some particular thing. The latter necessity does not remove merit when a man does voluntarily that which is necessary in this way. It does however exclude the credit of supererogation, according to 1 Corinthians ix. 16, "If I preach the Gospel, it is no glory to me, for a necessity lieth upon me."

19. *Metaph.* ix.
20. *Moral.* ii. 49.
21. D. F.: *Eth.* ii. 6.
22. *De offic.* i. 7.
23. Wis. viii. 7.

Reply Obj. 3. Justice is concerned about external things, not by making them, which pertains to art, but by using them in our dealings with other men.

Fourth Article

Whether Justice Is in the Will as Its Subject?

We proceed thus to the Fourth Article:

Objection 1. It would seem that justice is not in the will as its subject. For justice is sometimes called truth. But truth is not in the will, but in the intellect. Therefore justice is not in the will as its subject.

Obj. 2. Further, justice is about our dealings with others. Now it belongs to the reason to direct one thing in relation to another. Therefore justice is not in the will as its subject but in the reason.

Obj. 3. Further, justice is not an intellectual virtue, since it is not directed to knowledge; wherefore it follows that it is a moral virtue. Now the subject of moral virtue is the faculty which is "rational by participation," viz. the irascible and the concupiscible, as the Philosopher declares.[24] Therefore justice is not in the will as its subject, but in the irascible and concupiscible.

On the contrary, Anselm says that "justice is rectitude of the will observed for its own sake."[25]

I answer that, The subject of a virtue is the power whose act that virtue aims at rectifying. Now justice does not aim at directing an act of the cognitive power, for we are not said to be just through knowing something aright. Hence the subject of justice is not the intellect or reason, which is a cognitive power. But since we are said to be just through doing something aright, and because the proximate principle of action is the appetitive power, justice must needs be in some appetitive power as its subject.

Now the appetite is twofold; namely, the will which is in the reason, and the sensitive appetite which follows on sensitive apprehension, and is divided into the irascible and the concupiscible, as stated in the First Part.[26] Again the act of rendering his due to each man cannot proceed from the sensitive appetite, because sensitive apprehension does not go so far as to be able to consider the relation of one thing to another; but this is

24. *Eth.* i. 13.
25. *De verit.* xii.
26. *S.* I, Q. 81, A. 2.

proper to the reason. Therefore justice cannot be in the irascible or concupiscible as its subject, but only in the will; hence the Philosopher defines justice by an act of the will,[27] as may be seen above (A. 1).

Reply Obj. 1. Since the will is the rational appetite, when the rectitude of the reason which is called truth is imprinted on the will on account of its nighness to the reason, this imprint retains the name of truth; and hence it is that justice sometimes goes by the name of truth.

Reply Obj. 2. The will is borne toward its object consequently on the apprehension of reason; wherefore, since the reason directs one thing in relation to another, the will can will one thing in relation to another, and this belongs to justice.

Reply Obj. 3. Not only the irascible and concupiscible parts are "rational by participation," but the entire "appetitive" faculty, as stated in *Ethics* i. 13, because all appetite is subject to reason. Now the will is contained in the appetitive faculty, wherefore it can be the subject of moral virtue.

Fifth Article

Whether Justice Is a General Virtue?

We proceed thus to the Fifth Article:

Objection 1. It would seem that justice is not a general virtue. For justice is specified with the other virtues, according to Wisdom viii. 7: "She teacheth temperance, and prudence, and justice, and fortitude." Now the "general" is not specified or reckoned together with the species contained under the same "general." Therefore justice is not a general virtue.

Obj. 2. Further, as justice is accounted a cardinal virtue, so are temperance and fortitude. Now neither temperance nor fortitude is reckoned to be a general virtue. Therefore neither should justice in any way be reckoned a general virtue.

Obj. 3. Further, justice is always toward others, as stated above (A. 2). But a sin committed against one's neighbor cannot be a general sin, because it is condivided with sin committed against oneself. Therefore neither is justice a general virtue.

On the contrary, The Philosopher says that "justice is every virtue."[28]

I answer that, Justice, as stated above (A. 2), directs man in his relations with other men. Now this may happen in two ways: first, as regards his relations with individuals; secondly, as regards his relations

27. *Eth.* v. 1.
28. *Ibid.*

with others in general, in so far as a man who serves a community serves all those who are included in that community. Accordingly justice in its proper acceptation can be directed to another in both these senses. Now it is evident that all who are included in a community stand in relation to that community as parts to a whole; while a part, as such, belongs to a whole, so that whatever is the good of a part can be directed to the good of the whole. It follows, therefore, that the good of any virtue, whether such virtue directs man in relation to himself or in relation to certain other individual persons, is referable to the common good to which justice directs; so that all acts of virtue can pertain to justice, in so far as it directs man to the common good. It is in this sense that justice is called a general virtue. And since it belongs to the law to direct to the common good, as stated above (I–II, Q. 90, A. 2), it follows that the justice which is in this way styled general, is called "legal justice," because thereby man is in harmony with the law which directs the acts of all the virtues to the common good.

Reply Obj. 1. Justice is specified or enumerated with the other virtues, not as a general but as a special virtue, as we shall state further on (AA. 7, 12).

Reply Obj. 2. Temperance and fortitude are in the sensitive appetite, viz. in the concupiscible and irascible. Now these powers are appetitive of certain particular goods, even as the senses are cognitive of particulars. On the other hand justice is in the intellective appetite as its subject, which can have the universal good as its object, knowledge whereof belongs to the intellect. Hence justice can be a general virtue rather than temperance or fortitude.

Reply Obj. 3. Things referable to oneself are referable to another, especially in regard to the common good. Wherefore legal justice, in so far as it directs to the common good, may be called a general virtue, and in like manner injustice may be called a general sin; hence it is written that all "sin is iniquity."[29]

Sixth Article

Whether Justice, as a General Virtue, Is Essentially the Same as All Virtue?

We proceed thus to the Sixth Article:

Objection 1. It would seem that justice, as a general virtue, is essentially the same as all virtue. For the Philosopher says that "virtue and legal jus-

---

29. I John iii. 4.

tice are the same as all virtue, but differ in their mode of being."[30] Now things that differ merely in their mode of being or [logically] do not differ essentially. Therefore justice is essentially the same as every virtue.

Obj. 2. Further, every virtue that is not essentially the same as all virtue is a part of virtue. Now the aforesaid justice, according to the Philosopher, "is not a part but the whole of virtue."[31] Therefore the aforesaid justice is essentially the same as all virtue.

Obj. 3. Further, the essence of a virtue does not change through that virtue directing its act to some higher end, even as the habit of temperance remains essentially the same even though its act be directed to a divine good. Now it belongs to legal justice that the acts of all the virtues are directed to a higher end, namely, the common good of the multitude, which transcends the good of one single individual. Therefore it seems that legal justice is essentially all virtue.

Obj. 4. Further, every good of a part can be directed to the good of the whole, so that if it be not thus directed it would seem without use or purpose. But that which is in accordance with virtue cannot be so. Therefore it seems that there can be no act of any virtue that does not belong to general justice, which directs to the common good; and so it seems that general justice is essentially the same as all virtue.

On the contrary, The Philosopher says that "many are able to be virtuous in matters affecting themselves, but are unable to be virtuous in matters relating to others,"[32] and that "the virtue of the good man is not strictly the same as the virtue of the good citizen."[33] Now the virtue of a good citizen is general justice, whereby a man is directed to the common good. Therefore general justice is not the same as virtue in general, and it is possible to have one without the other.

I answer that, A thing is said to be "general" in two ways. First, by "predication": thus "animal" is general in relation to man and horse and the like; and in this sense that which is general must needs be essentially the same as the things in relation to which it is general, for the reason that the genus belongs to the essence of the species and forms part of its definition. Secondly, a thing is said to be general [virtually]: thus a universal cause is general in relation to all its effects—the sun, for instance, in relation to all bodies that are illumined or transmuted by its power; and in

30. *Eth.* v. 1.
31. *Ibid.*
32. *Ibid.*
33. *Pol.* iii. 2.

this sense there is no need for that which is "general" to be essentially the same as those things in relation to which it is general, since cause and effect are not essentially the same. Now it is in the latter sense that, according to what has been said (A. 5), legal justice is said to be a general virtue, inasmuch, to wit, as it directs the acts of the other virtues to its own end, and this is to move all the other virtues by its command; for just as charity may be called a general virtue in so far as it directs the acts of all the virtues to the divine good, so, too, is legal justice in so far as it directs the acts of all the virtues to the common good. Accordingly, just as charity which regards the divine good as its proper object is a special virtue in respect of its essence, so, too, legal justice is a special virtue in respect of its essence in so far as it regards the common good as its proper object. And thus it is in the sovereign principally and by way of a master-craft, while it is secondarily and administratively in his subjects.

However, the name of legal justice can be given to every virtue in so far as every virtue is directed to the common good by the aforesaid legal justice, which though special essentially is nevertheless [virtually general]. Speaking in this way, legal justice is essentially the same as all virtue, but differs therefrom logically; and it is in this sense that the Philosopher speaks.

Wherefore the *Replies* to the *First* and *Second Objections* are manifest.

Reply Obj. 3. This argument again takes legal justice for the virtue commanded by legal justice.

Reply Obj. 4. Every virtue, strictly speaking, directs its act to that virtue's proper end; that it should happen to be directed to a further end either always or sometimes does not belong to that virtue considered strictly, for it needs some higher virtue to direct it to that end. Consequently there must be one supreme virtue essentially distinct from every other virtue, which directs all the virtues to the common good; and this virtue is legal justice.

Seventh Article

Whether There Is a Particular Besides a General Justice?

We proceed thus to the Seventh Article:

Objection 1. It would seem that there is not a particular besides a general justice. For there is nothing superfluous in the virtues, as neither is there in nature. Now general justice directs man sufficiently in all his relations with other men. Therefore there is no need for a particular justice.

Obj. 2. Further, the species of a virtue does not vary according to "one" and "many." But legal justice directs one man to another in matters relating to the multitude, as shown above (AA. 5, 6). Therefore there is not another species of justice directing one man to another in matters relating to the individual.

Obj. 3. Further, between the individual and the general public stands the household community. Consequently, if in addition to general justice there is a particular justice corresponding to the individual, for the same reason there should be a domestic justice directing man to the common good of a household; and yet this is not the case. Therefore neither should there be a particular besides a legal justice.

On the contrary, Chrysostom in his commentary on Matthew v. 6, "Blessed are they that hunger and thirst after justice," says: "By justice He signifies either the general virtue or the particular virtue which is opposed to covetousness."[34]

I answer that, As stated above (A. 6), legal justice is not essentially the same as every virtue, and besides legal justice, which directs man immediately to the common good, there is need for other virtues to direct him immediately in matters relating to particular goods; and these virtues may be relative to himself or to another individual person. Accordingly, just as in addition to legal justice there is a need for particular virtues to direct man in relation to himself, such as temperance and fortitude, so, too, besides legal justice there is need for particular justice to direct man in his relations to other individuals.

Reply Obj. 1. Legal justice does indeed direct man sufficiently in his relations toward others. As regards the common good it does so immediately, but as to the good of the individual, it does so mediately. Wherefore there is need for particular justice to direct a man immediately to the good of another individual.

Reply Obj. 2. The common good of the realm and the particular good of the individual differ not only in respect of the "many" and the "few," but also under a formal [aspect]. For the aspect of the "common" good differs from the aspect of the "individual" good, even as the aspect of "whole" differs from that of "part." Wherefore the Philosopher says that "they are wrong who maintain that the State and the home and the like differ only as many and few and not specifically."[35]

Reply Obj. 3. The household community, according to the Philoso-

34. *Hom. in Matth.* xxv.
35. *Pol.* i. 1.

pher, differs in respect of a threefold fellowship; namely, "of husband and wife, father and son, master and slave,"[36] in each of which one person is, as it were, part of the other. Wherefore between such persons there is not justice simply, but a species of justice, viz. "domestic" justice, as stated in *Ethics* v. 6.

Eighth Article

Whether Particular Justice Has a Special Matter?

We proceed thus to the Eighth Article:

Objection 1. It would seem that particular justice has no special matter. Because a gloss on Genesis ii. 14, "The fourth river is Euphrates," says: "Euphrates signifies 'fruitful'; nor is it stated through what country it flows, because justice pertains to all the parts of the soul." Now this would not be the case if justice had a special matter, since every special matter belongs to a special power. Therefore particular justice has no special matter.

Obj. 2. Further, Augustine says that "the soul has four virtues whereby, in this life, it lives spiritually, viz. temperance, prudence, fortitude and justice"; and he says that "the fourth is justice, which pervades all the virtues."[37] Therefore particular justice, which is one of the four cardinal virtues, has no special matter.

Obj. 3. Further, justice directs man sufficiently in matters relating to others. Now a man can be directed to others in all matters relating to this life. Therefore the matter of justice is general and not special.

On the contrary, The Philosopher reckons particular justice to be specially about those things which belong to social life.[38]

I answer that, Whatever can be rectified by reason is the matter of moral virtue, for this is defined in reference to right reason, according to the Philosopher.[39] Now the reason can rectify not only the internal passions of the soul, but also external actions, and also those external things of which man can make use. And yet it is in respect of external actions and external things by means of which men can communicate with one another that the relation of one man to another is to be considered;

36. *Ibid.*, 2.
37. *Qq*, qu. 61.
38. *Eth.* v. 2.
39. *Ibid.*, ii. 6.

whereas it is in respect of internal passions that we consider man's rectitude in himself. Consequently, since justice is directed to others, it is not about the entire matter of moral virtue, but only about external actions and things, under a certain special aspect of the object, in so far as one man is related to another through them.

Reply Obj. 1. It is true that justice belongs essentially to one part of the soul, where it resides as in its subject; and this is the will which moves by its command all the other parts of the soul; and, accordingly, justice belongs to all the parts of the soul, not directly but by a kind of diffusion.

Reply Obj. 2. As stated above,[40] the cardinal virtues may be taken in two ways: first, as special virtues, each having a determinate matter; secondly, as certain general modes of virtue. In this latter sense Augustine speaks in the passage quoted; for he says that "prudence is knowledge of what we should seek and avoid, temperance is the curb on the lust for fleeting pleasures, fortitude is strength of mind in bearing with passing trials, justice is the love of God and our neighbor which pervades the other virtues, that is to say, is the common principle of the entire order between one man and another."

Reply Obj. 3. A man's internal passions which are a part of moral matter are not in themselves directed to another man, which belongs to the specific nature of justice; yet their effects, i.e., external actions, are capable of being directed to another man. Consequently it does not follow that the matter of justice is general.

Ninth Article

Whether Justice Is About the Passions

We proceed thus to the Ninth Article:

Objection 1. It would seem that justice is about the passions. For the Philosopher says that "moral virtue is about pleasure and pain."[41] Now pleasure or delight, and pain are passions, as stated above[42] when we were treating of the passions. Therefore justice, being a moral virtue, is about the passions.

Obj. 2. Further, justice is the means of rectifying a man's operations in relation to another man. Now suchlike operations cannot be rectified un-

40. *S.* I–II, Q. 61, Aa. 3, 4.
41. *Eth.* ii. 3.
42. D. F.: *S.* I–II, Q. 23, A. 4; Q. 31, A. 1; Q. 35, A. 1.

less the passions be rectified, because it is owing to disorder of the passions that there is disorder in the aforesaid operations; thus sexual lust leads to adultery, and overmuch love of money leads to theft. Therefore justice must needs be about the passions.

Obj. 3. Further, even as particular justice is toward another person, so is legal justice. Now legal justice is about the passions, else it would not extend to all the virtues, some of which are evidently about the passions. Therefore justice is about the passions.

On the contrary, The Philosopher says that justice is about operations.[43]

I answer that, The true answer to this question may be gathered from a twofold source. First from the subject of justice, i.e. from the will, whose movements or acts are not passions, as stated above,[44] for it is only the sensitive appetite whose movements are called passions. Hence justice is not about the passions, as are temperance and fortitude, which are in the irascible and concupiscible parts. Secondly, on the part of the matter, because justice is about a man's relations with another, and we are not directed immediately to another by the internal passions. Therefore justice is not about the passions.

Reply Obj. 1. Not every moral virtue is about pleasure and pain as its proper matter, since fortitude is about fear and daring; but every moral virtue is directed to pleasure and pain, as to ends to be acquired, for, as the Philosopher says, "pleasure and pain are the principal end in respect of which we say that this is an evil and that a good,"[45] and in this way, too, they belong to justice, since "a man is not just unless he rejoice in just actions."[46]

Reply Obj. 2. External operations are, as it were, between external things which are their matter and internal passions which are their origin. Now it happens sometimes that there is a defect in one of these, without there being a defect in the other. Thus a man may steal another's property, not through the desire to have the thing, but through the will to hurt the man; or vice versa, a man may covet another's property without wishing to steal it. Accordingly, the directing of operations in so far as they tend toward external things belongs to justice, but in so far as they arise from the passions it belongs to the other moral virtues which are about the passions. Hence justice hinders theft of another's property in so far as

43. *Eth.* v. 1.
44. *S.* I–II, Q. 22, A. 3; Q. 59, A. 4.
45. *Eth.* vii. 2.
46. *Ibid.*, i. 8.

stealing is contrary to the equality that should be maintained in external things, while liberality hinders it as resulting from an immoderate desire for wealth. Since, however, external operations take their species, not from the internal passions, but from external things as being their objects, it follows that external operations are essentially the matter of justice rather than of the other moral virtues.

Reply Obj. 3. The common good is the end of each individual member of a community, just as the good of the whole is the end of each part. On the other hand the good of one individual is not the end of another individual; wherefore legal justice which is directed to the common good is more capable of extending to the internal passions whereby man is disposed in some way or other in himself, than particular justice which is directed to the good of another individual; although legal justice extends chiefly to other virtues in the point of their external operations, in so far, to wit, as "the law commands us to perform the actions of a courageous person . . . the actions of a temperate person . . . and the actions of a gentle person."[47]

Tenth Article

Whether the Mean of Justice is the Real Mean?

We proceed thus to the Tenth Article:

Objection 1. It would seem that the mean of justice is not the real mean. For the generic nature remains entire in each species. Now moral virtue is defined[48] to be *an elective habit which observes the mean fixed, in our regard, by reason.* Therefore justice observes the rational and not the real mean.

Obj. 2. Further, in things that are good simply, there is neither excess nor defect, and consequently neither is there a mean, as is clearly the case with the virtues, according to *Ethics* ii. 6. Now justice is about things that are good simply, as stated in *Ethics* v. Therefore justice does not observe the real mean.

Obj. 3. Further, the reason why the other virtues are said to observe the rational and not the real mean is because in their case the mean varies according to different persons, since what is too much for one is too

47. *Ibid.*, v. 5.
48. *Ibid.*, ii. 6.

little for another.[49] Now this is also the case in justice; for one who strikes a prince does not receive the same punishment as one who strikes a private individual. Therefore justice also observes, not the real, but the rational mean.

On the contrary, The Philosopher says that the mean of justice is to be taken according to "arithmetical" proportion,[50] so that it is the real mean.

I answer that, As stated above (A. 9; I–II, Q. 59, A. 4), the other moral virtues are chiefly concerned with the passions, the regulation of which is gauged entirely by a comparison with the very man who is the subject of those passions, in so far as his anger and desire are vested with their various due circumstances. Hence the mean in suchlike virtues is measured not by the proportion of one thing to another, but merely by comparison with the virtuous man himself, so that with them the mean is only that which is fixed by reason in our regard.

On the other hand, the matter of justice is external operation in so far as an operation or the thing used in that operation is duly proportionate to another person; wherefore the mean of justice consists in a certain proportion of equality between the external thing and the external person. Now equality is the real mean between greater and less, as stated in *Metaphysics* x;[51] wherefore justice observes the real mean.

Reply Obj. 1. This real mean is also the rational mean, wherefore justice satisfies the conditions of a moral virtue.

Reply Obj. 2. We may speak of a thing being good simply in two ways. First, a thing may be good in every way: thus the virtues are good, and there is neither mean nor extremes in things that are good simply in this sense. Secondly, a thing is said to be good simply through being good absolutely, i.e. in its nature, although it may become evil through being abused. Such are riches and honors; and in the like it is possible to find excess, deficiency, and mean, as regards men who can use them well or ill; and it is in this sense that justice is about things that are good simply.

Reply Obj. 3. The injury inflicted bears a different proportion to a prince from that which it bears to a private person; wherefore each injury requires to be equalized by vengeance in a different way, and this implies a real and not merely a rational diversity.

49. *Ibid.*
50. *Ibid.*, ii. 6; v. 4.
51. D. F.: Didot ed., ix. 5. Cf. *Eth*. v. 4.

Eleventh Article

Whether the Act of Justice Is to Render to Each One His Own?

We proceed thus to the Eleventh Article:

Objection 1. It would seem that the act of justice is not to render to each one his own. For Augustine ascribes to justice the act of succoring the needy.[52] Now in succoring the needy we give them what is not theirs but ours. Therefore the act of justice does not consist in rendering to each one his own.

Obj. 2. Further, Cicero says that "beneficence, which we may call kindness or liberality, belongs to justice."[53] Now it pertains to liberality to give to another of one's own, not of what is his. Therefore the act of justice does not consist in rendering to each one his own.

Obj. 3. Further, it belongs to justice not only to distribute things duly, but also to repress injurious actions, such as murder, adultery, and so forth. But the rendering to each one of what is his seems to belong solely to the distribution of things. Therefore the act of justice is not sufficiently described by saying that it consists in rendering to each one his own.

On the contrary, Ambrose says: "It is justice that renders to each one what is his, and claims not another's property; it disregards its own profit in order to preserve the common equity."[54]

I answer that, As stated above (AA. 8, 10), the matter of justice is an external operation in so far as either it or the thing we use by it is made proportionate to some other person to whom we are related by justice. Now each man's own is that which is due to him according to equality of proportion. Therefore the proper act of justice is nothing else than to render to each one his own.

Reply Obj. 1. Since justice is a cardinal virtue, other secondary virtues, such as mercy, liberality, and the like, are connected with it, as we shall state further on.[55] Wherefore to succor the needy, which belongs to mercy or pity, and to be liberally beneficent, which pertains to liberality, are by a kind of reduction ascribed to justice as to their principal virtue.

This suffices for the *Reply* to the *Second Objection*.

Reply Obj. 3. As the Philosopher states, in matters of justice the name

52. *De Trin.* xiv. 9.
53. *De offic.* i. 7.
54. *De offic. min.* i. 24.
55. *S.* II–II, Q. 80, A. I.

of "profit" is extended to whatever is excessive, and whatever is deficient is called "loss."[56] The reason for this is that justice is first of all and more commonly exercised in voluntary interchanges of things, such as buying and selling, wherein those expressions are properly employed; and yet they are transferred to all other matters of justice. The same applies to the rendering to each one of what is his own.

Twelfth Article

Whether Justice Stands Foremost Among All Moral Virtues?

We proceed thus to the Twelfth Article:

Objection 1. It would seem that justice does not stand foremost among all the moral virtues. Because it belongs to justice to render to each one what is his, whereas it belongs to liberality to give of one's own, and this is more virtuous. Therefore liberality is a greater virtue than justice.

Obj. 2. Further, nothing is adorned by a less excellent thing than itself. Now magnanimity is the ornament both of justice and of all the virtues, according to *Ethics* iv. 3. Therefore magnanimity is more excellent than justice.

Obj. 3. Further, virtue is about that which is "difficult" and "good," as stated in *Ethics* ii. 3. But fortitude is about more difficult things than justice is, since it is about dangers of death, according to *Ethics* iii. 6. Therefore fortitude is more excellent than justice.

On the contrary, Cicero says: "Justice is the most resplendent of the virtues and gives its name to a good man."[57]

I answer that, If we speak of legal justice, it is evident that it stands foremost among all the moral virtues, for as much as the common good transcends the individual good of one person. In this sense the Philosopher declares that "the most excellent of the virtues would seem to be justice, and more glorious than either the evening or the morning star."[58] But even if we speak of particular justice, it excels the other moral virtues for two reasons. The first reason may be taken from the subject, because justice is in the more excellent part of the soul, viz. the rational appetite or will, whereas the other moral virtues are in the sensitive appetite, whereunto appertain the passions which are the matter of the other moral virtues.

56. *Eth.* v. 4.
57. *De offic.* i. 7.
58. *Eth.* v. 1.

The second reason is taken from the object, because the other virtues are commendable in respect of the sole good of the virtuous person himself, whereas justice is praiseworthy in respect of the virtuous person being well disposed toward another, so that justice is somewhat the good of another person, as stated in *Ethics* v. 1. Hence the Philosopher says: "The greatest virtues must needs be those which are most profitable to other persons, because virtue is a faculty of doing good to others. For this reason the greatest honors are accorded the brave and the just, since bravery is useful to others in warfare, and justice is useful to others both in warfare and in time of peace."[59]

Reply Obj. 1. Although the liberal man gives of his own, yet he does so in so far as he takes into consideration the good of his own virtue, while the just man gives to another what is his, through consideration of the common good. Moreover justice is observed toward all, whereas liberality cannot extend to all. Again liberality which gives of a man's own is based on justice, whereby one renders to each man what is his.

Reply Obj. 2. When magnanimity is added to justice it increases the latter's goodness; and yet without justice it would not even be a virtue.

Reply Obj. 3. Although fortitude is about the most difficult things, it is not about the best, for it is only useful in warfare, whereas justice is useful both in war and in peace, as stated above.

59. *Rhet.* i. 9.

7

G. W. Leibniz,
"Reflections on the Common
Concept of Justice,"
from *Philosophical Papers and Letters*

According to Bertrand Russell, the seventeenth-century philosopher Leibniz (1646–1716) "was one of the supreme intellects of all time." Leibniz made numerous contributions to the fields of mathematics, physics, and metaphysics. These discoveries include calculus, modular arithmetic, the concepts of the kinetic energy and the preestablished harmony. In Leibniz's often-repeated formulation:

Wisdom is the science of happiness.

Virtue is the habit of acting in accord with wisdom.

Justice is the charity of the wise man, i.e., that which is congruent with the will of the good and prudent man.

It is generally agreed that whatever God wills is good and just. But there remains the question whether it is good and just because God wills it or whether God wills it because it is good and just; in other words, whether justice and goodness are arbitrary or whether they belong to the necessary and eternal truths about the nature of things, as do numbers and proportions. The former opinion has been held by certain philosophers and by theologians, both Roman and Reformed. But the Reformed theologians of today usually reject this teaching, as do also all our own theologians and most of those of the Roman church as well.

As a matter of fact it would destroy the justice of God. For why praise him for acting justly if the concept of justice adds nothing to his act? And to say, *Stat pro ratione voluntas*—'Let my will stand for the reason'— is definitely the motto of a tyrant. Moreover, this opinion would hardly distinguish God from the devil. For if the devil, that is, an intelligent,

From G. W. Leibniz, *Philosophical Papers and Letters*, translated by Leroy E. Loemker, 1956. Reprinted by permission of Kluwer Academic Publishers.

Bracketed footnotes are those of Loemker.

invisible power who is very great and very evil, were the master of the world, this devil or this god would still be evil even if we were forced to honor him, just as certain people honor imaginary gods of this kind in the hope of bringing them to do less evil. Consequently, some people, overly devoted to the absolute right of God, have believed that he could justly condemn innocent people and even that this may actually happen. This does violence to those attributes which make God love-worthy and destroys our love for God, leaving only fear. Those who believe, for example, that infants who die without baptism are cast into the eternal flames must in effect have a very weak idea of the goodness and the justice of God and thus thoughtlessly injure what is most essential to religion.

The Sacred Scriptures also give us an entirely different idea of this sovereign substance, speaking, as they so often and so clearly do, of the goodness of God and presenting him as a person who justifies himself against complaints. In the story of the creation of the world, the Scripture says that God considered all that he had done and found it good; that is, he was content with his work and had reason to be so. This is a human way of speaking which seems to be used explicitly to point out that the goodness of the acts and products of God does not depend on his will but on their nature. Otherwise he would only have to see what he willed and did to determine if it is good and to justify himself to himself as a wise sovereign. All our theologians, therefore, and most of those of the Roman church, as well as the ancient Church Fathers and the wisest and most esteemed philosophers, have favored the second view, which holds that goodness and justice have grounds independent of will and of force.

In his dialogues Plato introduces and refutes a certain Thrasymachus who tried to explain what justice is by a definition which, if acceptable, would strongly support the view which we are opposing.[1] That is just, he says, which suits or pleases the most powerful. If this were true, the sentence of a sovereign court or a supreme judge would never be unjust, nor would an evil but powerful man ever deserve condemnation. What is more, the same action could be just and unjust depending on the judges who decide, which is ridiculous. It is one thing to *be* just, another to *pass* for just and to take the place of justice.

A celebrated English philosopher named Hobbes, who has a reputation for his paradoxes, has tried to maintain almost the same thing as

1. [*Republic* 338c ff. Note the change in Leibniz's opinion since 1666, when he applied Hobbes' theory of justice to God.]

Thrasymachus.[2] He holds that God has the right to do anything because he is all-powerful. This fails to distinguish between *right* and *fact*. For what *can* be is one thing; what *ought* to be is another. This same Hobbes believes, for almost the same reason, that the true religion is that of the state.[3] It would follow that if the emperor Claudius, who decreed in an edict that "in libera re publica crepitus atque ructus liberos esse debere,"[4] had established the god Crepitus among the authorized gods, he would have been a true god worthy of worship.

This amounts to saying, in concealed terms, that there is no true religion and that religion is merely an invention of men. And in the same vein, the remark that justice is that which pleases the most powerful is nothing but saying that there is no certain and determined rule of justice which prevents our doing what we wish to do and can do with impunity, however evil it may be. Thus treason, assassination, poisoning, the torture of innocents, would all be just if they succeeded. This is essentially to change the meaning of terms and to speak a language different from that of other men. Until now we have meant by justice something different from that which always prevails. We have believed that a happy man can be evil and that an unpunished act can nevertheless be unjust, that is, it may deserve punishment, so that the issue is solely to know why it deserves punishment, without raising the question of whether the punishment will actually follow or not, or whether there is any judge to impose it.

There were once two tyrants in Sicily named Denis, father and son. The father was more evil than the son. He had established his tyranny by destroying many honorable men. His son was less cruel but more addicted to disorders and luxuries. The father was happy and kept himself in power; the son was overthrown and finally made himself schoolmaster at Corinth in order to have the pleasure of ruling always and of carrying a scepter, after a fashion at least, by wielding the switches used in punishing the children. Should we say that the actions of the father were more just than those of the son because he was happy and unpunished? Would such a view permit history to condemn a happy tyrant? We see too, every day, that men, whether interested or disinterested, complain of the actions of certain powerful people and find them unjust. So the question is only

2. *De cive* xv. 5.

3. *Ibid*, 16.

4. ["In a free state the passing of wind and belching should be free." The ruling of Claudius is reported by Suetonius, chap. 32.]

whether they have reason to complain and whether history can justly blame the inclinations and acts of any prince. If this be granted, we must acknowledge that men mean something else by justice and right than that which pleases a powerful being who remains unpunished because there is no judge capable of mending matters.

In the universe as a whole, or in the government of the world, it is fortunately true that he who is the most powerful is at the same time just and does nothing against which anyone has a right to complain. We must hold for certain that if we understood that universal order, we should find it impossible to do anything better than he has done it. Yet his power is not the formal reason which makes him just. Otherwise, if power were the formal reason for justice, all powerful beings would be just, each in proportion to his power, which is contrary to experience.

We must therefore search after this formal reason, that is, the 'wherefore' of this attribute or the concept which should teach us what justice is and what men mean when they call an act just or unjust. And this formal reason must be common to God and man. Otherwise we should be wrong in seeking to ascribe the same attribute to both without equivocation. These are fundamental rules for reasoning and discourse.

I grant that there is a great difference between the way in which men are just and the way in which God is just, but this difference is only one of degree. For God is perfectly and entirely just, while the justice of men is mixed with injustice, with faults and sins, because of the imperfection of human nature. The perfections of God are infinite; ours are limited. Anyone, therefore, who tries to maintain that the justice and goodness of God have entirely different rules from those of men must at the same time admit that two entirely different concepts are involved and that to ascribe justice to both is either deliberate equivocation or gross self-deceit. But if we choose one of the two concepts as the proper conception of justice, it must follow either that there is no true justice in God or that there is none in man, or perhaps that there is none in either God or man, so that in the end we do not know what we are talking about when we speak of justice. This would in effect destroy justice and leave nothing but the name, as do those who make it arbitrary and dependent on the whim of a judge or ruler, since the same act will appear just and unjust to different judges.

This is somewhat as if we should try to maintain that our science—for example, arithmetic, or the science of numbers—does not agree with the science of God or the angels, or perhaps that all truth is arbitrary and based on a whim. For example, 1, 4, 9, 16, 25, etc., are square numbers produced by multiplying 1, 2, 3, 4, 5, etc., by themselves. Thus 1 times 1 is 1; 2 times 2 is 4; 3 times 3 is 9, etc. We discover that the successive odd numbers are the differences between successive square numbers. Thus the difference between 1 and 4 is 3, that between 4 and 9 is 5, between 9 and 16 is 7, etc. . . . Now would one have any reason to maintain that this is not true for God and the angels and that they see or discover something in numbers entirely contrary to what we find in them? Would we not be right in laughing at a man who maintained this and who did not know the difference between eternal and necessary truths, which must be the same for all, and truths that are contingent and changeable or arbitrary?

This same thing is true about justice. If it is a fixed term with determinate meaning—in a word, if it is not a simple sound without sense, like *blitiri*—the term or word *justice* will have some definition or intelligible meaning. And, by using the incontestable rules of logic, one can draw definite consequences from every definition. This is precisely what we do in building the necessary and demonstrative sciences which do not depend at all on facts but solely on reason; such are logic, metaphysics, arithmetic, geometry, the science of motion and the science of Right [*droit*] as well, which are not at all based on experience or facts but serve rather to give reasons for facts and to control them in advance. This would be true in regard to Right, even if there were no law [*loi*] in the world.[5] The error of those who have made justice depend upon power comes in part from their confusion of *Right* with *law*. Right cannot be unjust; this would be a contradiction. But law can be, for it is power which gives and maintains law; and if this power lacks wisdom or good will, it can give and maintain very bad laws. But happily for the world, the laws of God are always just, and he is in a position to maintain them, as he without a doubt does, even though this has not always happened visibly and at once—for which he assuredly has good reasons.

We must determine, then, the formal principle of justice and the measure by which we should judge acts to know if they are just or unjust. After what has been said we can already foresee what this must be. Justice is nothing but what conforms to wisdom and goodness combined. The end of goodness [*bonté*] is the greatest good [*bien*]. But to recognize this we need wisdom, which is merely the knowledge of the good, as goodness is merely the inclination to do good to all and to prevent evil, at least if evil is not necessary for a greater good or to prevent a greater evil. Thus wisdom is in the understanding, and goodness is in the will, and as a result justice is in both. Power is another matter. But if power is added, it brings

5. [This reaffirms the position taken in the Mainz period around 1670.]

to pass the Right and causes that which should be to exist really as well, insofar as the nature of things permits. And this is what God does in the world.

But since justice aims at the good, and wisdom and goodness together form justice and so refer to the good, we may ask what is the true good. I reply that it is merely whatever serves the perfection of intelligent substances. It is obvious, therefore, that order, contentment, joy, wisdom, goodness, and virtue are goods in an essential sense and can never be bad and that power is a good in a natural sense, that is, by itself, because, other things being equal, it is better to have it than not to have it. But power does not become an assured good until it is joined with wisdom and goodness. For the power of an evil man serves only sooner or later to plunge him further into misery, since it gives him the means of doing more evil and of earning a greater punishment, from which he will not escape, since the universe has a perfectly just monarch whose infinite penetration and sovereign power one cannot avoid.

Since experience shows us that God, for reasons unknown to us but surely very wise and based on a greater good, permits many evil persons to be happy in this life and many good persons to be unhappy, a fact which would not conform to the rules of a perfect government such as God's if it had not been corrected, it follows necessarily that there will be another life and that souls will not perish with the visible bodies. Otherwise there would be crimes unpunished and good deeds unrewarded, which is contrary to order.

There are demonstrative proofs, besides, of the immortality of the soul, for the principle of action and of consciousness could not derive from a purely passive extended thing indifferent to all motion, as is matter. Therefore action and consciousness must necessarily come from something simple or immaterial, without extension and without parts, which is called the soul. But whatever is simple and without parts is not subject to dissolution and as a result, cannot be destroyed. There are people who imagine that we are too small a thing in the sight of an infinite God for him to be concerned about us. It is thought that we are to God as are the worms which we crush without thinking, in relation to us. But this is to imagine that God is like man and that he cannot think of everything. God, according to this reasoning, being infinite, does things without work in a way that results from his will, just as it results from my will and that of my friend that we are in accord, without needing some action to produce the accord after our resolutions are made. But if mankind, or even the smallest thing, were not well governed, the whole universe would not be well governed, for the whole consists of its parts.

We also find order and wonders in the smallest whole things when we are capable of distinguishing their parts and at the same time of seeing the whole, as we do in looking at insects and other small things in the microscope. There are thus the strongest reasons for holding that the same craftsmanship and harmony would be found in great things if we were capable of seeing them as a whole. Above all, they would be found in the whole economy of the government of spirits, which are the substances most similar to God because they are themselves capable of recognizing and inventing order and craftsmanship. As a result we must conclude that the Author of things who is so inclined to order will be concerned for those creatures who are naturally sources of order in the measure of their perfection and who are alone capable of imitating his workmanship. But it is impossible that this should seem so to us, in this small portion of life which we live here below, which is but a small bit of the life without bounds which no spirit can fail to achieve. To consider this bit separately is to consider things like a broken stick or like the bits of flesh of an animal taken separately, so that the craftsmanship of its organs cannot be made apparent.

This is also true when one looks at the brain, which must undoubtedly be one of the greatest wonders of nature, since it contains the most immediate organs of sense. Yet one finds there only a confused mass in which nothing unusual appears but which nevertheless conceals some kind of filaments of a fineness much greater than that of a spider's web which are thought to be the vessels for that very subtle fluid called the animal spirits. Thus this mass of brain contains a very great multitude of passages—and of passages too small for us to overcome the labyrinth with our eyes, whatever microscope we may use. For the subtlety of the spirits contained in these passages is equal to that of light rays themselves. Yet our eyes and our sense of touch show us nothing extraordinary in the appearance of the brain.

We may say that it is the same in the government of intelligent substances under the kingship of God, in which everything seems confused to our eyes. Nevertheless, it must be the most beautiful and most marvelous arrangement of the world, since it comes from an Author who is the source of all perfection. But it is too great and too beautiful for spirits with our present range to be able to perceive it so soon. To try to see it here is like wishing to take a novel by the tail and to claim to have deciphered the plot from the first book; the beauty of a novel, instead, is great in the degree that order emerges from very great apparent confusion. The composition would thus contain a fault if the reader could divine the entire issue at once. But what is only suspense [*curiosité*] and beauty in novels, which imitate creation, so to speak, is also utility and wisdom in this great and true poem, this word-by-word creation, the universe. The beauty and justice of the divine government have been hidden in part from our eyes, not only because it could not be otherwise without changing the entire harmony of the world, but also because it is proper in order that there may be more exercise of free virtue, wisdom, and a love of God which is not mercenary, since the rewards and punishments are still outwardly invisible and appear only to the eyes of our reason or faith. This I find to be a good thing here, since the true faith is based on reason. And since the wonders of nature show us that God's operations are admirably beautiful whenever we can envisage a whole in its setting, even though this beauty is not apparent when we consider things detached or torn from their whole, we must likewise conclude that all that we cannot yet disentangle or envisage as a whole with all its parts must no less have justice and beauty. To recognize this point is to have a natural foundation for faith, hope, and the love of God, since these virtues are based on a knowledge of the divine perfections.

Now nothing better corroborates the incomparable wisdom of God than the structure of the works of nature, particularly the structure which appears when we study them more closely with a microscope. It is for this reason, as well as because of the great light which could be thrown upon bodies for the use of medicine, food, and mechanical ends, that it should be most necessary to push our knowledge further with the aid of microscopes. There are scarcely ten men in the world who are carefully at work on this, and if there were a hundred thousand, there would not be too many to discover the important wonders of this new world which makes up the interior of ours and which is capable of making our knowledge a hundred thousand times greater than it is. It is for this reason that I have more than once hoped that the great princes might be led to arrange for this and to induce men to work at it. Observatories have been founded for watching the stars, whose structures are spectacular and demand great apparatus, but telescopes are far from being as useful and from revealing the beauties and varieties of knowledge which microscopes reveal. A man in Delft has accomplished wonders at it, and if there were many others like him, our knowledge of physics would be advanced far beyond its present state. It behooves great princes to arrange this for the public welfare, in which they are most interested. And since this matter involves little cost and display, is very easy to direct, and needs very little but good will and attention to accomplish it, there is little reason to neglect it. As for me I have no other motive in recommending this research than to advance our knowledge of truth and the public good, which is strongly interested in the increase of the treasure of human knowledge.

Most of the questions of Right, but especially of the right of sovereigns and nations, are confused because they do not agree on a *common conception of justice*, with the result that we do not understand the same thing by the same word, and this opens the way to endless dispute. Everyone would agree, perhaps, on this nominal definition—that justice is a constant will to act in such a way that no person has reason to complain of us. But this is not enough unless the method is given for determining these reasons. Now I observe that some people restrict the reasons for human complaints very narrowly and that others extend them. There are those who believe that it is enough if no harm is done to them and if no one has deprived them of their possessions, holding that no one is obligated to seek the good of others or prevent evil for them, even if it should cost us nothing and give us no pain. Many who pass in the world for great judges keep themselves within these limits. They content themselves with harming no one, but they are not inclined to improve people's conditions. In a word, they believe one can be just without being charitable.

There are others in the world who have greater and more beautiful views and who would not wish anyone to complain of their lack of goodness. They would approve what I have said in my preface to the *Codex juris gentium*—that justice is the charity of the wise man, that is, a goodness toward others which ought to conform to wisdom. And wisdom, in my opinion, is nothing but the knowledge of happiness. Men may be permitted to vary in their use of words, and if anyone wants to insist on limiting the term *just* to what is the opposite of charitable, there is no way to force him to change his language, since names are arbitrary. Yet we have a right to learn the reasons which he has for being what he calls just, in order to see whether these same reasons will not bring him also to be good and to do good.

I believe we will agree that those who are charged with the conduct of others, like tutors, the directors of societies, and certain magistrates, are obligated not merely to prevent evil but also to secure the good. But it might perhaps be questioned whether a man free from commitments, or the sovereign of a state, has such obligations, the former in relation to others involved in the situation, the latter in relation to his subjects.

On top of this I shall ask that whoever can sustain a person must not do evil to others. One can give more than one reason for this. The most pressing will be the fear that someone will do the same thing to us. But are we not also subject to the fear that men will hate us if we refuse them aid which does not at all inconvenience us and if we neglect to prevent an evil which is about to crush them? Someone may say, 'I am content that others should not harm me. I do not ask at all for their aid and their good deeds and have no wish either to give or to claim more.' But can one sincerely maintain this? Let him ask himself what he would say or hope for if he should find himself actually on the point of falling into an evil which someone could help him avoid by a turn of his hand? Would one not hold him for a bad man and even for an enemy if he refused to save us in such a situation? . . . It will be granted, then, that one ought to prevent evil for another if it can be done conveniently. But perhaps it will not be granted that justice orders us to do positive good to others. I now ask if one is not at least obligated to relieve others' ills. And I return again to the proof, that is, to the rule, *quod tibi non vis fieri.*[6] Suppose that you were plunged into misery. Would you not complain about someone who did not help you, if he could easily do so? You have fallen into the water. If he refuses to throw a rope to you to give you a way of saving yourself, would you not judge him to be an evil man and even an enemy? Suppose that you suffered from violent pains and that someone had in his house, under his lock and key, a healing fountain capable of relieving your ills. What would you say and what would you do if he refused to give you a few glasses of its water?

Led by degrees,[7] people will agree not only that men ought to abstain from doing evil but also that they ought to prevent evil from being done and even to alleviate it when it is done, at least as far as they can without inconvenience to themselves. I am not now examining how far this inconvenience can go. Yet it will still be doubted, perhaps, that one is obligated to secure the good of another, even when this can be done without difficulty. Someone may say, 'I am not obligated to help you achieve. Each for himself, God for all.' But let me again suggest an intermediate case. A great good comes to you, but an obstacle arises, and I can remove that obstacle without pain. Would you not think it right to ask me to do so and to remind me that I would ask it of you if I were in a similar plight? If you

6. ["What you do not wish to have done to you." This is the Golden Rule in its negative formulation (cf. Matt. 7:12; Luke 6:31).]

7. [Leibniz's method of reasoning is an application if his law of continuity to cases of justice, arranged from the narrowest legal concept (*nemimem laedere*) in a continuous scale to the highest religious demands. Hence his device of seeking middle cases between the given cases, in which there may be disagreement; this approximates the method this he employed, for example, in his criticism of Descartes's laws of motion.]

grant this point, as you can hardly help doing, how can you refuse the only remaining request, that is, to procure a great good for me when you can do this without inconvenience of any kind to yourself and without being able to offer any reason for not doing it except a simple, 'I do not want to'? You could make me happy, and you refuse to do so. I complain, and you would complain in the same circumstances; therefore, I complain with justice.

This gradation shows us that the same grounds for complaint subsist throughout. Whether one does evil or refuses to do good is a matter of degree, or more or less, but this does not alter the nature of the matter. It can also be said that the absence of the good is an evil and the absence of the evil a good. In general, if someone asks you to do something or not to do something, and you refuse his request, he has reason to complain if he can judge that you would make the same request if you were in his place. And this is the principle of *equity* or, what is the same thing, of equality or of the identity of reasons, which holds that one should grant to others whatever one would himself wish in a similar situation, without claiming any privilege contrary to reason or without claiming to be able to allege one's will as a reason.

Perhaps we can say, then, that not to do evil to another, *neminem laedere*, is the precept of the Law which is called *strict Right* [*jus strictum*] but that *equity* demands that one also do good when this is fitting and that it is in this that the precept consists which orders us to give each one his due, *suum cuique tribuere*. But what determines fitness [*convenance*] or what each one is due can be known by the rule of equity or of equality: *quod tibi non vis fieri aut quod tibi vis fieri, neque aliis facito aut negato.*[8] This is the rule of reason and of our Master. Put yourself in the place of another, and you will have the true point of view to judge what is just or not.

Certain objections have been made against this great rule, but they come from the fact that it is not applied universally. For example, it has been objected that by virtue of this maxim a criminal can claim a pardon from the sovereign judge because the judge would wish the same thing if he were in a similar position. The reply is easy. The judge must put himself not only in the place of the criminal but also in that of the others whose interest lies in the crime being punished. And he must determine the greater good in which the lesser evil is included. The same is true of the objection that distributive justice demands an inequality among men,

8. ["What you do not wish to have done to you (or what you do wish to have done to you), do not do to others (or do not deny to others)". The advance of the argument beyond the negative statement in note 6 above is obvious.]

that a society ought to divide gains in proportion to what each has contributed, and that merit and lack of merit must be considered. Here the reply is also easy. Put yourself in the place of all and assume that they are well informed and enlightened. You will gather this conclusion from their votes: they will regard it fitting to their own interest that distinctions be made between one another. For example, if profits were not divided proportionately in a commercial society, some would not enter it at all, and others would quickly leave it, which is contrary to the interest of the whole society.

We may say, then, that *justice*, at least among men, is the constant will to act as far as possible in such a way that no one can complain of us if we would not complain of others in a similar situation. From this it is evident that when it is impossible to act so that the whole world is satisfied, we should try to satisfy people as much as possible. What is just thus conforms to the charity of the wise man.

So wisdom, which is a knowledge of our own good, brings us to justice, that is to say, to a reasonable advance toward the good of others. So far we have proposed as a reason for this the fear that we will be harmed if we do otherwise. But there is also the hope that others will do the same for us. Nothing is surer than the proverbs, *homo homini deus, homo homini lupus*.[9] Nothing can contribute more to the happiness, or to the misery, of man than men themselves. If they were all wise and knew how to treat each other, they would all be happy, as far as happiness can be obtained by human reason. But we may be permitted to use fictions for a better insight into the nature of things. Assume a person who has nothing to fear from others; such a person as would be a superior power in relation to men—some higher spirit; some substance which pagans would have called a divinity; some immortal, invulnerable, invincible man—in short, a person who can neither hope for nor fear anything from us. Shall we say that such a person is nonetheless obligated to do us no harm and even to do us good? Mr. Hobbes would say 'No.' He would even add that this person would have an absolute right in making us his conquest, because we could not complain of such a conqueror on the grounds which we have just pointed out, since there is another condition which exempts him from all consideration for us. But without needing a fiction, what shall we say of the supreme divinity whom reason makes us recognize? Christians agree, and others should agree, that this great God is supremely just and

9. ["Man is a god to man; man is a wolf to man." Symmachus *Epistle* ix, 114; Plautus *Asin.* ii, 4. 90.]

supremely good. But it cannot be for his own repose or to maintain peace with us that he shows us so much goodness, for we should be unable to wage war against him. What then is the principle of his justice, and what is its law? It cannot be this equity or equality which exists among men and makes them envisage the common end of our human condition, 'to do unto others what we wish others to do unto us'.

One cannot envisage any other motives in God than that of perfection or if you like, of his pleasure. Assuming, according to my definition, that *pleasure* is nothing but the feeling of perfection, he has nothing to consider outside of himself; on the contrary, everything depends upon him. But his happiness would not be supreme if he did not aim at as much good and perfection as possible. But what will you say if I show that this same motive is found in truly virtuous and generous men, whose highest function is to imitate divinity so far as human nature is able? The earlier reasons of fear and hope can bring men to be just in public and when necessary for their own interest. They will even obligate them to exercise and practice the rules of justice from childhood in order to acquire habits, out of fear of betraying themselves too easily, and so harming themselves along with others. Yet if there were no other motive, this would merely be political at bottom. And if someone who is just in this sense should find opportunity to make a great fortune through a great crime which would remain unknown, or at least unpunished, he would say as did Julius Caesar, following Euripides:

> Si violandum est jus, regnandi gratia
> Violandum est.[10]

But he whose justice is proof against such a temptation cannot have any motive but that of his own inclination, acquired by birth or exercise and regulated by reason, which makes him find so much pleasure in the practice of justice and so much ugliness in unjust acts that other pleasures and displeasures are compelled to give way.

One can say that this serenity of spirit, which finds the greatest pleasure in *virtue* and the greatest evil in *vice*, that is, in the perfection and imperfection of the will, would be the greatest good of which man is capable here below, even if he had nothing to expect beyond this life. For

10. [According to Suetonius, chap. 30; Euripides' original lines are in the *Phoenissae* v. 524–25. Way translates, "If wrong e'er be right, for a throne's sake were wrong most right."]

what can be preferred to this internal harmony, this continual pleasure in the purest and greatest, of which one is always master and which one need never abandon? Yet it must also be said that it is difficult to attain this disposition of spirit and that the number of those who have achieved it is small, most men remaining insensible to this motive, great and beautiful though it be. This seems to be why the Siamese believed that those who attain this degree of perfection receive divinity as a reward. The goodness of the Author of things has therefore provided for it through a motive more nearly within the reach of all men, by making himself known to the human race, as he has done by the eternal light of reason which he has given us and by the wonderful effects which he has placed before our eyes of his power, wisdom, and infinite goodness. This knowledge should make us see God as the sovereign Monarch of the universe, whose government is the most perfect state conceivable, in which nothing is neglected, in which all the hairs on our heads are counted, in which everything right becomes a fact, either in itself or in some equivalent form, in such a way that justice coincides with the good pleasure of God and no divorce ever arises between the honorable [*l'honnête*] and the useful. After this it must be imprudent not to be just, because, according as he is just or unjust, a man will certainly experience good or bad for himself from what he has done.

But there is something still more beautiful than all this in the government of God. What Cicero has said allegorically of ideal justice is really true in reference to this substantial justice—that if we could see it, we should be inflamed by its beauty.[11] One can compare the divine Monarchy to a kingdom whose sovereign would be a queen more spiritual and more learned than Queen Elizabeth; more judicious, more happy, and in a word, greater than Queen Anne; cleverer, wiser, and more beautiful than the Queen of Prussia—in short, as accomplished as it is possible to be.[12] Conceive that the perfections of this queen make such an impression upon the minds of her subjects that it is their greatest pleasure to obey and to please her. In this case the whole world would be virtuous and just by inclination. It is this which occurs literally and beyond all description in relation to God and to those who know him. It is in him that wisdom, vir-

---

11. [*De officiis* iii. 6. 17.]

12. [This flattering example is obviously addressed to the Electress Sophia, for the three queens are those in whom that ambitious sovereign might well be most interested—her mother, the English ruler to whose throne her own right had been established, and her daughter, the Queen of Prussia.]

tue, justice, and grandeur are accompanied by sovereign beauty. One cannot know God as one should without loving him above all things, and one cannot love him thus without willing what he wills. His perfections are infinite and cannot cease. This is why the pleasure which consists in the feeling of his perfections is the greatest and most durable possible; that is, it is the greatest felicity. And that which causes one to love him at the same time makes one happy and virtuous. . . .

This shows that justice can be taken in different ways. It can be opposed to charity, and then it is only the *jus strictum*. It can be opposed to the wisdom of him who must exercise justice, and then it conforms to the general good, but there will be cases in which the particular good will not be found in it. God and immortality would not enter into account. When one considers them, however, one always finds his own good in the general good.

While justice is merely a particular virtue, moreover, when we leave out of consideration God or a government which imitated that of God, and while this virtue so limited includes only what is called commutative and distributive justice, it can be said that as soon as it is based on God or on the imitation of God it becomes *universal justice* and contains all the virtues. For when we are vicious not only do we harm ourselves but we also diminish, so far as depends on us, the perfection of the great state of which God is the monarch. And although the evil is in fact redressed by the wisdom of the sovereign Lord this is partly through our punishment. Universal justice is distinguished by the supreme precept—*honeste (hoc est probe, pie) vivere*; as *suum cuique tribuere* conforms to particular justice, whether in general or taken more narrowly as the distributive justice which distinguishes men in particular; and as *neminem laedere* stands for commutative justice or for *jus strictum* as opposed to equity, as one takes these terms.[13]

It is true that Aristotle has recognized this universal justice, though he has not related it to God; even so, I find it beautiful that he had so lofty an idea.[14] But a well-formed government or state takes the place of God on earth for him, and this government will do what it can to require men to be virtuous. But as I have already said, one cannot compel men to be always virtuous by the principle solely of self-interest in this life; even less can one find the rare secret of lifting them up so that virtue constitutes

13. ["To live honorably (i.e., uprightly, piously), to give to each his due, to injure no one."]

14. [*Nic. Ethics* v. 1. 19.]

their greatest pleasure, in the way I have just finished describing. Aristotle seems to have hoped for this rather than shown it. Yet I do not find it impossible that there should be times and places where one attains this, especially if piety is added.

We can still distinguish *jus strictum*, equity, and piety when we are considering the right of sovereigns and of peoples. Hobbes and Filmer seem to have considered only *jus strictum*.[15] The Roman jurisconsults also sometimes adhere to this level of right alone. It can even be said that piety and equity regularly demand the *jus strictum* when they do not supply an exception to it. In insisting upon *jus strictum*, however, one must always add, 'except for the demands of equity and of piety.' Otherwise the proverb would hold: *summum jus summa est injuria.*[16]

In examining the *jus strictum*, it is important to consider the origin of kingdoms or states. Hobbes seems to think that men are something like beasts at first and became more tractable little by little but that, as long as they were free, they were in a state of war of all against all and thus had no *jus strictum*, since each had a right in everything and was able, without injustice, to seize the possessions of his neighbor as he saw fit. For there was then no security or judge, and anyone had the right to forestall those whom one had grounds to fear greatly. But as this state of crude nature was a state of misery, men agreed upon the means to secure their safety, transferring their right to judge to the person of the state, represented by an individual or by some assembly.[17] However, Hobbes acknowledges somewhere that a man has not, for this reason, lost the right to judge what is most agreeable to him and that a criminal is allowed to do what he can to save himself. But the citizens of a state must submit to the judgment of the state.[18] The same author must also recognize, however, that these same citizens, who have not lost their power of judgment, also cannot let their own safety be endangered in some situation where many of them are mistreated.[19] So in the end, in spite of what Hobbes says, each one has retained his right and his liberty regardless of the transfer to the state, and

15. [Robert Filmer's *Patriarchia, or the Natural Power of Kings*, derived royal sovereignty from patriarchal authority. His theory evoked Locke's *Treatises on Government* (1689).]

16. ["The more law, the more injustice." Cicero (*De officiis* i. 10. 33) has *summum ius, summa iniuria.*]

17. [*De cive* ii, 5.]

18. [*Leviathan*, chap. 21.]

19. [*Ibid.*, chap. 29.]

this transfer will be provisional and limited, that is, it will take place to the degree that we believe our safety is involved. The reasons which this illustrious author gives to prevent subjects from resisting their sovereign are nothing but plausible considerations based on the true principle that ordinarily such a remedy is worse than the evil itself. But what is ordinarily the case is not absolutely so. The one is like the *jus strictum*, the other like equity.

It seems to me also that this author makes the mistake of confusing right with its factual application. A man who has acquired a good, who has built a house or forged a sword, is the proprietary master of it, although someone else, in time of war, has the right to drive him from his house and to take away his sword. And although there are cases where one cannot enjoy his right for want of a judge and of enforcement, the right does not cease to subsist. To try to destroy something because there is no way at once to prove it and to enjoy it is to confuse matters.

Mr. Filmer seems to me to have recognized rightly that there is a right, even a *jus strictum*, before the foundation of states. Whoever produces something new or gains possession of something already existing but which no one has possessed before, and improves and adapts it to his use, cannot as a rule be deprived of it without injustice. This is also true if one acquires a thing from such an owner, either directly or through intermediates. The right of acquisition is a *jus strictum* which even equity approves. Hobbes believes that by virtue of this right children are the property of their mother unless society orders differently, and Filmer, assuming the superiority of the father, gives him the right of property over his children as well as over the children of his slaves. Since all men from the beginning until now are, according to sacred history, descended from Adam and also from Noah, it follows, according to Filmer, that if Noah were living, he would have the right of an absolute monarch over all men. In his absence fathers always are, or should be, the sovereign masters of their descendants. This paternal power is the origin of kings, who replace progenitors, in the last analysis, either by force or by consent. And since the power of fathers is absolute, that of kings is absolute also.

This conception ought not entirely to be condemned, but I think we can say that it has been pushed too far. We must admit that a father or a mother acquires a great power over children by their procreation and education. But I do not think that we can conclude from this that children are the property of their progenitors, as are the horses or dogs which are born to us and the works which we create. The objection may be raised that we can acquire slaves and that the children of slaves are also slaves. And according to the law of nations, slaves are the property of their masters, and no reason can be seen why children whom we have produced and nurtured by education should not be our slaves by an even juster title than those whom we have bought or captured.

To this I reply that even if I were to agree that there is a right of slavery among men which conforms to natural reason, and that according to *jus strictum* the bodies of slaves and their infants are under the power of their masters, it will always be true that another stronger right opposes the abuse of this one. This is the right of reasonable souls, which are naturally and inalienably free. It is the Law of God who is the sovereign master of bodies and souls and under whom masters are the fellow-citizens of their slaves, since slaves have the right of citizenship in the kingdom of God as well as their masters. So it can be said that a man's body is the property of his soul and ought not to be taken from him as long as he lives. Since a man's soul cannot be acquired, neither can ownership of his body be acquired, so that the right of a master over his slave can be in the nature only of what is called servitude to another, or a kind of usufruct. But usufruct has its limits; it must be practiced without destroying itself, *salva re*, so that this right cannot be extended to the point of making a slave evil or unhappy. But even if I were to agree, contrary to the nature of things, that an enslaved man is the property of another man, the right of the master, however rigorous, would be limited by *equity*, which demands that one man shall care for another as he would wish another to care for himself in a similar situation, and by *charity*, which orders us to work for the happiness of others. And these obligations are perfected by *piety*, that is, by what we owe to God. If we wished to stop with *jus strictum* alone, the American cannibals would have a right to eat their prisoners. There are those among them who demand even more; they use their prisoners to have children, then fatten and eat the children, and afterward, when she produces no more, the mother. Such are the consequences of a pretended right of masters over slaves and of fathers over children. . . .

8

David Hume,
"Of Justice," from *An Enquiry*
Concerning the Principles of Morals

David Hume (1711–1776) was a skeptic in the theory of knowledge but not in politics. It has been said of him, "He is rightly regarded as the founder of utilitarianism, though, like many founders, he is less uncompromising than most of his successors" (John Plamenatz, The English Utilitarians, *1949).*

I

That Justice is useful to society, and consequently that *part* of its merit, at least, must arise from that consideration, it would be a superfluous undertaking to prove. That public utility is the *sole* origin of justice, and that reflections on the beneficial consequences of this virtue are the *sole* foundation of its merit; this proposition, being more curious and important, will better deserve our examination and enquiry.

Let us suppose that nature has bestowed on the human race such profuse *abundance* of all *external* conveniencies, that, without any uncertainty in the event, without any care or industry on our part, every individual finds himself fully provided with whatever his most voracious appetites can want, or luxurious imagination wish or desire. His natural beauty, we shall suppose, surpasses all acquired ornaments: the perpetual clemency of the seasons renders useless all clothes or covering: the raw herbage affords him the most delicious fare; the clear fountain, the richest beverage. No laborious occupation required: no tillage: no navigation. Music, poetry, and contemplation form his sole business: conversation, mirth, and friendship his sole amusement.

It seems evident that, in such a happy state, every other social virtue would flourish, and receive tenfold increase; but the cautious, jealous virtue of justice would never once have been dreamed of. For what purpose make a partition of goods, where every one has already more than enough?

From David Hume, *An Enquiry Concerning the Principles of Morals*, edited by J. B. Schneewind, 1983, Hackett Publishing Company, Inc.

Why give rise to property, where there cannot possibly be any injury? Why call this object *mine*, when upon the seizing of it by another, I need but stretch out my hand to possess myself to what is equally valuable? Justice, in that case, being totally useless, would be an idle ceremonial, and could never possibly have place in the catalogue of virtues.

We see, even in the present necessitous condition of mankind, that, wherever any benefit is bestowed by nature in an unlimited abundance, we leave it always in common among the whole human race, and make no subdivisions of right and property. Water and air, though the most necessary of all objects, are not challenged as the property of individuals; nor can any man commit injustice by the most lavish use and enjoyment of these blessings. In fertile extensive countries, with few inhabitants, land is regarded on the same footing. And no topic is so much insisted on by those, who defend the liberty of the seas, as the unexhausted use of them in navigation. Were the advantages, procured by navigation, as inexhaustible, these reasoners had never had any adversaries to refute; nor had any claims ever been advanced of a separate, exclusive dominion over the ocean.

It may happen, in some countries, at some periods, that there be established a property in water, none in land;[1] if the latter be in greater abundance than can be used by the inhabitants, and the former be found, with difficulty, and in very small quantities.

Again; suppose, that, though the necessities of human race continue the same as at present, yet the mind is so enlarged, and so replete with friendship and generosity, that every man has the utmost tenderness for every man, and feels no more concern for his own interest than for that of his fellows; it seems evident, that the use of justice would, in this case, be suspended by such an extensive benevolence, nor would the divisions and barriers of property and obligation have ever been thought of. Why should I bind another, by a deed or promise, to do me any good office, when I know that he is already prompted, by the strongest inclination, to seek my happiness, and would, of himself, perform the desired service; except the hurt, he thereby receives, be greater than the benefit accruing to me? in which case, he knows, that, from my innate humanity and friendship, I should be the first to oppose myself to his imprudent generosity. Why raise land-marks between my neighbour's field and mine, when my heart has made no division between our interests; but shares all his joys and sorrows with the same force and vivacity as if originally my own? Every

1. Genesis, chaps. xiii and xxi.

man, upon this supposition, being a second self to another, would trust all his interests to the discretion of every man; without jealousy, without partition, without distinction. And the whole human race would form only one family; where all would lie in common, and be used freely, without regard to property; but cautiously too, with as entire regard to the necessities of each individual, as if our own interests were most intimately concerned.

In the present disposition of the human heart, it would, perhaps, be difficult to find complete instances of such enlarged affections; but still we may observe, that the case of families approaches towards it; and the stronger the mutual benevolence is among the individuals, the nearer it approaches; till all distinction of property be, in a great measure, lost and confounded among them. Between married persons, the cement of friendship is by the laws supposed so strong as to abolish all division of possessions; and has often, in reality, the force ascribed to it. And it is observable, that, during the ardour of new enthusiasms, when every principle is inflamed into extravagance, the community of goods has frequently been attempted; and nothing but experience of its inconveniencies, from the returning or disguised selfishness of men, could make the imprudent fanatics adopt anew the ideas of justice and of separate property. So true is it, that this virtue derives its existence entirely from its necessary *use* to the intercourse and social state of mankind.

To make this truth more evident, let us reverse the foregoing suppositions; and carrying everything to the opposite extreme, consider what would be the effect of these new situations. Suppose a society to fall into such want of all common necessaries, that the utmost frugality and industry cannot preserve the greater number from perishing, and the whole from extreme misery; it will readily, I believe, be admitted, that the strict laws of justice are suspended, in such a pressing emergence, and give place to the stronger motives of necessity and self-preservation. Is it any crime, after a shipwreck, to seize whatever means or instrument of safety one can lay hold of, without regard to former limitations of property? Or if a city besieged were perishing with hunger; can we imagine, that men will see any means of preservation before them, and lose their lives, from a scrupulous regard to what, in other situations, would be the rules of equity and justice? The use and tendency of that virtue is to procure happiness and security, by preserving order in society: but where the society is ready to perish from extreme necessity, no greater evil can be dreaded from violence and injustice; and every man may now provide for himself by all the means, which prudence can dictate, or humanity permit. The public, even in less urgent necessities, opens granaries, without the consent of proprietors; as justly supposing, that the authority of magistracy may, consistent with equity, extend so far: but were any number of men to assemble, without the tie of laws or civil jurisdiction; would an equal partition of bread in a famine, though effected by power and even violence, be regarded as criminal or injurious?

Suppose likewise, that it should be a virtuous man's fate to fall into the society of ruffians, remote from the protection of laws and government; what conduct must he embrace in that melancholy situation? He sees such a desperate rapaciousness prevail; such a disregard to equity, such contempt of order, such stupid blindness to future consequences, as must immediately have the most tragical conclusion, and must terminate in destruction to the greater number, and in a total dissolution of society to the rest. He, meanwhile, can have no other expedient than to arm himself, to whomever the sword he seizes, or the buckler, may belong: To make provision of all means of defence and security: And his particular regard to justice being no longer of use to his own safety or that of others, he must consult the dictates of self-preservation alone, without concern for those who no longer merit his care and attention.

When any man, even in political society, renders himself by his crimes, obnoxious to the public, he is punished by the laws in his goods and person; that is, the ordinary rules of justice are, with regard to him, suspended for a moment, and it becomes equitable to inflict on him, for the *benefit* of society, what otherwise he could not suffer without wrong or injury.

The rage and violence of public war; what is it but a suspension of justice among the warring parties, who perceive, that this virtue is now no longer of any *use* or advantage to them? The laws of war, which then succeed to those of equity and justice, are rules calculated for the *advantage* and *utility* of that particular state, in which men are now placed. And were a civilized nation engaged with barbarians, who observed no rules even of war, the former must also suspend their observance of them, where they no longer serve to any purpose; and must render every action or rencounter as bloody and pernicious as possible to the first aggressors.

Thus, the rules of equity or justice depend entirely on the particular state and condition in which men are placed, and owe their origin and existence to that utility, which results to the public from their strict and regular observance. Reverse, in any considerable circumstance, the condition of men: Produce extreme abundance or extreme necessity: Implant in the human breast perfect moderation and humanity, or perfect rapaciousness and malice: By rendering justice totally *useless*, you thereby totally destroy its essence, and suspend its obligation upon mankind.

The common situation of society is a medium amidst all these extremes. We are naturally partial to ourselves, and to our friends; but are capable of learning the advantage resulting from a more equitable conduct. Few enjoyments are given us from the open and liberal hand of nature; but by art, labour, and industry, we can extract them in great abundance. Hence the ideas of property become necessary in all civil society: Hence justice derives its usefulness to the public: And hence alone arises its merit and moral obligation.

These conclusions are so natural and obvious, that they have not escaped even the poets, in their descriptions of the felicity attending the golden age or the reign of Saturn. The seasons, in that first period of nature, were so temperate, if we credit these agreeable fictions, that there was no necessity for men to provide themselves with clothes and houses, as a security against the violence of heat and cold: The river flowed with wine and milk: The oaks yielded honey; and nature spontaneously produced her greatest delicacies. Nor were these the chief advantages of that happy age. Tempests were not alone removed from nature; but those more furious tempests were unknown to human breasts, which now cause such uproar, and engender such confusion. Avarice, ambition, cruelty, selfishness, were never heard of: Cordial affection, compassion, sympathy, were the only movements with which the mind was yet acquainted. Even in the punctilious distinction of *mine* and *thine* was banished from among that happy race of mortals, and carried with it the very notion of property and obligation, justice and injustice.

This *poetical* fiction of the *golden age* is, in some respects, of a piece with the *philosophical* fiction of the *state of nature*; only that the former is represented as the most charming and most peaceable condition, which can possibly be imagined; whereas the latter is painted out as a state of mutual war and violence, attended with the most extreme necessity. On the first origin of mankind, we are told, their ignorance and savage nature were so prevalent, that they could give no mutual trust, but must each depend upon himself and his own force or cunning for protection and security. No law was heard of: No rule of justice known: No distinction of property regarded: Power was the only measure of right; and a perpetual war of all against all was the result of men's untamed selfishness and barbarity.[2]

Whether such a condition of human nature could ever exist, or if it did,

2. This fiction of a state of nature, as a state of war, was not first started by Mr. Hobbes, as is commonly imagined. Plato endeavours to refute an hypothesis very like it in the second, third, and fourth books de republica. Cicero, on the contrary, supposes it certain and universally acknowledged in the following passage. [Can

could continue so long as to merit the appellation of a *state*, may justly be doubted. Men are necessarily born in a family-society, at least; and are trained up by their parents to some rule of conduct and behaviour. But this must be admitted, that, if such a state of mutual war and violence was ever real, the suspension of all laws of justice, from their absolute inutility, is a necessary and infallible consequence.

The more we vary our views of human life, and the newer and more unusual the lights are in which we survey it, the more shall we be convinced, that the origin here assigned for the virtue of justice is real and satisfactory.

Were there a species of creatures intermingled with men, which, though rational, were possessed of such inferior strength, both of body and mind, that they were incapable of all resistance, and could never, upon the highest provocation, make us feel the effects of their resentment; the necessary consequence, think, is that we should be bound by the laws of humanity to give gentle usage to these creatures, but should not, properly speaking, lie under any restraint of justice with regard to them, nor could they possess any right or property, exclusive of such arbitrary lords. Our intercourse with them could not be called society, which supposes a degree of equality; but absolute command on the one side, and servile obedience on the other. Whatever we covet, they must instantly resign: Our permission is the only tenure, by which they hold their possessions: Our compassion and kindness the only check, by which they curb our lawless will: And as no inconvenience ever results from the exercise of a power, so firmly established in nature, the restraints of justice and

---

there be anyone among you, jurors, who does not know that nature had brought things about so that, at one time, before natural or civil law was discerned, scattered and landless men roamed the country-side, men who had just as much as they had been able to snatch by force and defend by bloodshed and violence? Then those men who first stood out for their exceptional virtue and judgment, having recognized men's natural talent for training and ingenuity, brought the nomads together and led them from savagery into justice and mildness. And after human and divine law were discovered, then matters were arranged for the general good, which we call public affairs, then common meeting places, which were later called communities, and eventually homes were brought within walls, which we call cities. And so there is no more difference between this orderly civilized life, and that former savagery, than there is between LAW and VIOLENCE. If we prefer not to use one of these, we must use the other. Do we want violence eradicated? Then the law must prevail, i.e., the verdicts in which all law is contained. Are the verdicts disliked or ignored? Then violence must prevail. Everyone understands this.]

property, being totally *useless*, would never have place in so unequal a confederacy.

This is plainly the situation of men, with regard to animals; and how far these may be said to possess reason, I leave it to others to determine. The great superiority of civilized Europeans above barbarous Indians, tempted us to imagine ourselves on the same footing with regard to them, and made us throw off all restraints of justice, and even of humanity, in our treatment of them. In many nations, the female sex are reduced to like slavery, and are rendered incapable of all property, in opposition to their lordly masters. But though the males, when united, have in all countries bodily force sufficient to maintain this severe tyranny, yet such are the insinuation, address, and charms of their fair companions, that women are commonly able to break the confederacy, and share with the other sex in all the rights and privileges of society.

Were the human species so framed by nature as that each individual possessed within himself every faculty, requisite both for his own preservation and for the propagation of his kind: Were all society and intercourse cut off between man and man, by the primary intention of the supreme Creator: It seems evident, that so solitary a being would be as much incapable of justice, as of social discourse and conversation. Where mutual regards and forbearance serve to no manner of purpose, they would never direct the conduct of any reasonable man. The headlong course of the passions would be checked by no reflection on future consequences. And as each man is here supposed to love himself alone, and to depend only on himself and his own activity for safety and happiness, he would, on every occasion, to the utmost of his power, challenge the preference above every other being, to none of which he is bound by any ties, either of nature or of interest.

But suppose the conjunction of the sexes to be established in nature, a family immediately arises; and particular rules being found requisite for its subsistence, these are immediately embraced; though without comprehending the rest of mankind within their prescriptions. Suppose that several families unite together into one society, which is totally disjoined from all others, the rules, which preserve peace and order, enlarge themselves to the utmost extent of that society; but becoming then entirely useless, lose their force when carried one step farther. But again suppose, that several distinct societies maintain a kind of intercourse for mutual convenience and advantage, the boundaries of justice still grow larger, in proportion to the largeness of men's views, and the force of their mutual connexions. History, experience, reason sufficiently instruct us in this natural progress of human sentiments, and in the gradual enlargement of our regards to justice, in proportion as we become acquainted with the extensive utility of that virtue.

II

If we examine the *particular* laws, by which justice is directed, and property determined; we shall still be presented with the same conclusion. The good of mankind is the only object of all these laws and regulations. Not only it is requisite, for the peace and interest of society, that men's possessions should be separated; but the rules, which we follow, in making the separation, are such as can best be contrived to serve farther the interests of society.

We shall suppose that a creature, possessed of reason, but unacquainted with human nature, deliberates with himself what rules of justice or property would best promote public interest, and establish peace and security among mankind: His most obvious thought would be, to assign the largest possessions to the most extensive virtue, and give every one the power of doing good, proportioned to his inclination. In a perfect theocracy, where a being, infinitely intelligent, governs by particular volitions, this rule would certainly have place, and might serve to the wisest purposes: But were mankind to execute such a law; so great is the uncertainty of merit; both from its natural obscurity, and from the self-conceit of each individual, that no determinate rule of conduct would ever result from it; and the total dissolution of society must be the immediate consequence. Fanatics may suppose, *that dominion is founded in grace*, and *that saints alone inherit the earth*; but the civil magistrate very justly puts these sublime theorists on the same footing with common robbers, and teaches them by the severest discipline, that a rule, which, in speculation, may seem the most advantageous to society, may yet be found, in practice, totally pernicious and destructive.

That there were *religious* fanatics of this kind in England, during the civil wars, we learn from history; though it is probable, that the obvious *tendency* of these principles excited such horror in mankind, as soon obliged the dangerous enthusiasts to renounce, or at least conceal their tenets. Perhaps the *levellers*, who claimed an equal distribution of property, were a kind of *political* fanatics, which arose from the religious species, and more openly avowed their pretensions; as carrying a more plausible appearance, of being practicable in themselves, as well as useful to human society.

It must, indeed, be confessed, that nature is so liberal to mankind, that, were all her presents equally divided among the species, and improved by art and industry, every individual would enjoy all the necessaries, and even most of the comforts of life; nor would ever be liable to any ills, but such as might accidentally arise from the sickly frame and constitution of his body. It must also be confessed, that, wherever we depart from this equality, we rob the poor of more satisfaction than we add to the rich, and that the slight gratification of a frivolous vanity, in one individual, frequently costs more than bread to many families, and even provinces. It may appear withal, that the rule of equality, as it would be highly *useful*, is not altogether *impracticable*; but has taken place, at least in an imperfect degree, in some republics; particularly that of Sparta; where it was attended, it is said, with the most beneficial consequences. Not to mention that the Agrarian laws, so frequently claimed in Rome, and carried into execution in many Greek cities, proceeded, all of them, from a general idea of the utility of this principle.

But historians, and even common sense, may inform us, that, however specious these ideas of *perfect* equality may seem, they are really, at bottom, *impracticable*; and were they not so, would be extremely *pernicious* to human society. Render possessions ever so equal, men's different degrees of art, care, and industry will immediately break that equality. Of if you check these virtues, you reduce society to the most extreme indigence; and instead of preventing want and beggary in a few, render it unavoidable to the whole community. The most rigorous inquisition too is requisite to watch every inequality on its first appearance; and the most severe jurisdiction, to punish and redress it. But besides, that so much authority must soon degenerate into tyranny, and be exerted with great partialities; who can possibly be possessed of it, in such a situation as is here supposed? Perfect equality of possessions, destroying all subordination, weakens extremely the authority of magistracy, and must reduce all power nearly to a level, as well as property.

We may conclude, therefore, that, in order to establish laws for the regulation of property, we must be acquainted with the nature and situation of man; must reject appearances, which may be false, though specious; and must search for those rules, which are, on the whole, most *useful* and *beneficial*. Vulgar sense and slight experience are sufficient for this purpose; where men give not way to too selfish avidity, or too extensive enthusiasm.

Who sees not, for instance, that whatever is produced or improved by a man's art or industry ought, for ever, to be secured to him, in order to give encouragement to such *useful* habits and accomplishments? That the property ought also to descend to children and relations, for the same *useful* purpose? That it may be alienated by consent, in order to beget that commerce and intercourse, which is so *beneficial* to human society? And that all contracts and promises ought carefully to be fulfilled, in order to secure mutual trust and confidence, by which the general *interest* of mankind is so much promoted?

Examine the writers on the laws of nature; and you will always find, that, whatever principles they set out with, they are sure to terminate here at last, and to assign, as the ultimate reason for every rule which they establish, the convenience and necessities of mankind. A concession thus extorted, in opposition to systems, has more authority than if it had been made in prosecution of them.

What other reason, indeed, could writers ever give, why this must be *mine* and that *yours*; since uninstructed nature surely never made any such distinction? The objects which receive those appellations are, of themselves, foreign to us; they are totally disjoined and separated from us; and nothing but the general interests of society can form the connexion.

Sometimes the interests of society may require a rule of justice in a particular case; but may not determine any particular rule, among several, which are all equally beneficial. In that case, the slightest *analogies* are laid hold of, in order to prevent that indifference and ambiguity, which would be the source of perpetual dissension. Thus possession alone, and first possession, is supposed to convey property, where no body else has any preceding claim and pretension. Many of the reasonings of lawyers are of this analogical nature, and depend on very slight connexions of the imagination.

Does any one scruple, in extraordinary cases, to violate all regard to the private property of individuals, and sacrifice to public interest a distinction, which had been established for the sake of that interest? The safety of the people is the supreme law: All other particular laws are subordinate to it, and dependent on it: And if, in the *common* course of things, they be followed and regarded; it is only because the public safety and interest *commonly* demand so equal and impartial an administration.

Sometimes both *utility* and *analogy* fail, and leave the laws of justice in total uncertainty. Thus, it is highly requisite, that prescription or long possession should convey property; but what number of days or months or years should be sufficient for that purpose, it is impossible for reason alone to determine. *Civil laws* here supply the place of the natural *code*, and assign different terms for prescription, according to the different *utili-*

ties, proposed by the legislator. Bills of exchange and promissory notes, by the laws of most countries, prescribe sooner than bonds, and mortgages, and contracts of a more formal nature.

In general we may observe that all questions of property are subordinate to the authority of civil laws, which extend, restrain, modify, and alter the rules of natural justice, according to the particular *convenience* of each community. The laws have, or ought to have, a constant reference to the constitution of government, the manners, the climate, the religion, the commerce, the situation of each society. A late author of genius, as well as learning, has prosecuted this subject at large, and has established, from these principles, a system of political knowledge, which abounds in ingenious and brilliant thoughts, and is not wanting in solidity.[3]

---

3. The author of *L'Esprit des Loix*. This illustrious writer, however, sets out with a different theory, and supposes all right to be founded on certain *rapports* or relations; which is a system, that, in my opinion, never will be reconciled with true philosophy. Father Malebranche, as far as I can learn, was the first that started this abstract theory of morals, which was afterwards adopted by Cudworth, Clarke, and others; and as it excludes all sentiment, and pretends to found everything on reason, it has not wanted followers in this philosophic age. With regard to justice, the virtue here treated of, the inference against this theory seems short and conclusive. Property is allowed to be dependent on civil laws; civil laws are allowed to have no other object, but the interest of society: This therefore must be allowed to be the sole foundation of property and justice. Not to mention, that our obligation itself to obey the magistrate and his laws is founded on nothing but the interests of society.

If the ideas of justice, sometimes, do not follow the dispositions of civil law; we shall find, that these cases, instead of objections, are confirmations of the theory delivered above. Where a civil law is so perverse as to cross all the interests of society, it loses all its authority, and men judge by the ideas of natural justice, which are conformable to those interests. Sometimes also civil laws, for useful purposes, require a ceremony or form to any deed; and where that is wanting, their decrees run contrary to the usual tenour of justice; but one who takes advantage of such chicanes, is not commonly regarded as an honest man. Thus, the interests of society require, that contracts be fulfilled; and there is not a more material article either of natural or civil justice: But the omission of a trifling circumstance will often, by law, invalidate a contract, *in foro humano*, but not *in foro conscientiae*, as divines express themselves. In these cases, the magistrate is supposed only to withdraw his power of enforcing the right, not to have altered the right. Where his intention extends to the right, and is conformable to the interests of society, it never fails to alter the right; a clear proof of the origin of justice and of property, as assigned above.

What is a man's property? Anything which it is lawful for him, and for him alone, to use. *But what rule have we, by which we can distinguish these objects?* Here we must have recourse to statutes, customs, precedents, analogies, and a hundred other circumstances; some of which are constant and inflexible, some variable and arbitrary. But the ultimate point, in which they all professedly terminate, is the interest and happiness of human society. Where this enters not into consideration, nothing can appear more whimsical, unnatural, and even superstitious, than all or most of the laws of justice and of property.

Those who ridicule vulgar superstitions, and expose the folly of particular regards to meats, days, places, postures, apparel, have an easy task; while they consider all the qualities and relations of the objects, and discover no adequate cause for that affection or antipathy, veneration or horror, which have so mighty an influence over a considerable part of mankind. A Syrian would have starved rather than taste pigeon; an Egyptian would not have approached bacon: But if these species of food can be examined by the senses of sight, smell, or taste, or scrutinized by the sciences of chemistry, medicine, or physics, no difference is ever found between them and any other species, nor can that precise circumstance be pitched on, which may afford a just foundation for the religious passion. A fowl on Thursday is lawful food; on Friday abominable: Eggs in this house and in this diocese, are permitted during Lent; a hundred paces farther, to eat them is a damnable sin. This earth or building, yesterday was profane; to-day, by the muttering of certain words, it has become holy and sacred. Such reflections as these, in the mouth of a philosopher, one may safely say, are too obvious to have any influence; because they must always, to every man, occur at first sight; and where they prevail not, of themselves, they are surely obstructed by education, prejudice, and passion, not by ignorance or mistake.

It may appear to a careless view, or rather a too abstracted reflection, that there enters a like superstition into all the sentiments of justice; and that, if a man expose its object, or what we call property, to the same scrutiny of sense and science, he will not, by the most accurate enquiry, find any foundation for the difference made by moral sentiment. I may lawfully nourish myself from this tree; but the fruit of another of the same species, ten paces off, it is criminal for me to touch. Had I worn this apparel an hour ago, I had merited the severest punishment; but a man, by pronouncing a few magical syllables, has now rendered it fit for my use and service. Were this house placed in the neighbouring territory, it had been immoral for me to dwell in it; but being built on this side the river, it is subject to a different municipal law, and by its becoming mine I incur no blame or censure. The same species of reasoning it may be thought, which so successfully exposes superstition, is also applicable to justice; nor is it possible, in the one case more than in the other, to point out, in the object, that precise quality or circumstance, which is the foundation of the sentiment.

But there is this material difference between *superstition* and *justice*, that the former is frivolous, useless, and burdensome; the latter is absolutely requisite to the well-being of mankind and existence of society. When we abstract from this circumstance (for it is too apparent ever to be overlooked) it must be confessed, that all regards to right and property, seem entirely without foundation, as much as the grossest and most vulgar superstition. Were the interests of society nowise concerned, it is as unintelligible why another's articulating certain sounds implying consent, should change the nature of my actions with regard to a particular object, as why the reciting of a liturgy by a priest, in a certain habit and posture, should dedicate a heap of brick and timber, and render it, thenceforth and for ever, sacred.[4]

4. It is evident, that the will or consent alone never transfers property, nor causes the obligations of a promise (for the same reasoning extends to both) but the will must be expressed by words or signs, in order to impose a tie upon any man. The expression being once brought in as subservient to the will, soon becomes the principal part of the promise; nor will a man be less bound by his word, though he secretly give a different direction to his intention, and withhold the assent of his mind. But though the expression makes, on most occasions, the whole of the promise, yet it does not always so; and one who should make use of any expression, of which he knows not the meaning, and which he uses without any sense of the consequences, would not certainly be bound by it. Nay, though he knows its meaning, yet if he use it in jest only, and which such signs as evidently show, that he has no serious intention of binding himself, he would not lie under any obligation of performance; but it is necessary, that the words be a perfect expression of the will, without any contrary signs. Nay, even this we must not carry so far as to imagine, that one, whom, by our quickness of understanding, we conjecture, from certain signs, to have an intention of deceiving us, is not bound by his expression or verbal promise, if we accept of it; but must limit this conclusion to those cases where the signs are of a different nature from those of deceit. All these contradictions are easily accounted for, if justice arise entirely from its usefulness to society; but will never be explained on any other hypothesis.

It is remarkable, that the moral decisions of the *Jesuits* and other relaxed casuists, were commonly formed in prosecution of some such subtleties of reasoning as are here pointed out, and proceed as much from the habit of scholastic

These reflections are far from weakening the obligations of justice, or diminishing anything from the most sacred attention to property. On the contrary, such sentiments must acquire new force from the present reasoning. For what stronger foundation can be desired or conceived for any duty, than to observe, that human society, or even human nature, could not subsist without the establishment of it; and will still arrive at greater degrees of happiness and perfection, the more inviolable the regard is, which is paid to that duty?

The dilemma seems obvious: As justice evidently tends to promote public utility and to support civil society, the sentiment of justice is either derived from our reflecting on that tendency, or like hunger, thirst, and other appetites, resentment, love of life, attachment to offspring, and other passions, arises from a simple original instinct in the human breast, which nature has implanted for like salutary purposes. If the latter be the case, it follows, that property, which is the object of justice, is also distinguished by a simple original instinct, and is not ascertained by any argu-

---

refinement as from any corruption of the heart, if we may follow the authority of Mons. Bayle. See his Dictionary, article LOYOLA. And why has the indignation of mankind risen so high against these casuists; but because every one perceived, that human society could not subsist were such practices authorized, and that morals must always be handled with a view to public interest, more than philosophical regularity? If the secret direction of the intention, said every man of sense, could invalidate a contract; where is our security? And yet a metaphysical schoolman might think, that, where an intention was supposed to be requisite, if that intention really had not place, no consequence ought to follow, and no obligation be imposed. The casuistical subtleties may not be greater than the subtleties of lawyers, hinted at above; but as the former are *pernicious*, and the latter *innocent* and even *necessary*, this is the reason of the very different reception they meet with from the world.

It is a doctrine of the Church of Rome, that the priest, by a secret direction of his intention, can invalidate any sacrament. This position is derived from a strict and regular prosecution of the obvious truth, that empty words alone, without any meaning or intention in the speaker, can never be attended with any effect. If the same conclusion be not admitted in reasonings concerning civil contracts, where the affair is allowed to be of so much less consequence than the eternal salvation of thousands, it proceeds entirely from men's sense of the danger and inconvenience of the doctrine in the former case: And we may thence observe, that however positive, arrogant, and dogmatical any superstition may appear, it never can convey any thorough persuasion of the reality of its objects, or put them, in any degree, on a balance with the common incidents of life, which we learn from daily observation and experimental reasoning.

ment or reflection. But who is there that ever heard of such an instinct? Or is this a subject in which new discoveries can be made? We may as well expect to discover, in the body, new senses, which had before escaped the observation of all mankind.

But farther, though it seems a very simple proposition to say, that nature, by an instinctive sentiment, distinguishes property, yet in reality we shall find, that there are required for that purpose ten thousand different instincts, and these employed about objects of the greatest intricacy and nicest discernment. For when a definition of *property* is required, that relation is found to resolve itself into any possession acquired by occupation, by industry, by prescription, by inheritance, by contract, &c. Can we think that nature, by an original instinct, instructs us in all these methods of acquisition?

These words too, inheritance and contract, stand for ideas infinitely complicated; and to define them exactly, a hundred volumes of laws, and a thousand volumes of commentators, have not been found sufficient. Does nature, whose instincts in men are all simple, embrace such complicated and artificial objects, and create a rational creature, without trusting anything to the operation of his reason?

But even though all this were admitted, it would not be satisfactory. Positive laws can certainly transfer property. It is by another original instinct, that we recognize the authority of kings and senates, and mark all the boundaries of their jurisdiction? Judges too, even though their sentence be erroneous and illegal, must be allowed, for the sake of peace and order, to have decisive authority, and ultimately to determine property. Have we original innate ideas of praetors and chancellors and juries? Who sees not, that all these institutions arise merely from the necessities of human society?

All birds of the same species in every age and country, built their nests alike: In this we see the force of instinct. Men, in different times and places, frame their houses differently: Here we perceive the influence of reason and custom. A like inference may be drawn from comparing the instinct of generation and the institution of property.

How great soever the variety of municipal laws, it must be confessed, that their chief out-lines pretty regularly concur; because the purposes, to which they tend, are everywhere exactly similar. In like manner, all houses have a roof and walls, windows and chimneys; though diversified in their shape, figure, and materials. The purposes of the latter, directed to the convenience of human life, discover not more plainly their origin from reason and reflection, than do those of the former, which point all to a like end.

I need not mention the variations, which all the rules of property receive from the finer turns and connexions of the imagination, and from the subtilties and abstractions of law-topics and reasonings. There is no possibility of reconciling this observation to the notion of original instincts.

What alone will beget a doubt concerning the theory, on which I insist, is the influence of education and acquired habits, by which we are so accustomed to blame injustice, that we are not, in every instance, conscious of any immediate reflection on the pernicious consequences of it. The views the most familiar to us are apt, for that very reason, to escape us; and what we have very frequently performed from certain motives, we are apt likewise to continue mechanically, without recalling, on every occasion, the reflections, which first determined us. The convenience, or rather necessity, which leads to justice is so universal, and everywhere points so much to the same rules, that the habit takes place in all societies; and it is not without some scrutiny, that we are able to ascertain its true origin. The matter, however, is not so obscure, but that even in common life we have every moment recourse to the principle of public utility, and ask, *What must become of the world, if such practices prevail? How could society subsist under such disorders?* Were the distinction or separation of possessions entirely useless, can any one conceive, that it ever should have obtained in society?

Thus we seem, upon the whole, to have attained a knowledge of the force of that principle here insisted on, and can determine what degree of esteem or moral approbation may result from reflections on public interest and utility. The necessity of justice to the support of society is the sole foundation of that virtue; and since no moral excellence is more highly esteemed, we may conclude that this circumstance of usefulness has, in general, the strongest energy, and most entire command over our sentiments. It must, therefore, be the source of a considerable part of the merit ascribed to humanity, benevolence, friendship, public spirit, and other social virtues of that stamp; as it is the sole source of the moral approbation paid to fidelity, justice, veracity, integrity, and those other estimable and useful qualities and principles. It is entirely agreeable to the rules of philosophy, and even of common reason; where any principle has been found to have a great force and energy in one instance, to ascribe to it a like energy in all similar instances. This indeed is Newton's chief rule of philosophizing.[5]

5. Principia, Lib. iii.

9

Immanuel Kant,
"A Definition of Justice,"
from *The Metaphysical Elements of Justice*

The philosophy of Immanuel Kant (1724–1804) incorporated two major ethical principles: People should be treated as ends and not merely as means, and the principle behind each act should be capable of being willed as a universal law, the so-called categorical imperative. According to Kant, the demand of morality is unconditional.

What Jurisprudence Is

The body of these laws that are susceptible of being made into external laws, that is, externally legislated, [constitutes justice and here] is called jurisprudence (*Jus*). Where these laws have actually been externally legislated, the body of them is called positive Law. A specialist in the latter, or a jurist (*Jurisconsultus*), is said to be skilled in the law (*Jurisperitus*) if he knows these external laws also "externally," in the sense that he knows how to apply them to concrete cases presented in experience. Such knowledge can also be called legal knowledge (*Jurisprudentia*). Without the two together, however, it is pure juridical science (*Jurisscientia*). The last designation applies to the systematic knowledge of natural Law (*Jus naturae*), although a specialist in natural Law must provide the immutable principles for all positive legislation.[1]

From Kant, *The Metaphysical Elements of Justice*, translated by John Ladd. © 1965. Reprinted by permission of Prentice-Hall, Inc., Upper Saddle River, N.J. The footnotes are those of Ladd.

  1. [The construction of the last three sentences is so ambiguous that it is not clear whether Kant intends the term "juridical science" to apply to the science of positive Law, of natural Law, or of both. But the nomenclature introduced here

What Is Justice?

This question can be just as perplexing for a jurist as the well-known question "What is truth?" is for a logician, assuming, that is, that he does not want to lapse into a mere tautology or to refer us to the laws of a particular country at a particular time. A jurist can, of course, tell us what the actual Law of the land is (*quid sit juris*), that is, what the laws say or have said at a certain time and at a certain place. But whether what these laws prescribe is also just and the universal criterion that will in general enable us to recognize what is just or unjust (*justum et injustum*)—the answer to such questions will remain hidden from him unless, for a while, he abandons empirical principles and searches for the sources of these judgments in pure reason. [To do so is necessary] in order to lay the foundations of any possible positive legislation. (Although [the empirical knowledge of these actual laws] can provide us with helpful clues), a purely empirical theory of justice and Law (like the wooden head in Phaedrus'[2] fable) is very beautiful, but, alas, it has no brain!

The concept of justice, insofar as it relates to an obligation corresponding to it (that is, the moral concept of justice), applies [only under the following three conditions]. First, it applies only to the external and—what is more—practical relationship of one person to another in which their actions can in fact exert an influence on each other (directly or indirectly). Second, the concept applies only to the relationship of a will to another person's will, not to his wishes or desires (or even just his needs), which are the concern of acts of benevolence and charity. Third, the concept of justice does not take into consideration the matter [content] of the will, that is, the end that a person intends to accomplish by means of the object that he wills; for example, we do not ask whether someone who buys wares from me for his own business will profit from the transaction. Instead, in applying the concept of justice we take into consideration only the form of the relationship between the wills insofar as they are regarded as free, and whether the action of one of them can be con-

---

has little significance for the rest of this treatise. The German terms are as follows:

"jurisprudence"—*Rechtslehre*	"jurist"—*Rechtsgelehrte*
"positive Law"—*positives Recht*	"legally skilled"—*rechtserfahren*
"legal specialist"—*Rechtskundige*	"legal knowledge"—*Rechtsklugkeit*
	"juridical science"—*Rechtswissenschaft*.]

2. [A Roman fabulist of the early first century after Christ.]

joined with the freedom of the other in accordance with a universal law.

Justice is therefore the aggregate of those conditions under which the will of one person can be conjoined with the will of another in accordance with a universal law of freedom.

Universal Principle of Justice

"Every action is just [right] that in itself or in its maxim is such that the freedom of the will of each can coexist together with the freedom of everyone in accordance with a universal law."

If, therefore, my action or my condition in general can coexist with the freedom of everyone in accordance with a universal law, then anyone who hinders me in performing the action or in maintaining the condition does me an injustice, inasmuch as this hindrance (this opposition) cannot coexist with freedom in accordance with universal laws.

It also follows that I cannot be required to adopt as one of my maxims this principle of all maxims, that is, to make this principle a maxim of my action. For anyone can still be free, even though I am quite indifferent to his freedom or even though I might in my heart wish to infringe on his freedom, as long as I do not through an external action violate his freedom. That I adopt as a maxim the maxim of acting justly is a requirement that Ethics [rather than jurisprudence] imposes on me.

Hence, the universal law of justice is: act externally in such a way that the free use of your will is compatible with the freedom of everyone according to a universal law. Admittedly, this law imposes an obligation on me, but I am not at all expected, much less required, to restrict my freedom to these conditions for the sake of this obligation itself. Rather, reason says only that, in its very Idea, freedom is restricted in this way and may be so restricted by others in practice. Moreover, it states this as a postulate not susceptible of further proof. Given that we do not intend to teach virtue, but only to give an account of what is just, we may not and ought not to represent this law of justice as being itself an incentive.

Justice is United with the Authorization to Use Coercion

Any opposition that counteracts the hindrance of an effect promotes that effect and is consistent with it. Now, everything that is unjust is a hindrance to freedom according to universal laws. Coercion, however, is a hindrance or opposition to freedom. Consequently, if a certain use of freedom is itself a hindrance to freedom according to universal laws (that is, is unjust), then the use of coercion to counteract it, inasmuch as it is the prevention of a hindrance to freedom, is consistent with freedom according to universal laws; in other words, this use of coercion is just. It follows by the law of contradiction that justice [a right] is united with the authorization to use coercion against anyone who violates justice [or a right].

Strict Justice Can Also Be Represented as the Possibility of a General Reciprocal Use of Coercion that is Consistent with the Freedom of Everyone in Accordance with Universal Laws

This statement amounts to saying that justice [or a right] cannot be conceived of as composed of two separate parts, namely, the obligation implied by a law and the authorization that someone has, by virtue of obligating another through his will, to use coercion to make the other fulfill [his obligation]. Instead, the concept of justice [or of a right] can be held to consist immediately of the possibility of the conjunction of universal reciprocal coercion with the freedom of everyone. Just as justice in general has as its object only what is external in actions, so strict justice, inasmuch as it contains no ethical elements, requires no determining grounds of the will besides those that are purely external, for only then is it pure and not confused with any prescriptions of virtue. Consequently, strict (narrow) justice is that which alone can be called wholly external. Strict justice is admittedly founded on the consciousness of each person's obligation under the law; but, if it is to remain pure, this consciousness may not and cannot be invoked as an incentive in order to determine the will to act in accordance with it. For this reason, strict justice relies instead on the principle of the possibility of external coercion that is compatible with the freedom of everyone in accordance with universal laws.

Accordingly, when it is said that a creditor has a right to demand from his debtor the payment of a debt, this does not mean that he can persuade the debtor that his own reason itself obligates him to this performance; on the contrary, to say that he has such a right means only that the use of coercion to make anyone do this is entirely compatible with everyone's freedom, including the freedom of the debtor, in accordance with universal laws. Thus "right" [or "justice"] and "authorization to use coercion" mean the same thing.

The law of a reciprocal use of coercion that is necessarily consistent with everyone's freedom under the principle of universal freedom may in certain respects be regarded as the *construction* of this concept [of justice]; that is, it exhibits this concept in a pure a priori intuition on the analogy of the possibility of the free movement of bodies under the law of the equality of action and reaction. Just as in pure mathematics we cannot immediately deduce the properties of the object from a concept, but can only discover them by means of the construction of the concept, so likewise the exhibition and description of the concept of justice is not made possible so much by the concept itself as by the general reciprocal and equal use of coercion that comes under a universal law and is consistent with it. In the same way that this dynamic concept [of the equality of action and reaction] still has a ground in a purely formal concept of pure mathematics (for example, of geometry), reason has also taken as much care as possible to provide the understanding with a priori intuitions to aid in the construction of the concept of justice.[3]

[A geometrical analogy may also throw light on the concept of justice and right. In geometry, there are two uses of the term "right" (*rectum*).] On the one hand, we may speak of a right line [straight line], in which case the opposite of "right" is "curved" [or "crooked"]; or on the other hand, we may speak of a right angle, in which case the opposite is "oblique."[4]

3. [This passage is complicated because Kant seems in fact to be calling attention to three distinct analogies. First, there is an analogy between the free movements of human beings and those of bodies, in that the law of the equality of action and reaction, reciprocal coercion, makes "freedom" possible in both cases. Another analogy appears in the introduction of the typical Kantian concept of a "construction of a concept." "To *construct* a concept means to exhibit *a priori* the intuition which corresponds to a concept. . . . Thus I construct a triangle by representing the object which corresponds to this concept either by imagination alone, in pure intuition, or in accordance therewith also on paper, in empirical intuition—in both cases completely *a priori*, without having borrowed the pattern from any experience. The single figure which we draw is empirical, and yet it serves to express the concept, without impairing its universality"—*Critique of Pure Reason*, trans. Kemp Smith, B 741–742. According to Kant, all mathematical knowledge is gained from the construction of concepts. In other words, in order to accomplish a complete analysis of the concept of justice, we need to resort to more concrete phenomena (for example, the use of coercion). Finally, at the end of this passage, Kant introduces a third analogy which points up the necessity for having "intermediate" concepts; thus, geometry provides "intermediate concepts" for physics, and similarly there must be "intermediate concepts" in Law.]

4. [The translation into English of the new few lines is rendered difficult because of the various uses of the German word *Recht*. I have consequently translated rather freely, without, however, fundamentally changing the sense of the original. It may be pointed out that Kant was without doubt deliberately making puns in this passage, because he goes out of his way to use certain expressions.

The unique feature of a right line is that only one such line can be drawn between two points; similarly, where two lines intersect or join each other, there can be only one right angle. The perpendicular forming the right angle may not incline more to one side than to the other, and it divides the space on both sides equally. This bears an analogy to jurisprudence, which wants to know exactly (with mathematical precision) what the property of everyone is. In ethics, in contrast, such narrow exactitude should not be expected, since it cannot refuse to make some room for exceptions (*latitudinem*).

But, without having to enter the field of Ethics, we are confronted with two cases that claim to be decidable by justice, but for which no one can be found who could decide them and which, as it were, belong to Epicurus' *intermundia* ["spaces between the worlds"]. These two cases must first be excluded from jurisprudence proper, to which we shall presently proceed, so that their shaky principles will not acquire any influence on the fixed basic principles of that discipline itself.

Appendix to the Introduction to the Elements of Justice

Equivocal Rights (*Jus aequivocum*) All justice and every right in the narrower sense (*jus strictum*) are united with the authorization to use coercion. But one can also think of justice or rights in a wider sense (*jus latum*), where the authorization to use coercion cannot be stipulated by any law. Now, there are two true or supposed rights of this kind—equity and the right of necessity. The first admits a right without any coercion; the second, coercion without any right. It can be easily seen that this equivocation arises from the fact that there are cases in which a right with regard to which no judge could be appointed to render a decision is called into question.

I

Equity (*Aequitas*) When one appeals to equity (regarded objectively) as the ground of a demand, he is by no means basing this demand solely on the ethical duties of others (their benevolence and kindness); on the contrary, he is basing it on his right. In the case of a right of equity, however,

---

Thus, besides punning on *Recht*, he was punning on *krumm* ("curved"), which also means "crooked" or "dishonest," and on *schief* ("oblique"), which may mean "askew" or "crooked."]

the requisite conditions according to which the judge is able to stipulate how much or what kind of remedy should be allowed for the claim in question are absent. [For example,] when one of the partners of a mercantile company formed under the condition of sharing the profits equally has nevertheless done more for the company than the other members and through various mishaps has thereby lost more than the others, then on the grounds of equity he can demand that he receive more than an equal share. If he rests his case solely on justice proper (strict Law), his request will be refused, because—if one imagines a judge in his case—the judge has no definite particulars (data) to serve as a guide in rendering a decision as to how much he should receive according to the contract. Again, a domestic servant whose wages through the end of the year have been paid in a currency that has in the intervening period become depreciated, with the result that he can no longer buy what he could have bought with the same money at the time of concluding the contract, cannot appeal to a right to be compensated for the loss caused by the fact that the same amount of money no longer has the same value. He can only appeal to equity (a silent goddess who cannot be heard), because nothing was stipulated about this in the contract, and a judge cannot pronounce in accordance with unstipulated conditions.

From this it follows that a court of equity (for disputes with others over their rights) contains a self-contradiction. Only when the rights of the judge himself are involved and over matters of which he can dispose for his own person may and should there be any hearing for equity. For example, this might happen in a case in which the Crown itself takes over the loss that others have suffered in its service and for which remedy is requested, although by strict justice it has a strict right to reject the claim on the grounds that they undertook the service at their own risk.

Indeed, the motto (*dictum*) of equity is: "The strictest justice is the greatest injustice" (*summum jus summa injuria*); there is, however, no remedy for this evil in actual legal proceedings, even though a claim of justice is involved. The claim belongs solely to the court of conscience (*forum poli*), whereas every question regarding the actual Law of the land must be taken before a civil court (*forum soli*).[5]

5. [*Das Gewissensgericht; das bürgerliche Recht. Forum poli* means "the court of heaven" (*polus* = "heaven"), and *forum soli* means "the court of the earth" (*solum* = "earth").]

II

The Right of Necessity (Jus necessitatis)

This imagined right is supposed to give me permission to take the life of another person when my own life is in danger, even if he has done me no harm. It is quite obvious that this conception implies a self-contradiction within jurisprudence, since the point in question here has nothing to do with an unjust assailant on my own life, which I defend by taking his life (*jus inculpatae tutelae*), for even in such a situation the recommendation of moderation (*moderamen*) is not part of justice, but belongs only to Ethics. The question under discussion is whether I am permitted to use violence against someone who himself has not used it against me.

It is clear that this allegation [of a right based on necessity] is not to be understood objectively, according to what a law might prescribe, but merely subjectively, as the sentence might be pronounced in a court of law. There could be no penal law assigning the death penalty to a man who has been shipwrecked and finds himself struggling with another man—both in equal danger of losing their lives—and who, in order to save his own life, pushes the other man off the plank on which he had saved himself. For the first man, no punishment threatened by the law could be greater than losing his life. A penal law applying to such a situation could never have the effect intended, for the threat of an evil that is still uncertain (being condemned to death by a judge) cannot outweigh the fear of an evil that is certain (being drowned). Hence, we must judge that, although an act of self-preservation through violence is not inculpable (*inculpabile*) [*unsträflich*], it still is unpunishable (*impunibilie*) [*unstrafbar*], and this subjective immunity from punishment, through a strange confusion among jurists, is identified with an objective (legal) immunity from punishment.

The motto of the right of necessity is: "Necessity has no law" (*necessitas non habet legem*); but there still cannot be any necessity that will make what is unjust legal.

It is apparent that, in both kinds of judgment concerning justice and rights (equity and the right of necessity), the equivocation arises from a confusion of the objective with the subjective grounds of the exercise of justice (before reason and before a court). Thus, on the one hand, what one himself recognizes on good grounds to be just will not receive confirmation in a court of justice, and, on the other hand, what he must judge unjust in itself will be treated with indulgence by the court. This is a consequence of the fact that the term "justice" [or "right"] is not used with the same meaning in the two cases.

10

John Stuart Mill, "On the Connexion between Justice and Utility," from *Utilitarianism*

John Stuart Mill (1806–1873), philosopher and political and social theorist, was the author of On Liberty *(1859),* Utilitarianism *(1861),* Representative Government *(1861), and* Subjection of Women *(1860), a defense of women's rights. Utilitarian ethics states that "the foundation of morals (is) 'utility' or the greatest happiness principle (which) holds that actions are right in proportion as they tend to promote happiness; wrong as they tend to produce the reverse of happiness." Mill was the son of philosopher James Mill and godfather to Bertrand Russell (1872–1970).*

In all ages of speculation one of the strongest obstacles to the reception of the doctrine that Utility or Happiness is the criterion of right and wrong has been drawn from the idea of Justice. The powerful sentiment, and apparently clear perception, which that word recalls with a rapidity and certainty resembling an instinct, have seemed to the majority of thinkers to point to an inherent quality in things; to show that the Just must have an existence in Nature as something absolute, generically distinct from every variety of the Expedient, and, in idea, opposed to it, though (as is commonly acknowledged) never, in the long run, disjoined from it in fact.

In the case of this, as of our other moral sentiments, there is no necessary connexion between the question of its origin, and that of its binding force. That a feeling is bestowed on us by Nature does not necessarily legitimate all its promptings. The feeling of justice might be a peculiar instinct, and might yet require, like our other instincts, to be controlled and enlightened by a higher reason. If we have intellectual instincts, leading us to judge in a particular way, as well as animal instincts that prompt us to act in a particular way, there is no necessity that the former should be more infallible in their sphere than the latter in theirs: it may as well hap-

From John Stuart Mill, *Utilitarianism*, London, 1863.

pen that wrong judgments are occasionally suggested by those, as wrong actions by these. But though it is one thing to believe that we have natural feelings of justice, and another to acknowledge them as an ultimate criterion of conduct, these two opinions are very closely connected in point of fact. Mankind are always predisposed to believe that any subjective feeling, not otherwise accounted for, is a revelation of some objective reality. Our present object is to determine whether the reality, to which the feeling of justice corresponds, is one which needs any such special revelation; whether the justice or injustice of an action is a thing intrinsically peculiar, and distinct from all its other qualities, or only a combination of certain of those qualities, presented under a peculiar aspect.

For the purpose of this inquiry it is practically important to consider whether the feeling itself, of justice and injustice, is *sui generis* like our sensations of colour and taste, or a derivative feeling, formed by a combination of others. And this it is the more essential to examine, as people are in general willing enough to allow, that objectively the dictates of Justice coincide with a part of the field of General Expediency; but inasmuch as the subjective mental feeling of Justice is different from that which commonly attaches to simple expediency, and, except in the extreme cases of the latter, is far more imperative in its demands, people find it difficult to see, in Justice, only a particular kind or branch of general utility, and think that its superior binding force requires a totally different origin.

To throw light upon this question it is necessary to attempt to ascertain what is the distinguishing character of justice, or of injustice: what is the quality, or whether there is any quality, attributed in common to all modes of conduct designated as unjust (for justice, like many other moral attributes, is best defined by its opposite), and distinguishing them from such modes of conduct as are disapproved, but without having that particular epithet of disapprobation applied to them. If in everything which men are accustomed to characterize as just or unjust some one common attribute or collection of attributes is always present, we may judge whether this particular attribute or combination of attributes would be capable of gathering round it a sentiment of that peculiar character and intensity by virtue of the general laws of our emotional constitution, or whether the sentiment is inexplicable, and requires to be regarded as a special provision of Nature. If we find the former to be the case, we shall, in resolving this question, have resolved also the main problem: if the latter, we shall have to seek for some other mode of investigating it.

To find the common attributes of a variety of objects it is necessary to begin by surveying the objects themselves in the concrete. Let us therefore advert successively to the various modes of action, and arrangements of human affairs, which are classed, by universal or widely spread opinion, as Just or as Unjust. The things well known to excite the sentiments associated with those names, are of a very multifarious character. I shall pass them rapidly in review, without studying any particular arrangement.

In the first place, it is mostly considered unjust to deprive any one of his personal liberty, his property, or any other thing which belongs to him by law. Here, therefore, is one instance of the application of the terms just and unjust in a perfectly definite sense, namely that it is just to respect, unjust to violate, the *legal rights* of any one. But this judgment admits of several exceptions, arising from the other forms in which the notions of justice and injustice present themselves. For example, the person who suffers the deprivation may (as the phrase is) have *forfeited* the rights which he is so deprived of: a case to which we shall return presently. But also,

Secondly: the legal rights of which he is deprived, may be rights which *ought* not to have belonged to him; in other words, the law which confers on him these rights, may be a bad law. When it is so, or when (which is the same thing for our purpose) it is supposed to be so, opinions will differ as to the justice or injustice of infringing it. Some maintain that no law, however bad, ought to be disobeyed by an individual citizen; that his opposition to it, if shown at all, should be shown only in endeavouring to get it altered by competent authority.

This opinion (which condemns many of the most illustrious benefactors of mankind, and would often protect pernicious institutions against the only weapons which, in the state of things existing at the time, have any chance of succeeding against them) is defined by those who hold it on grounds of expediency; principally on that of the importance, to the common interest of mankind, of maintaining inviolate the sentiment of submission to law. Other persons, again, hold the directly contrary opinion, that any law, judged to be bad, may blamelessly be disobeyed, even though it be not judged to be unjust, but only inexpedient; while others would confine the licence of disobedience to the case of unjust laws: but again, some say, that all laws which are inexpedient are unjust; since every law imposes some restriction on the natural liberty of mankind, which restriction is an injustice, unless legitimated by tending to their good. Among these diversities of opinion, it seems to be universally admitted that there may be unjust laws, and that law, consequently, is not the ultimate criterion of justice, but may give to one person a benefit, or impose on another an evil, which justice condemns. When, however, a law is thought to be unjust, it seems always to be regarded as being so in the same way in which a breach of law is unjust, namely, by infringing somebody's right; which, as it cannot in this case be a legal right, receives a different appellation, and is called a moral right. We may say, therefore, that a second case of injustice consists in taking or withholding from any person that to which he has a *moral right*.

Thirdly: It is universally considered just that each person should obtain that (whether good or evil) which he *deserves*; and unjust that he should obtain a good, or be made to undergo an evil, which he does not deserve. This is, perhaps, the clearest and most emphatic form in which the idea of justice is conceived by the general mind. As it involves the notion of desert, the question arises, what constitutes desert? Speaking in a general way, a person is understood to deserve good if he does right, evil if he does wrong; and in a more particular sense, to deserve good from those to whom he does or has done good, and evil from those to whom he does or has done evil. The precept of returning good for evil has never been regarded as a case of the fulfilment of justice, but as one in which the claims of justice are waved, in obedience to other considerations.

Fourthly: it is confessedly unjust to *break faith* with any one: to violate an engagement, either express or implied, or disappoint expectations raised by our own conduct, at least if we have raised those expectations knowingly and voluntarily. Like the other obligations of justice already spoken of, this one is not regarded as absolute, but as capable of being overruled by a stronger obligation of justice on the other side; or by such conduct on the part of the person concerned as is deemed to absolve us from our obligation to him, and to constitute a *forfeiture* of the benefit which he has been led to expect.

Fifthly: it is, by universal admission, inconsistent with justice to be *partial*; to show favour or preference to one person over another, in matters to which favour and preference do not properly apply. Impartiality, however, does not seem to be regarded as a duty in itself, but rather as instrumental to some other duty; for it is admitted that favour and preference are not always censurable, and indeed the cases in which they are condemned are rather the exception than the rule. A person would be more likely to be blamed than applauded for giving his family or friends no superiority in good offices over strangers, when he could do so without violating any other duty; and no one thinks it unjust to seek one person in preference to another as a friend, connexion, or companion. Impartiality where rights are concerned, is of course obligatory, but this is involved in the more general obligation, of giving to every one his right. A tribunal, for example, must be impartial, because it is bound to award, without regard to any other consideration, a disputed object to the one of two parties who has the right to it. There are other cases in which impartiality means, being solely influenced by desert; as with those who, in the capacity of judges, preceptors, or parents, administer reward and punishment as such. There are cases, again, in which it means, being solely influenced by consideration for the public interest; as in making a selection among candidates for a government employment. Impartiality, in short, as an obligation of justice, may be said to mean, being exclusively influenced by the considerations which it is supposed ought to influence the particular case in hand; and resisting the solicitation of any motives which prompt to conduct different from what those considerations would dictate.

Nearly allied to the idea of impartiality, is that of *equality*; which often enters as a component part both into the conception of justice and into the practice of it, and, in the eyes of many persons, constitutes its essence. But in this, still more than in any other case, the notion of justice varies in different persons, and always conforms in its variations to their notion of utility. Each person maintains that equality is the dictate of justice, except where he thinks that expediency requires inequality. The justice of giving equal protection to the rights of all, is maintained by those who support the most outrageous inequality in the rights themselves. Even in slave countries it is theoretically admitted that the rights of the slave, such as they are, ought to be as sacred as those of the master; and that a tribunal which fails to enforce them with equal strictness is wanting in justice; while, at the same time, institutions which leave to the slave scarcely any rights to enforce, are not deemed unjust, because they are not deemed inexpedient. Those who think that utility requires distinctions of rank, do not consider it unjust that riches and social privileges should be unequally dispensed; but those who think this inequality inexpedient, think it unjust also. Whoever thinks that government is necessary, sees no injustice in as much inequality as is constituted by giving to the magistrate powers not granted to other people. Even among those who hold levelling doctrines, there are as many questions of justice as there are differences of opinion about expediency. Some Communists consider it unjust that the produce of the labour of the community should be shared on any other principle than that of exact equality; others think it just that those should receive most whose wants are greatest; while others hold that those who work harder, or who produce more, or whose services are more valuable to the community, may justly claim a larger quota in the division of the produce. And the sense of natural justice may be plausibly appealed to in behalf of every one of these opinions.

Among so many diverse applications of the term Justice, which yet is not regarded as ambiguous, it is a matter of some difficulty to seize the mental link which holds them together, and on which the moral sentiment adhering to the term essentially depends. Perhaps, in this embarrassment, some help may be derived from the history of the word, as indicated by its etymology.

In most, if not in all, languages, the etymology of the word which corresponds to Just, points distinctly to an origin connected with the ordinances of law. *Justum* is a form of *jussum*, that which has been ordered. Δίκαιον comes directly from δίκη, a·suit at law. *Recht*, from which came *right* and *righteous*, is synonymous with law. The courts of justice, the administration of justice, are the courts and the administration of law. *La justice*, in French, is the established term for judicature. I am not committing the fallacy, imputed with some show of truth to Horne Tooke, of assuming that a word must still continue to mean what it originally meant. Etymology is slight evidence of what the idea now signified is, but the very best evidence of how it sprang up. There can, I think, be no doubt that the *idée mère*, the primitive element, in the formation of the notion of justice, was conformity to law. It constituted the entire idea among the Hebrews, up to the birth of Christianity; as might be expected in the case of a people whose laws attempted to embrace all subjects on which precepts were required, and who believed those laws to be a direct emanation from the Supreme Being. But other nations, and in particular the Greeks and Romans, who knew that their laws had been made originally, and still continued to be made, by men, were not afraid to admit that those men might make bad laws; might do, by law, the same things, and from the same motives, which if done by individuals without the sanction of law, would be called unjust. And hence the sentiment of injustice came to be attached, not to all violations of law, but only to violations of such laws as *ought* to exist, including such as ought to exist, but do not; and to laws themselves, if supposed to be contrary to what ought to be law. In this manner the idea of law and of its injunctions was still predominant in the notion of justice, even when the laws actually in force ceased to be accepted as the standard of it.

It is true that mankind consider the idea of justice and its obligations as applicable to many things which neither are, nor is it desired that they should be, regulated by law. Nobody desires that laws should interfere with the whole detail of private life; yet every one allows that in all daily conduct a person may and does show himself to be either just or unjust. But even here, the idea of the breach of what ought to be law, still lingers in a modified shape. It would always give us pleasure, and chime in with our feelings of fitness, that acts which we deem unjust should be punished, though we do not always think it expedient that this should be done by the tribunals. We forego that gratification on account of incidental inconveniences. We should be glad to see just conduct enforced and injustice repressed, even in the minutest details, if we were not, with reason, afraid of trusting the magistrate with so unlimited an amount of power over individuals. When we think that a person is bound in justice to do a thing, it is an ordinary form of language to say that he ought to be compelled to do it. We should be gratified to see the obligation enforced by anybody who had the power. If we see that its enforcement by law would be inexpedient, we lament the impossibility, we consider the impunity given to injustice as an evil, and strive to make amends for it by bringing a strong expression of our own and the public disapprobation to bear upon the offender. Thus the idea of legal constraint is still the generating idea of the notion of justice, though undergoing several transformations before that notion, as it exists in an advanced state of society, becomes complete.

The above is, I think, a true account, as far as it goes, of the origin and progressive growth of the idea of justice. But we must observe, that it contains, as yet, nothing to distinguish that obligation from moral obligation in general. For the truth is, that the idea of penal sanction, which is the essence of law, enters not only into the conception of injustice, but into that of any kind of wrong. We do not call anything wrong, unless we mean to imply that a person ought to be punished in some way or other for doing it, if not by law, by the opinion of his fellow creatures; if not by opinion, by the reproaches of his own conscience. This seems the real turning point of the distinction between morality and simple expediency. It is a part of the notion of Duty in every one of its forms, that a person may rightfully be compelled to fulfil it. Duty is a thing which may be *exacted* from a person, as one exacts a debt. Unless we think that it may be exacted from him, we do not call it his duty. Reasons of prudence, or the interest of other people, may militate against actually exacting it; but the person himself, it is clearly understood, would not be entitled to complain. There are other things, on the contrary, which we wish that people should do, which we like or admire them for doing, perhaps dislike or despise them for not doing, but yet admit that they are not bound to do; it is not a case of moral obligation; we do not blame them, that is, we do not think that they are proper objects of punishment. How we come by these ideas of deserving and not deserving punishment, will appear, perhaps, in the sequel; but I think there is no doubt that this distinction lies at the bottom of the notions of right and wrong; that we call any conduct wrong, or employ, instead, some other term of dislike or disparagement, according as we think that the person ought, or ought not, to be punished for it; and we say, it would be right to do so and so, or merely that it would be desirable or laudable, according as we would wish to see the person whom it concerns, compelled, or only persuaded and exhorted, to act in that manner.[1]

This, therefore, being the characteristic difference which marks off, not justice, but morality in general, from the remaining provinces of Expediency and Worthiness; the character is still to be sought which distinguishes justice from other branches of morality. Now it is known that ethical writers divide moral duties into two classes, denoted by the ill-chosen expressions, duties of perfect and of imperfect obligation; the latter being those in which, though the act is obligatory, the particular occasions of performing it are left to our choice; as in the case of charity or beneficence, which we are indeed bound to practise, but not towards any definite person, nor at any prescribed time. In the more precise language of philosophic jurists, duties of perfect obligation are those duties in virtue of which a correlative *right* resides in some person or persons; duties of imperfect obligations are those moral obligations which do not give birth to any right. I think it will be found that this distinction exactly coincides with that which exists between justice and the other obligations of morality.

In our survey of the various popular acceptations of justice, the term appeared generally to involve the idea of a personal right—a claim on the part of one or more individuals, like that which the law gives when it confers a proprietary or other legal right. Whether the injustice consists in depriving a person of a possession, or in breaking faith with him, or in treating him worse than he deserves, or worse than other people who have no greater claims, in each case the supposition implies two things—a wrong done, and some assignable person who is wronged. Injustice may also be done by treating a person better than others; but the wrong in this

---

1. See this point enforced and illustrated by Professor Bain, in an admirable chapter (entitled *The Ethical Emotions, or the Moral Sense*) of the second of the two treatises composing his elaborate and profound work on the Mind.

case is to his competitors; who are also assignable persons. It seems to me that this feature in the case—a right in some person, correlative to the moral obligation—constitutes the specific difference between justice, and generosity or beneficence. Justice implies something which it is not only right to do, and wrong not to do, but which some individual person can claim from us as his moral right. No one has a moral right to our generosity or beneficence, because we are not morally bound to practise those virtues towards any given individual. And it will be found with respect to this as to every correct definition, that the instances which seem to conflict with it are those which most confirm it. For if a moralist attempts, as some have done, to make out that mankind generally, though not any given individual, have a right to all the good we can do them, he at once, by that thesis, includes generosity and beneficence within the category of justice. He is obliged to say that our utmost exertions are *due* to our fellow creatures, thus assimilating them to a debt; or that nothing less can be a sufficient *return* for what society does for us, thus classing the case as one of gratitude; both of which are acknowledged cases of justice. Wherever there is a right, the case is one of justice, and not of the virtue of beneficence: and whoever does not place the distinction between justice and morality in general, where we have now placed it, will be found to make no distinction between them at all, but to merge all morality in justice.

Having thus endeavoured to determine the distinctive elements which enter into the composition of the idea of justice, we are ready to enter on the inquiry, whether the feeling which accompanies the idea is attached to it by a special dispensation of nature, or whether it could have grown up, by any known laws, out of the idea itself; and in particular, whether it can have originated in considerations of general expediency.

I conceive that the sentiment itself does not arise from anything which would commonly, or correctly, be termed an idea of expediency; but that, though the sentiment does not, whatever is moral in it does.

We have seen that the two essential ingredients in the settlement of justice are the desire to punish a person who has done harm, and the knowledge or belief that there is some definite individual or individuals to whom harm has been done.

Now it appears to me, that the desire to punish a person who has done harm to some individual, is a spontaneous outgrowth from two sentiments, both in the highest degree natural, and which either are or resemble instincts; the impulse of self-defence, and the feeling of sympathy.

It is natural to resent, and to repel or retaliate, any harm done or attempted against ourselves, or against those with whom we sympathize. The origin of this sentiment it is not necessary here to discuss. Whether it be an instinct or a result of intelligence, it is, we know, common to all animal nature; for every animal tries to hurt those who have hurt, or who it thinks are about to hurt, itself or its young. Human beings, on this point, only differ from other animals in two particulars. First, in being capable of sympathizing, not solely with their offspring, or, like some of the more noble animals, with some superior animal who is kind to them, but with all human, and even with all sentient, beings. Secondly, in having a more developed intelligence, which gives a wider range to the whole of their sentiments, whether self-regarding or sympathetic. By virtue of his superior intelligence, even apart from his superior range of sympathy, a human being is capable of apprehending a community of interest between himself and the human society of which he forms a part, such that any conduct which threatens the security of the society generally, is threatening to his own, and calls forth his instinct (if instinct it be) of self-defence. The same superiority of intelligence, joined to the power of sympathizing with human beings generally, enables him to attach himself to the collective idea of his tribe, his country, or mankind, in such a manner that any act hurtful to them, raises his instinct of sympathy, and urges him to resistance.

The sentiment of justice, in that one of its elements which consists of the desire to punish, is thus, I conceive, the natural feeling of retaliation or vengeance, rendered by intellect and sympathy applicable to those injuries, that is, to those hurts, which wound us through, or in common with, society at large. This sentiment, in itself, has nothing moral in it; what is moral is, the exclusive subordination of it to the social sympathies, so as to wait on and obey, their call. For the natural feeling would make us resent indiscriminately whatever any one does that is disagreeable to us; but when moralized by the social feeling, it only acts in the directions conformable to the general good: just persons resenting a hurt to society, though not otherwise a hurt to themselves, and not resenting a hurt to themselves, however painful, unless it be of the kind which society has a common interest with them in the repression of.

It is no objection against this doctrine to say, that when we feel our sentiment of justice outraged, we are not thinking of society at large, or of any collective interest, but only of the individual case. It is common enough certainly, though the reverse of commendable, to feel resentment merely because we have suffered pain; but a person whose resentment is really a moral feeling, that is, who considers whether an act is blameable before he allows himself to resent it—such a person, though he may not say expressly to himself that he is standing up for the interest of society, certainly does feel that he is asserting a rule which is for the benefit of others as well as for his own. If he is not feeling this—if he is regarding the act solely as it affects him individually—he is not consciously just; he is not concerning himself about the justice of his actions. This is admitted even by anti-utilitarian moralists. When Kant (as before remarked) propounds as the fundamental principle of morals, 'So act, that thy rule of conduct might, be adopted as a law by all rational beings', he virtually acknowledges that the interest of mankind collectively, or at least of mankind indiscriminately, must be in the mind of the agent when conscientiously deciding on the morality of the act. Otherwise he uses words without a meaning; for, that a rule even of utter selfishness could not *possibly* be adopted by all rational beings—that there is any insuperable obstacle in the nature of things to its adoption—cannot be even plausibly maintained. To give any meaning to Kant's principle, the sense put upon it must be, that we ought to shape our conduct by a rule which all rational beings might adopt *with benefit to their collective interest.*

To recapitulate: the idea of justice supposes two things; a rule of conduct, and a sentiment which sanctions the rule. The first must be supposed common to all mankind, and intended for their good. The other (the sentiment) is a desire that punishment may be suffered by those who infringe the rule. There is involved, in addition, the conception of some definite person who suffers by the infringement; whose rights (to use the expression appropriated to the case) are violated by it. And the sentiment of justice appears to me to be, the animal desire to repel or retaliate a hurt or damage to oneself, or to those with whom one sympathizes, widened so as to include all persons, by the human capacity of enlarged sympathy, and the human conception of intelligent self-interest. From the latter elements, the feeling derives its morality; from the former, its peculiar impressiveness, and energy of self-assertion.

I have, throughout, treated the idea of a *right* residing in the injured person, and violated by the injury, not as a separate element in the composition of the idea and sentiment, but as one of the forms in which the other two elements clothe themselves. These elements are a hurt to some assignable person or persons on the one hand, and a demand for punishment on the other. An examination of our own minds, I think, will show that these two things include all that we mean when we speak of violation of a right. When we call anything a person's right, we mean that he has a valid claim on society to protect him in the possession of it, either by the force of law, or by that of education and opinion. If he has what we consider a sufficient claim, on whatever account, to have something guaranteed to him by society, we say that he has a right to it. If we desire to prove that anything does not belong to him by right, we think this done as soon as it is admitted that society ought not to take measures for securing it to him, but should leave him to chance, or to his own exertions. Thus, a person is said to have a right to what he can earn in fair professional competition; because society ought not to allow any other person to hinder him from endeavouring to earn in that manner as much as he can. But he has not a right to three hundred a-year, though he may happen to be earning it; because society is not called on to provide that he shall earn that sum. On the contrary, if he owns ten thousand pounds three per cent stock, he *has* a right to three hundred a-year; because society has come under an obligation to provide him with an income of that amount.

To have a right, then, is, I conceive, to have something which society ought to defend me in the possession of. If the objector goes on to ask, why it ought? I can give him no other reason than general utility. If that expression does not seem to convey a sufficient feeling of the strength of the obligation, nor to account for the peculiar energy of the feeling, it is because there goes to the composition of the sentiment, not a rational only but also an animal element, the thirst for retaliation; and this thirst derives its intensity, as well as its moral justification, from the extraordinarily important and impressive kind of utility which is concerned. The interest involved is that of security, to every one's feelings the most vital of all interests. All other earthly benefits are needed by one person, not needed by another; and many of them can, if necessary, be cheerfully foregone, or replaced by something else; but security no human being can possibly do without; on it we depend for all our immunity from evil, and for the whole value of all and every good, beyond the passing moment; since nothing but the gratification of the instant could be of any worth to us, if we could be deprived of everything the next instant by whoever was momentarily stronger than ourselves. Now this most indispensable of all necessaries, after physical nutriment, cannot be had, unless the machinery for providing it is kept unintermittedly in active play. Our notion, therefore, of the claim we have on our fellow creatures to join in making safe for us the very groundwork of our existence, gathers feelings around it so much more intense than those concerned in any of the more common cases of utility, that the difference in degree (as is often the case in psychology) becomes a real difference in kind. The claim assumes that character of absoluteness, that apparent infinity, and incommensurability with all other considerations, which constitute the distinction between the feeling of right and wrong and that of ordinary expediency and inexpediency. The feelings concerned are so powerful, and we count so positively on finding a responsive feeling in others (all being alike interested), that *ought* and *should* grow into *must*, and recognized indispensability becomes a moral necessity, analogous to physical, and often not inferior to it in binding force.

If the preceding analysis, or something resembling it, be not the correct account of the notion of justice; if justice be totally independent of utility, and be a standard *per se*, which the mind can recognize by simple introspection of itself, it is hard to understand why that internal oracle is so ambiguous, and why so many things appear either just or unjust, according to the light in which they are regarded.

We are continually informed that Utility is an uncertain standard, which every different person interprets differently, and that there is no safety but in the immutable, ineffaceable, and unmistakable dictates of Justice, which carry their evidence in themselves, and are independent of the fluctuations of opinion. One would suppose from this that on questions of justice there could be no controversy; that if we take that for our rule, its application to any given case could leave us in as little doubt as a mathematical demonstration. So far is this from being the fact, that there is as much difference of opinion, and as much discussion, about what is just, as about what is useful to society. Not only have different nations and individuals different notions of justice, but in the mind of one and the same individual, justice is not some one rule, principle or maxim, but many, which do not always coincide in their dictates, and in choosing between which, he is guided either by some extraneous standard, or by his own personal predilections.

For instance, there are some who say that it is unjust to punish any one for the sake of example to others; that punishment is just, only when intended for the good of the sufferer himself. Others maintain the extreme reverse, contending that to punish persons who have attained years of discretion, for their own benefit, is despotism and injustice, since if the matter at issue is solely their own good, no one has a right to control their own judgment of it; but that they may justly be punished to prevent evil to others, this being the exercise of the legitimate right of self-defence.

Mr. Owen, again, affirms that it is unjust to punish at all; for the criminal did not make his own character; his education, and the circumstances which surrounded him, have made him a criminal, and for these he is not responsible. All these opinions are extremely plausible; and, so long as the question is argued as one of justice simply, without going down to the principles which lie under justice and are the source of its authority, I am unable to see how any of these reasoners can be refuted. For in truth every one of the three builds upon rules of justice confessedly true.

The first appeals to the acknowledged injustice of singling out an individual, and making him a sacrifice, without his consent, for other people's benefit. The second relies on the acknowledged justice of self-defence, and the admitted injustice of forcing one person to conform to another's notions of what constitutes his good. The Owenite invokes the admitted principle that it is unjust to punish any one for what he cannot help. Each is triumphant so long as he is not compelled to take into consideration any other maxims of justice than the one he has selected; but as soon as their several maxims are brought face to face, each disputant seems to have exactly as much to say for himself as the others. No one of them can carry out his own notion of justice without trampling upon another equally binding. These are difficulties; they have always been felt to be such; and many devices have been invented to turn rather than to overcome them. As a refuge from the last of the three, men imagined what they called the freedom of the will; fancying that they could not justify punishing a man whose will is in a thoroughly hateful state, unless it be supposed to have come into that state through no influence of anterior circumstances. To escape from the other difficulties, a favourite contrivance has been the fiction of a contract, whereby at some unknown period all the members of society engaged to obey the laws, and consented to be punished for any disobedience to them; thereby giving to their legislators the right, which it is assumed they would not otherwise have had, of punishing them, either for their own good or for that of society.

This happy thought was considered to get rid of the whole difficulty, and to legitimate the infliction of punishment, in virtue of another received maxim of justice, *Volenti non fit injuria*; that is not unjust which is done with the consent of the person who is supposed to be hurt by it. I need hardly remark that even if the consent were not a mere fiction, this maxim is not superior in authority to the others which it is brought in to supersede. It is, on the contrary, an instructive specimen of the loose and irregular manner in which supposed principles of justice grow up. This particular one evidently came into use as a help to the coarse exigencies of courts of law, which are sometimes obliged to be content with very uncertain presumptions on account of the greater evils which would often arise from any attempt on their part to cut finer. But even courts of law are not able to adhere consistently to the maxim, for they allow voluntary engagements to be set aside on the ground of fraud, and sometimes on that of mere mistake or misinformation.

Again, when the legitimacy of inflicting punishment is admitted, how many conflicting conceptions of justice come to light in discussing the proper apportionment of punishments to offences. No rule on the subject recommends itself so strongly to the primitive and spontaneous sentiment of justice as the *lex talionis*, an eye for an eye and a tooth for a tooth. Though this principle of the Jewish and of the Mahomedan law has been generally abandoned in Europe as a practical maxim, there is, I suspect, in most minds, a secret hankering after it; and when retribution accidentally falls on an offender in that precise shape, the general feeling of satisfaction evinced, bears witness how natural is the sentiment to which this repayment in kind is acceptable. With many the test of justice in penal infliction is that the punishment should be proportioned to the offence; meaning that it should be exactly measured by the moral guilt of the culprit (whatever be their standard for measuring moral guilt): the consideration, what amount of punishment is necessary to deter from the offence, having nothing to do with the question of justice, in their estimation; while there are others to whom that consideration is all in all; who maintain that it is not just, at least for man, to inflict on a fellow-creature, whatever may be his offences, any amount of suffering beyond the least that will suffice to prevent him from repeating, and others from imitating, his misconduct.

To take another example from a subject already once referred to. In a co-operative industrial association is it just or not that talent or skill should give a title to superior remuneration? On the negative side of the question it is argued that whoever does the best he can deserves equally well, and ought not in justice to be put in a position of inferiority for no fault of his own; that superior abilities have already advantages more than enough, in the admiration they excite, the personal influence they command, and the internal sources of satisfaction attending them, without adding to these a superior share of the world's goods; and that society is bound in justice rather to make compensation to the less favoured, for this unmerited inequality of advantages, than to aggravate it. On the contrary side it is contended that society receives more from the more efficient labourer; that his services being more useful, society owes him a larger return for them; that a greater share of the joint result is actually his work, and not to allow his claim to it is a kind of robbery; that if he is only to receive as much as others, he can only be justly required to produce as much, and to give a smaller amount of time and exertion, proportioned to his superior efficiency. Who shall decide between these appeals to conflicting principles of justice? Justice has in this case two sides to it, which it is impossible to bring into harmony, and the two disputants have chosen opposite sides; the one looks to what it is just that the individual should receive, the other to what it is just that the community should give. Each from his own point of view is unanswerable; and any choice between them, on grounds of justice, must be perfectly arbitrary. Social utility alone can decide the preference.

How many, again, and how irreconcilable, are the standards of justice to which reference is made in discussing the repartition of taxation. One opinion is that payment to the State should be in numerical proportion to pecuniary means. Others think that justice dictates what they term graduated taxation; taking a higher per-centage from those who have more to spare. In point of natural justice a strong case might be made for disregarding means altogether, and taking the same absolute sum (whenever it could be got) from every one: as the subscribers to a mess, or to a club, all pay the same sum for the same privileges, whether they can all equally afford it or not. Since the protection (it might be said) of law and government is afforded to and is equally required by all, there is no injustice in making all buy it at the same price. It is reckoned justice, not injustice, that a dealer should charge to all customers the same price for the same article, not a price varying according to their means of payment. This doctrine, as applied to taxation, finds no advocates, because it conflicts so strongly with man's feelings of humanity and of social expediency; but the principle of justice which it invokes is as true and as binding as those which can be appealed to against it. Accordingly it exerts a tacit influence on the line of defence employed for other modes of assessing taxation. People feel obliged to argue that the State does more for the rich than for the poor, as a justification for its taking more from them: though this is in reality not true, for the rich would be far better able to protect themselves, in the absence of law or government, than the poor, and indeed would probably be successful in converting the poor into their slaves. Others, again, so far defer to the same conception of justice as to maintain that all should pay an equal capitation tax for the protection of their persons (these being of equal value to all), and an unequal tax for the protection of their property, which is unequal. To this others reply that the all of one man is as valuable to him as the all of another. From these confusions there is no other mode of extrication than the utilitarian.

Is, then, the difference between the Just and the Expedient a merely imaginary distinction? Have mankind been under a delusion in thinking that justice is a more sacred thing than policy, and that the latter ought only to be listened to after the former has been satisfied? By no means. The exposition we have given of the nature and origin of the sentiment, recognizes a real distinction; and no one of those who profess the most sublime contempt for the consequences of actions as an element in their morality, attaches more importance to the distinction than I do. While I dispute the pretensions of any theory which sets up an imaginary standard of justice not grounded on utility, I account the justice which is grounded on utility to be the chief part, and incomparably the most sacred and binding part, of all morality. Justice is a name for certain classes of moral rules, which concern the essentials of human well-being more nearly, and are therefore of more absolute obligation, than any other rules for the guidance of life; and the notion which we have found to be of the essence of the idea of justice, that of a right residing in an individual, implies and testifies to this more binding obligation.

The moral rules which forbid mankind to hurt one another (in which we must never forget to include wrongful interference with each other's freedom) are more vital to human well-being than any maxims, however important, which only point out the best mode of managing some department of human affairs. They have also the peculiarity, that they are the main element in determining the whole of the social feelings of mankind. It is their observance which alone preserves peace among human beings: if obedience to them were not the rule, and disobedience the exception, every one would see in every one else an enemy, against whom he must be perpetually guarding himself. What is hardly less important, these are the precepts which mankind have the strongest and the most direct inducements for impressing upon one another. By merely giving to each other prudential instruction or exhortation, they may gain, or think they gain, nothing: in inculcating on each other the duty of positive beneficence they have an unmistakable interest, but far less in degree: a person may possibly not need the benefits of others; but he always needs that they should not do him hurt.

Thus the moralities which protect every individual from being harmed by others, either directly or by being hindered in his freedom of pursuing his own good, are at once those which he himself has most at heart, and those which he has the strongest interest in publishing and enforcing by word and deed. It is by a person's observance of these that his fitness to exist as one of the fellowship of human beings is tested and decided; for on that depends his being a nuisance or not to those with whom he is in contact. Now it is these moralities primarily, which compose the obligations of justice. The most marked cases of injustice, and those which give the tone to the feeling of repugnance which characterizes the sentiment, are acts of wrongful aggression, or wrongful exercise of power over some one; the next are those which consist in wrongfully withholding from him something which is his due: in both cases, inflicting on him a positive hurt, either in the form of direct suffering, or of the privation of some good which he had reasonable ground, either of a physical or of a social kind, for counting upon.

The same powerful motives which command the observance of these primary moralities enjoin the punishment of those who violate them; and as the impulses of self-defence, of defence of others, and of vengeance, are all called forth against such persons, retribution, or evil for evil, becomes closely connected with the sentiment of justice, and is universally included in the idea. Good for good is also one of the dictates of justice; and this, though its social utility is evident, and though it carries with it a natural human feeling, has not at first sight that obvious connexion with hurt or injury, which, existing in the most elementary cases of just and unjust, is the source of the characteristic intensity of the sentiment. But the connexion, though less obvious, is not less real. He who accepts benefits, and denies a return of them when needed, inflicts a real hurt, by disappointing one of the most natural and reasonable of expectations, and one which he must at least tacitly have encouraged, otherwise the benefits would seldom have been conferred. The important rank, among human evils and wrongs, of the disappointment of expectation, is shown in the fact that it constitutes the principal criminality of two such highly immoral acts as a breach of friendship and a breach of promise. Few hurts which human beings can sustain are greater, and none wound more, than when that on which they habitually and with full assurance relied, fails them in the hour of need; and few wrongs are greater than this mere withholding of good; none excite more resentment, either in the person suffering, or in a sympathizing spectator. The principle, therefore, of giving to each what they deserve, that is, good for good as well as evil for evil, is not only included within the idea of Justice as we have defined it, but is a proper object of that intensity of sentiment, which places the Just, in human estimation, above the simply Expedient.

Most of the maxims of justice current in the world, and commonly appealed to in its transactions, are simply instrumental to carrying into effect the principles of justice which we have now spoken of. That a person is responsible only for what he has done voluntarily, or could voluntarily have avoided; that it is unjust to condemn any person unheard; that the punishment ought to be proportioned to the offence, and the like, are maxims intended to prevent the just principle of evil for evil from being perverted to the infliction of evil without that justification. The greater part of these common maxims have come into use from the practice of courts of justice, which have been naturally led to a more complete recognition and elaboration than was likely to suggest itself to others, of the rules necessary to enable them to fulfil their double function, of inflicting punishment when due, and of awarding to each person his right.

That first of judicial virtues, impartiality, is an obligation of justice, partly for the reason last mentioned; as being a necessary condition of the fulfilment of the obligations of justice. But this is not the only source of the exalted rank, among human obligations, of those maxims of equality and impartiality, which, both in popular estimation and in that of the most enlightened, are included among the precepts of justice. In one point of view, they may be considered as corollaries from the principles already laid down. If it is a duty to do to each according to his deserts, returning good for good as well as repressing evil by evil, it necessarily follows that we should treat all equally well (when no higher duty forbids) who have deserved equally well of *us*, and that society should treat all equally well who have deserved equally well of *it*, that is, who have deserved equally well absolutely. This is the highest abstract standard of social and distributive justice; towards which all institutions, and the efforts of all virtuous citizens, should be made in the utmost possible degree to converge.

But this great moral duty rests upon a still deeper foundation, being a direct emanation from the first principle of morals, and not a mere logical corollary from secondary or derivative doctrines. It is involved in the very meaning of Utility, or the Greatest-Happiness Principle. That principle is a mere form of words without rational signification, unless one person's happiness, supposed equal in degrees (with the proper allowance made for kind), is counted for exactly as much as another's. Those conditions being supplied, Bentham's dictum, 'everybody to count for one, nobody for more than one', might be written under the principle of utility as an explanatory commentary.[2] The equal claim of everybody to happiness in the

---

2. This implication, in the first principle of the utilitarian scheme of perfect impartiality between persons, is regarded by Mr. Herbert Spencer (in his *Social Statics*) as a disproof of the pretensions of utility to be a sufficient guide to right: since (he says) the principle of utility presupposes the anterior principle, that everybody has an equal right to happiness. It may be more correctly described as supposing that equal amounts of happiness are equally desirable whether felt by the same or

estimation of the moralist and the legislator, involves an equal claim to all the means of happiness, except in so far as the inevitable conditions of human life, and the general interest, in which that of every individual is included, set limits to the maxim; and those limits ought to be strictly construed. As every other maxim of justice, so this, is by no means applied or held applicable, universally; on the contrary, as I have already remarked, it bends to every person's ideas of social expediency. But in whatever case it is deemed applicable at all, it is held to be the dictate of justice. All persons are deemed to have a *right* to equality of treatment, except when some recognised social expediency requires the reverse. And hence all social inequalities which have ceased to be considered expedient, assume the character not of simple inexpediency, but of injustice, and appear so tyrannical, that people are apt to wonder how they ever could have been tolerated; forgetful that they themselves perhaps tolerate other inequalities under an equally mistaken notion of expediency, the correc-

---

by different persons. This, however, is not a *presupposition*: not a premise needful to support the principle of utility, but the very principle itself; for what is the principle of utility, if it be not that 'happiness' and 'desirable' are synonymous terms? If there is any anterior principle implied, it can be no other than this, that the truths of arithmetic are applicable to the valuation of happiness, as of all other measurable quantities.

[Mr. Herbert Spencer, in a private communication on the subject of the preceding Note, objects to being considered an opponent of Utilitarianism, and states that he regards happiness as the ultimate end of morality; but deems that end only partially attainable by empirical generalizations from the observed results of conduct, and completely attainable only by deducing, from the laws of life and the conditions of existence, what kinds of action necessarily tend to produce happiness, and what kinds to produce unhappiness. With the exception of the word 'necessarily' I have no dissent to express from this doctrine, and (omitting that word) I am not aware that any modern advocate of utilitarianism is of a different opinion. Bentham, certainly, to whom in the *Social Statics* Mr. Spencer particularly referred, is, least of all writers, chargeable with unwillingness to deduce the effect of actions on happiness from the laws of human nature and the universal conditions of human life. The common charge against him is of relying too exclusively upon such deductions, and declining altogether to be bound by the generalizations from specific experiences which Mr. Spencer thinks that utilitarians generally confine themselves to. My own opinion (and, as I collect, Mr. Spencer's) is, that in ethics, as in all other branches of scientific study, the consilience of the results of both these processes, each corroborating and verifying the other, is requisite to give to any general proposition the kind and degree of evidence which constitutes scientific proof.]

tion of which would make that which they approve, seem quite as monstrous as what they have at last learnt to condemn. The entire history of social improvement has been a series of transitions, by which one custom or institution after another, from being a supposed primary necessity of social existence, has passed into the rank of an universally stigmatized injustice and tyranny. So it has been with the distinctions of slaves and freemen, nobles and serfs, patricians and plebeians; and so it will be, and in part already is, with the aristocracies of colour, race, and sex.

It appears from what has been said that justice is a name for certain moral requirements, which, regarded collectively, stand higher in the scale of social utility, and are therefore of more paramount obligation, than any others: though particular cases may occur in which some other social duty is so important, as to overrule any one of the general maxims of justice. Thus, to save a life it may not only be allowable, but a duty, to steal, or take by force, the necessary food or medicine, or to kidnap, and compel to officiate, the only qualified medical practitioner. In such cases, as we do not call anything justice which is not a virtue, we usually say, not that justice must give way to some other moral principle, but that what is just in ordinary cases is, by reason of that other principle, not just in the particular case. By this useful accommodation of language, the character of indefeasibility attributed to justice is kept up, and we are saved from the necessity of maintaining that there can be laudable injustice.

The considerations which have now been adduced resolve, I conceive, the only real difficulty in the utilitarian theory of morals. It has always been evident that all cases of justice are also cases of expediency: the difference is in the peculiar sentiment which attaches to the former as contradistinguished from the latter. If this characteristic sentiment has been sufficiently accounted for; if there is no necessity to assume for it any peculiarity of origin; if it is simply the natural feeling of resentment, moralized by being made coextensive with the demands of social good; and if this feeling not only does but ought to exist in all the classes of cases to which the idea of justice corresponds; that idea no longer presents itself as a stumbling-block to the utilitarian ethics. Justice remains the appropriate name for certain social utilities which are vastly more important, and therefore more absolute and imperative, than any others are as a class (though not more so than others may be in particular cases); and which, therefore, ought to be, as well as naturally are, guarded by a sentiment not only different in degree, but also in kind; distinguished from the milder feeling which attaches to the mere idea of promoting human pleasure or convenience, at once by the more definite nature of its commands, and by the sterner character of its sanctions.

11

Karl Marx,
"To Each According to His Needs,"
from *Critique of the Gotha Program*

Karl Marx (1818–1883), German philosopher, political economist, social critic, and advocate of violent revolution, was the father of modern communism. His works include Economic and Philosophic Manuscripts of 1844, *the* Communist Manifesto, *with Friedrich Engels (1848), and* Capital, *of which the first volume was published in 1867. The* Critique of the Gotha Program, *from which the following extract is taken, was Marx's highly critical commentary on a program adopted by an 1875 political congress which took place in Gotha, Southern Germany, at which the modern Socialist Labour Party of Germany was formed from other political groups.*

"Promotion of the instruments of labour to the common property" ought obviously to read their "conversion into the common property"; but this only in passing.

What are "proceeds of labour"? The product of labour or its value? And in the latter case, is it the total value of the product or only that part of the value which labour has newly added to the value of the means of production consumed?

"Proceeds of labour" is a loose notion which Lassalle has put in the place of definite economic conceptions.

What is "a fair distribution"?

Do not the bourgeois assert that the present-day distribution is "fair"? And is it not, in fact, the only "fair" distribution on the basis of the present-day mode of production? Are economic relations regulated by legal conceptions or do not, on the contrary, legal relations arise from economic ones? Have not also the socialist sectarians the most varied notions about "fair" distribution?

To understand what is implied in this connection by the phrase "fair distribution," we must take the first paragraph and this one together. The

From Karl Marx, *The Critique of the Gotha Program*. Reprinted by permission of International Publishers Co., New York.

latter presupposes a society wherein "the instruments of labour are common property and the total labour is cooperatively regulated," and from the first paragraph we learn that "the proceeds of labour belong undiminished with equal right to all members of society."

"To all members of society"? To those who do not work as well? What remains then of the "undiminished proceeds of labour"? Only to those members of society who work? What remains then of the "equal right" of all members of society?

But "all members of society" and "equal right" are obviously mere phrases. The kernel consists in this, that in this communist society every worker must receive the "undiminished" Lassallean "proceeds of labour."

Let us take first of all the words "proceeds of labour" in the sense of the product of labour; then the co-operative proceeds of labour are the *total social product*.

From this must now be deducted:

First, cover for replacement of the means of production used up.

Secondly, additional portion for expansion of production.

Thirdly, reserve or insurance funds to provide against accidents, dislocations caused by natural calamities, etc.

These deductions from the "undiminished proceeds of labour" are an economic necessity and their magnitude is to be determined according to available means and forces, and partly by computation of probabilities, but they are in no way calculable by equity.

There remains the other part of the total product, intended to serve as means of consumption.

Before this is divided among the individuals, there has to be deducted, again, from it:

First, the general costs of administration not belonging to production.

This part will, from the outset, be very considerably restricted in comparison with present-day society and it diminishes in proportion as the new society develops.

Secondly, that which is intended for the common satisfaction of needs, such as schools, health services, etc.

From the outset this part grows considerably in comparison with present-day society and it grows in proportion as the new society develops.

Thirdly, funds for those unable to work, etc., in short, for what is included under so-called official poor relief today.

Only now do we come to the "distribution" which the programme, under Lasallean influence, alone has in view in its narrow fashion, namely, to that part of the means of consumption which is divided among the individual producers of the co-operative society.

The "undiminished proceeds of labour" have already unnoticeably become converted into the "diminished" proceeds, although what the producer is deprived of in his capacity as a private individual benefits him directly or indirectly in his capacity as a member of society.

Just as the phrase of the "undiminished proceeds of labour" has disappeared, so now does the phrase of the "proceeds of labour" disappear altogether.

Within the co-operative society based on common ownership of the means of production, the producers do not exchange their products; just as little does the labour employed on the products appear here *as the value* of these products, as a material quality possessed by them, since now, in contrast to capitalist society, individual labour no longer exists in an indirect fashion but directly as a component part of the total labour. The phrase "proceeds of labour," objectionable also today on account of its ambiguity, thus loses all meaning.

What we have to deal with here is a communist society, not as it has *developed* on its own foundations, but, on the contrary, just as it *emerges* from capitalist society; which is thus in every respect, economically, morally and intellectually, still stamped with the birth marks of the old society from whose womb it emerges. Accordingly, the individual producer receives back from society—after the deductions have been made—exactly what he gives to it. What he has given to it is his individual quantum of labour. For example, the social working day consists of the sum of the individual hours of work; the individual labour time of the individual producer is the part of the social working day contributed by him, his share in it. He receives a certificate from society that he has furnished such and such an amount of labour (after deducting his labour for the common funds), and with this certificate he draws from the social stock of means of consumption as much as costs the same amount of labour. The same amount of labour which he has given to society in one form he receives back in another.

Here obviously the same principle prevails as that which regulates the exchange of commodities, as far as this is exchange of equal values. Content and form are changed, because under the altered circumstances no one can give anything except his labour, and because, on the other hand, nothing can pass to the ownership of individuals except individual means of consumption. But, as far as the distribution of the latter among the individual producers is concerned, the same principle prevails as in the exchange of commodity equivalents: a given amount of labour in one form is exchanged for an equal amount of labour in another form.

Hence, *equal right* here is still in principle—*bourgeois right*, although principle and practice are no longer at loggerheads, while the exchange of equivalents in commodity exchange only exists *on the average* and not in the individual case.

In spite of this advance, this *equal right* is still constantly stigmatised by a bourgeois limitation. The right of the producers is *proportional* to the labour they supply; the equality consists in the fact that measurement is made with an *equal standard*, labour.

But one man is superior to another physically or mentally and so supplies more labour in the same time, or can labour for a longer time; and labour, to serve as a measure, must be defined by its duration or intensity, otherwise it ceases to be a standard of measurement. This *equal* right is an unequal right for unequal labour. It recognises no class differences, because everyone is only a worker like everyone else; but it tacitly recognises unequal individual endowment and thus productive capacity as natural privileges. *It is, therefore, a right of inequality, in its content, like every right.* Right by its very nature can consist only in the application of an equal standard; but unequal individuals (and they would not be different individuals if they were not unequal) are measurable only by an equal standard in so far as they are brought under an equal point of view, are taken from one *definite* side only, for instance, in the present case, are regarded *only as workers* and nothing more is seen in them, everything else being ignored. Further, one worker is married, another not; one has more children than another, and so on and so forth. Thus, with an equal performance of labour, and hence an equal share in the social consumption fund, one will in fact receive more than another, one will be richer than another, and so on. To avoid all these defects, right instead of being equal would have to be unequal.

But these defects are inevitable in the first phase of communist society as it is when it has just emerged after prolonged birth pangs from capitalist society. Right can never be higher than the economic structure of society and its cultural development conditioned thereby.

In a higher phase of communist society, after the enslaving subordination of the individual to the division of labour, and therewith also the antithesis between mental and physical labour, has vanished; after labour has become not only a means of life but life's prime want; after the productive forces have also increased with the all-round development of the individual, and all the springs of co-operative wealth flow more abundantly—

only then can the narrow horizon of bourgeois right be crossed in its entirety and society inscribe on its banner: From each according to his ability, to each according to his needs!

I have dealt more at length with the "undiminished proceeds of labour," on the one hand, and with "equal right" and "fair distribution," on the other, in order to show what a crime it is to attempt, on the one hand, to force on our Party again, as dogmas, ideas which in a certain period had some meaning but have now become obsolete verbal rubbish, while again perverting, on the other, the realistic outlook, which it cost so much effort to instil into the Party but which has now taken root in it, by means of ideological nonsense about right and other trash so common among the democrats and French Socialists.

Quite apart from the analysis so far given, it was in general a mistake to make a fuss about so-called *distribution* and put the principal stress on it.

Any distribution whatever of the means of consumption is only a consequence of the distribution of the conditions of production themselves. The latter distribution, however, is a feature of the mode of production itself. The capitalist mode of production, for example, rests on the fact that the material conditions of production are in the hands of non-workers in the form of property in capital and land, while the masses are only owners of the personal condition of production, of labour power. If the elements of production are so distributed, then the present-day distribution of the means of consumption results automatically. If the material conditions of production are the co-operative property of the workers themselves, then there likewise results a distribution of the means of consumption different from the present one. Vulgar socialism (and from it in turn a section of the democracy) has taken over from the bourgeois economists the consideration and treatment of distribution as independent of the mode of production and hence the presentation of socialism as turning principally on distribution. After the real relation has long been made clear, why retrogress again?

12

Hans Kelsen,
"What Is Justice?"
from *What Is Justice?*

Hans Kelsen (1881–1973), author of Pure Theory of Law *(1967) was an international jurist and legal scholar. He is noted for his legal positivism and his criticism of the doctrine of a natural moral law behind the formally enacted law. He taught at the universities of Vienna, Prague, Cologne, and Geneva and also at Harvard University and the University of California at Berkeley.*

When Jesus of Nazareth was brought before Pilate and admitted that he was a king, he said: "It was for this that I was born, and for this that I came to the world, to give testimony for truth." Whereupon Pilate asked, "What is truth?" The Roman procurator did not expect, and Jesus did not give, an answer to this question; for to give testimony for truth was not the essence of his divine mission as the Messianic King. He was born to give testimony for justice, the justice to be realized in the Kingdom of God, and for this justice he died on the cross. Thus, behind the question of Pilate, "What is truth?" arises, out of the blood of Christ, another still more important question, the eternal question of mankind: What is justice?

No other question has been discussed so passionately; no other question has caused so much precious blood and so many bitter tears to be shed; no other question has been the object of so much intensive thinking by the most illustrious thinkers from Plato to Kant; and yet, this question is today as unanswered as it ever was. It seems that it is one of those questions to which the resigned wisdom applies that man cannot find a definitive answer, but can only try to improve the question.

From Hans Kelsen, *What Is Justice?*, 1957, University of California Press. Reprinted with the kind authorization of the Hans-Kelsen Institute, Vienna.

This essay is based on the author's farewell lecture as an active member of the University of California, Berkeley, May 27, 1952.

Page references in footnotes 2, 12, 18, 19, and 20 refer to later essays in Kelsen's book.

I

Justice is primarily a possible, but not a necessary, quality of a social order regulating the mutual relations of men. Only secondarily it is a virtue
of man, since a man is just, if his behavior conforms to the norms of a social order supposed to be just. But what does it really mean to say that a
social order is just? It means that this order regulates the behavior of men
in a way satisfactory to all men, that is to say, so that all men find their
happiness in it. The longing for justice is men's eternal longing for happiness. It is happiness that man cannot find alone, as an isolated individual, and hence seeks in society. Justice is social happiness. It is
happiness guaranteed by a social order. In this sense Plato, identifying
justice with happiness, maintains that only a just man is happy, and an
unjust man unhappy. The statement that justice is happiness is evidently
not a final answer; it is only shifting the question. For, now, we must ask:
What is happiness?

It is obvious that there can be no "just" order, that is, one affording
happiness to everyone, as long as one defines the concept of happiness in
its original, narrow sense of individual happiness, meaning by a man's
happiness, what he himself considers it to be. For it is then inevitable that
the happiness of one individual will, at some time, be directly in conflict
with that of another. For example, love is one of the most important
sources of happiness as well as of unhappiness. Let us suppose that two
men are in love with one and the same woman, and each believes, rightly
or wrongly, that he cannot be happy without having this woman exclusively for his own wife. However, according to law and perhaps also according to her own feelings, a woman can be only the wife of one of them.
Hence, the happiness of the one is inevitably the unhappiness of the other.
No social order can solve this problem in a satisfactory, that is to say, in a
just way, guaranteeing the happiness of both—not even the famous judgment of the wise King Solomon. He decided, as will be remembered, to
divide into two parts a child which each of two women claimed as her own;
but he was willing to attribute the child to the one who should withdraw
her claim in order to avoid the death of the child, because—so the king
assumed—she truly loved the child. If the Solomonic judgment was just
at all, it was so only under the condition that one woman only loved the
child. If both loved the child, which is quite possible and even probable
since both wished to have it, and if both had withdrawn their claim, the
dispute would have remained undecided; and if, despite the fact that both
women waived their claim, the child had been awarded one of them, the

judgment would certainly not have been just, since it would have made one party unhappy. Our happiness very often depends on the satisfaction of needs which no social order can satisfy.

Another example: The commander in chief of the army shall be appointed. Two men are in competition, but only one can be appointed. It seems to be evident that it is just to appoint the one who is more fit for the office. But what if the two are equally fit? Then, no just solution is possible. Let us suppose that the one is considered to be better than the other because he is tall and handsome, and has an impressive personality, whereas the other, although professionally absolutely equal, is small and plain and looks insignificant. If the first one gets the job, the other will not feel that the decision was just. He will ask, "Why am I not tall and handsome as the other, why has nature given me a less attractive body?" And, indeed, if we judge nature from the point of view of justice, we must admit that nature is not just; it makes the one healthy, and the other sick, the one intelligent, the other stupid. No social order can compensate completely for the injustice of nature.

If justice is happiness, a just social order is impossible if justice means individual happiness. But a just social order is impossible even on the supposition that it tries to bring about, not the individual happiness of each, but the greatest possible happiness of the greatest possible number of individuals. This is the famous definition of justice formulated by the English philosopher and jurist Jeremy Bentham. But Bentham's formula is not applicable, if by happiness is meant a subjective value, and if, consequently, different individuals have different ideas of what constitutes their happiness. The happiness that a social order is able to assure cannot be happiness in a subjective-individual sense; it must be happiness in an objective-collective sense, that is to say, by happiness we must understand the satisfaction of certain needs, recognized by the social authority, the lawgiver, as needs worthy of being satisfied, such as the need to be fed, clothed, housed, and the like. There can be little doubt that satisfaction of socially recognized needs is very different from the original meaning which the idea of happiness implies. That idea has, by its very nature, a highly subjective character. The desire for justice is so elementary, and so deeply rooted in the human mind, because it is a manifestation of man's indestructible desire for his own subjective happiness.

In order to become a social category—the happiness of justice—the idea of happiness must radically change its significance. The metamorphosis of individual happiness into satisfaction of socially recognized needs as the meaning of justice, is similar to the transformation which the idea of freedom must undergo in order to become a social principle; and the idea of freedom is sometimes identified with the idea of justice, so that a social order is considered just if it guarantees individual freedom. Since genuine freedom, that is, freedom from any kind of social authority or government, is incompatible with any kind of social organization, the idea of freedom must cease to mean absence of government; it must assume the meaning of a special form of government: government exercised by the majority—if necessary, against the minority of the governed individuals. The freedom of anarchy turns to the self-determination of democracy. In the same way and for the same reason, the idea of justice is transformed from a principle guaranteeing the individual happiness of all subjects, into a social order protecting certain interests socially recognized by the majority as worthy of being protected.

But which human interests are worthy of being satisfied and, especially, what is their proper order of rank? That is the question which arises when conflicting interest exist, and it is with respect to the possible conflict of interests that justice within a social order is required. Where there is no conflict of interests, there is no need for justice. A conflict of interests exists when one interest can be satisfied only at the expense of the other; or, what amounts to the same, when there is a conflict between two values, and when it is not possible to realize both at the same time; when the one can be realized only if the other is neglected; when it is necessary to prefer the realization of the one to that of the other; to decide which one is more important, or in other terms, to decide which is the higher value, and finally: which is the highest value. The problem of values is in the first place the problem of conflicts of values, and this problem cannot be solved by means of rational cognition. The answer to these questions is a judgment of value, determined by emotional factors, and, therefore, subjective in character—valid only for the judging subject, and therefore relative only. Some examples will illustrate this statement.

II

According to a certain ethical conviction, human life, the life of every human being, is the highest value. Consequently it is, according to this ethical conviction, absolutely forbidden to kill a human being, even in war, and even as capital punishment. This is, for instance, the opinion of so-called conscientious objectors who refuse to perform military service; and of those who repudiate in principle, and in any case, the death penalty. However, there is another ethical conviction, according to which the highest value is the interest and honor of the nation. Consequently, everybody is, according to this opinion, morally obliged to sacrifice his own life and to kill other human beings as enemies of the nation in war if the interest or the honor of the nation requires such action, and it is justified to kill human beings as criminals in inflicting capital punishment. It is impossible to decide between these two conflicting judgments of value in a rational scientific way. It is, in the last instance, our feeling, our will, and not our reason; the emotional, and not the rational element of our consciousness which decides this conflict.

If a man has been made a slave or a prisoner in a Nazi concentration camp, and it is impossible to escape, the question of whether suicide is justifiable in such a situation arises. This is a question which has been again and again discussed, since Socrates drank his poison cup. The decision depends on the answer to the question of which is the higher value: life or freedom. If life is the higher value, then suicide is not justifiable; if freedom is the higher value, if life without freedom is worthless, suicide is morally justified. It is the question of the order or rank of the values, life and freedom. Only a subjective answer is possible to this question, an answer valid only for the judging subject; no objective statement, valid for everybody, as for instance the statement that heat expands metallic bodies.

Let us suppose that it is possible to prove that the economic situation of a people can be improved so essentially by so-called planned economy that social security is guaranteed to everybody in an equal measure; but that such an organization is possible only if all individual freedom is abolished. The answer to the question whether planned economy is preferable to free economy depends on our decision between the values of individual freedom and social security. A man with strong self-confidence may prefer individual freedom, whereas one suffering from an inferiority complex may prefer social security. Hence, to the question of whether individual freedom is a higher value than social security or vice versa, only a subjective answer is possible, no objective judgment, as for instance, the statement that iron is heavier than water, and water heavier than wood. This is a judgment about reality verifiable by experiment, not a judgment of value which defies such verification.

A doctor, after a careful examination of a patient, diagnoses an incurable disease of which the patient shall probably die within a short time. Must the doctor tell the truth, or is he allowed, or even obliged, to lie and tell the patient that his disease is curable and that there is no imminent danger? The decision depends on the order of rank we recognize in the relationship between the value of truth and the value of freedom from fear. To tell the truth means to cause the patient's fear of death; to lie means to free him from fear. If the ideal of truth stands above the ideal of freedom from fear, the doctor has to tell the truth; if the ideal of freedom from fear stands above the ideal of truth, he has to lie. But the answer to the questions as to whether truth or freedom from fear is the higher value is not possible on the basis of a rational scientific consideration.

Plato advocates the opinion that a just man—that means in this connection, a man who obeys the law—and only a just man, is happy; whereas an unjust man—a man who violates the law—is unhappy. Plato says, that "the most just life is the most pleasant."[1] Plato, however, admits that perhaps in one case or another the just man may be unhappy and the unjust man happy. But, asserts the philosopher, it is absolutely necessary that the individuals, subject to the legal order, believe in the truth of the statement that only a just man is happy, even if it should not be true; for otherwise nobody would obey the law. Consequently the government has, according to Plato, the right to spread among the people by means of propaganda the doctrine that the just is happy and the unjust unhappy, even if this doctrine be a lie. If this is a lie, says Plato, it is a very useful lie, for it guarantees obedience to the law. "Could a lawgiver, who was worth his salt, find any more useful lie than this, or one more effective in persuading all men to act justly in all things willingly and without constraint? . . . If I were a legislator, I should endeavour to compel the poets and all the citizens to speak in this sense [that the most just life is the happiest]." The government, then, is fully justified in making use of a useful lie. Plato places justice—and that means here, what the government considers to be justice, namely, lawfulness—above truth; but there is no sufficient reason not to place truth above lawfulness and to repudiate as immoral a governmental propaganda based on lies, even if it serves a good purpose.

The answer to the question concerning the rank of the different values such as freedom, equality, security, truth, lawfulness, and others, is different according to whether the question is answered by a believing Christian, who holds his salvation—the fate of his soul in the hereafter—more important than earthly goods; or by a materialist who does not believe in an after life. And it will be just as different according to whether the decision is made by one who considers individual freedom as the highest good, that is by a liberal, or by one for whom social security and the equal treatment of all men is rated higher than freedom, by a socialist. The answer

1. Plato, *Laws*, 662b.

has always the character of a subjective, and therefore only relative, judgment of value.

III

The fact that value judgments are subjective and that very different value judgments are possible, does not mean that every individual has his own system of values. In fact, very many individuals agree in their judgments of value. A positive system of values is not an arbitrary creation of the isolated individual, but always the result of the mutual influences the individuals exercise upon one another within a given group, be it family, tribe, clan, caste, profession, and under certain political and economic circumstances. Every system of values, especially a system of morals and its central idea of justice, is a social phenomenon, the product of a society, and hence different according to the nature of the society within which it arises. The fact that there are certain values generally accepted in a certain society in no way contradicts the subjective and relative character of these judgments of value. That many individuals agree in their judgments of value is no proof that these judgments are correct, that is to say, valid in an objective sense. Just as the fact that most people believe or used to believe that the sun turns around the earth, is, or was, no proof of the truth of this idea. The criterion of justice, like the criterion of truth, is not dependent on the frequency with which judgments about reality or judgments of value are made. In the history of human civilization quite generally accepted value judgments have often been replaced by quite different value judgments no less generally accepted. In ancient times, blood revenge based on collective responsibility was generally considered as a just institution; but in modern times the opposite idea obtains that only individual responsibility is just. Nevertheless, it is not incompatible with the feeling of justice of most people that in some fields, as, for example, in international relations, the principle of collective responsibility is established; and in religious belief the idea of an original sin—which, too, implies collective responsibility—is still prevailing. And it is by no means impossible that in the future, if socialism should become victorious, a kind of collective responsibility again may generally be considered as adequate.

Although the question as to whether the individual or the nation, the material or the spiritual, freedom or security, truth or justice, represent the highest value, cannot be answered rationally, yet the subjective, and hence relative, judgment by which this question actually is answered, is usually presented as the assertion of an objective and absolute value, as a generally valid norm. It is a peculiarity of the human being that he has a deep need to justify his behavior, that he has a conscience. The need for justification or rationalization is perhaps one of the differences which exist between human beings and animals. Man's external behavior is not very different from that of animals. The big fish swallow the small ones, in the kingdom of animals as well as in that of men. But if a human fish, driven by his instincts, behaves in this way, he wishes to justify his behavior before himself as well as before society, to appease his conscience by the idea that his behavior in relation to his fellow man is right.

If man is more or less a rational being, he tries to justify his behavior, motivated by the emotions of his fear and desire, in a rational way, that is to say, through the function of his intellect. This, however, is possible only to a limited extent—only to the extent that his fear or desire refers to means by which some end is to be achieved; for the relationship of means to end is a relationship of cause and effect, and this can be determined on the basis of experience, which means in a scientific rational way. To be sure, even this is frequently not possible, if the means to achieve a certain end are specifically social measures. For the actual status of social science is such that we have no adequate insight into the causal nexus of social phenomena, and hence no sufficient experience which enables us to determine how certain social aims may best be attained. This is, for example, the case, when a legislator has to decide the question of whether he should provide capital punishment or only imprisonment in order to prevent certain crimes. This question may be formulated as the question of whether capital punishment or imprisonment is a "just" punishment. To decide this question the legislator must know the effect which the threat of these different penalties has on the mind of men inclined to commit the crimes the legislator wishes to prevent. But unfortunately, we have no exact knowledge of this effect and are not in a position to acquire such knowledge, since this is possible only by experiment, and experiment in the field of social life is possible only to a very limited extent. Hence, the problem of justice even as thus restricted to a question of the appropriate means to a presupposed end, cannot always be rationally answered. And even if it could be answered, the answer could not constitute a full justification of our behavior, that justification which our conscience requires. By most appropriate means, most inappropriate ends may be achieved. Think of the atomic bomb. The end—it is true—justifies the means, but the means do not justify the end; and it is the justification of the end, the end which is not itself a means to a further end, the ultimate end, which is the final justification of our behavior.

If something, especially a pattern of human behavior, is justified as means to a certain end, the inevitable question arises whether this end is justifiable. This train of ideas must finally lead to the assumption of an ultimate end, which is the very problem of morality in general and justice in particular. If some human behavior is justified only as an appropriate means to a presupposed end, this behavior is justified only conditionally—under the condition that the presupposed end is justifiable. Such a conditional—and in this sense relative—justification does not exclude the possibility of the opposite. For if the ultimate end is not justifiable, the means to this end is also not justifiable. Democracy is a just form of government only because it is a form of government by which individual freedom is preserved. That means that it is a just form of government under the condition that individual freedom is presupposed as an ultimate end. If instead of individual freedom, social security is presupposed as the ultimate end and if it can be proved that social security cannot be established under a democratic form of government, then not democracy, but another form of government may be considered as just, since another end requires another means. Hence democracy can be justified only as a relatively—not as an absolutely—just form of government.

Our conscience may not be satisfied with such a conditional—and that means relative—justification; it may require an unconditional—an absolute—justification, that is to say, our conscience may be appeased only if our behavior is justified not merely as an appropriate means to an end whose justification is doubtful, but as an end, an ultimate end, or, what amounts to the same, as an absolute value. However, such a justification is not possible in a rational way, because a rational justification is justification as an appropriate means; and an ultimate end is—by definition—not itself a means to a further end. If our conscience requires absolute justification of our behavior—and that means the validity of absolute values—human reason is not able to fulfill this requirement. The absolute in general, and absolute values in particular, are beyond human reason, for which only a conditional, and in this sense relative, solution of the problem of justice, as the problem of justification of human behavior, is possible.

But the need for absolute justification seems to be stronger than any rational consideration. Hence man tries to attain the satisfaction of this need through religion and metaphysics. That means that absolute justice is transferred from this world into the transcendental world. It becomes the essential quality, and its realization the essential function, of a superhuman being, of God, whose qualities and functions are, by definition, inaccessible to human cognition. Man must believe in the existence of God, and that means in the existence of absolute justice, but he is unable to understand it. Those who cannot accept this metaphysical solution of the problem of justice and nevertheless maintain the idea of absolute values in the hope of being able to determine them in a rational-scientific way deceive themselves with an illusion—namely, that it is possible to find in human reason certain fundamental principles from which absolute values may be deduced. But these values are, in truth, determined, in the last analysis, by the emotional elements of their mind. The determination of these absolute values, and in particular the definition of the idea of justice, achieved in this way, are but empty formulas by which any social order whatever may be justified as just.

Hence the many doctrines of justice that have been expounded from the oldest times of the past until today may easily be reduced to two basic types: a metaphysical-religious and a rationalistic or—more exactly formulated—a pseudorationalistic one.

IV

The classical representative of the metaphysical type is Plato.[2] The central problem of his whole philosophy is justice, and for the solution of this problem he developed his famous doctrine of ideas. The ideas are transcendental entities, existing in an ideal world; they represent the absolute values which should be, but never can be, realized entirely in this world. The main idea, the one to which all others are subordinated and from which they all receive their validity, is the idea of the absolute good. This idea plays in Plato's philosophy exactly the same role as the idea of God in the theology of any religion. The idea of the absolute good implies the justice, at whose cognition almost all Platonic dialogues aim. The question as to what is justice coincides with the question as to what is good. Plato makes numerous attempts to approach this problem in a rationalistic way, but none of them leads to a final result. If some definition seems to be reached, Plato immediately declares that it cannot be considered as definitive; that further investigations are necessary. Plato speaks frequently of a specific method of abstract thinking, the so-called dialectic, which, as he maintains, enables those who master it, to grasp, or rather to get a sight or vision of, the ideas. But he himself does not apply this method in his dialogues, or at least does not let us know the results of this

2. See "Platonic Justice," pp. 82 ff.

dialectic cognition. Of the idea of the absolute good, he even says expressly that it is beyond all rational cognition. In one of his epistles—*Epistle VII*, where he gives an account of the inner motives of his philosophy—he declares that the vision of the absolute good is possible only through a specifically mystic experience, which only very few are able to attain by divine grace; but that it is impossible to describe the object of their mystic vision, the absolute good, in words of human language. Hence there can be no answer to the question of what is justice. For justice is the secret which God reveals, if at all, only to a few select persons who cannot communicate it to others.

It is interesting to note how near Plato's philosophy of justice is to the teaching of Christ, whose main concern, too, was justice. After having rejected the rationalistic answer of the Old Testament, that justice is retribution—the principle of an eye for an eye, a tooth for a tooth—he proclaimed as the new justice the principle of love: Don't requite evil with evil, don't resist injury, pass no judgment upon others, love the wrongdoer, love even your enemy.[3] This justice is beyond any social order to be established in reality; and the love which is the essence of this justice is evidently not the human instinct we call love. Not only because it is against human nature to love one's enemy, but also because Jesus emphatically rejected human love uniting man with woman, parent with children. He who wants to enter the Kingdom of God must give up home and wife and brothers and sisters and parents and children.[4] Jesus goes even so far as to say: "If anyone comes to me without hating his own father and mother and wife and children and brothers and sisters, and his very life too, he cannot be a disciple of mine."[5] The love taught by Jesus is not human love. It is the love through which man shall become as perfect as his Father in heaven, who makes his sun rise on bad and good alike and makes the rain fall on the upright and the wrongdoer.[6] It is the love of God. It is supposed to be compatible with the cruel and even eternal punishment of the sinner in the Last Judgment, and hence with the deepest fear, the fear of God. Jesus did not and could not explain these contradictions; for contradictions they are only for the limited human reason, not for the absolute reason of God, which is incomprehensible to man. Hence, Paul, the first theologian of the Christian religion, taught that this world's

3. Matthew V:38, 44.
4. Luke XVIII:29, 30.
5. Luke XIV:26.
6. Matthew V:45, 48.

wisdom is foolishness to God,[7] that philosophy—that is logical-rationalistic cognition—is no way to the divine justice hidden in the mysterious wisdom of God,[8] that justice comes from God through faith,[9] faith acting through love.[10] Paul maintains Jesus' teaching of the new justice, the love of God. But he admits that the love taught by Jesus is far beyond our understanding.[11] It is a secret, one of the many secrets of faith.[12]

V

The rationalistic type, the one which tries to answer the question by defining the concept of justice by the means of human reason, is represented in the popular wisdom of all nations as well as in some famous philosophical systems. To one of the seven sages of ancient Greece, the well-known saying is attributed that justice is to give to each his own. This definition has been accepted by many outstanding thinkers and especially by legal philosophers. It is easy to show that this is an empty formula, because the decisive question, what is that which is everybody's own, is not answered, and hence the formula is applicable only under the condition that this question is already decided by a social order—legal or moral—established by custom or legislation, that is to say, by positive morality or positive law. Hence the formula can be used to justify any such order, whether it be capitalistic or communistic, democratic or autocratic—which probably explains its general acceptance, but which shows that it is useless as a definition of justice as an absolute value, different from the merely relative values guaranteed by positive law or positive morality.

The same holds true with respect to the principle which probably is most often presented as the essence of justice: like for like, that is, good for good and evil for evil, the principle of retribution. This principle is meaningless unless the answer to the question, what is good and what is evil, is presupposed as self-evident. But the answer to this question is not at all self-evident, since the ideas of good and evil are very different among different peoples and at different times. The principle of retribution expresses only the specific technique of the positive law, which reacts

7. 1 Corinthians III:19.
8. 1 Corinthians II:1 ff.
9. Philippians III:9.
10. Galatians V:6.
11. Ephesians III:19.
12. See "The Idea of Justice in the Holy Scriptures," pp. 72 ff.

against the evil of the delict with the evil of the sanction. Hence, any positive legal order corresponds to this principle. The question of justice, however, is the question of whether a positive legal order, attaching to the evil of the delict the evil of the sanction, is just, whether that which the lawmaker considers as an evil to society is indeed a behavior against which society should justly react, and whether the sanction with which society actually reacts is appropriate. To this question, which is the very question of the justice of the law, the principle of retribution is no answer at all.

So far as retribution means like for like, it is one of the many varieties of the principle of equality, which, too, is presented as the essence of justice. This idea of justice starts from the presupposition that men are by their very nature equal, and results in the postulate that all men shall be treated in an equal way. Since, however, the presupposition is evidently wrong, men being in fact very different, no two men being really equal, the only possible meaning of the postulate is that a social order, in conferring rights and imposing duties on men, should ignore certain differences—only certain, not all differences. It would be absurd to treat children in the same way as adults, insane people in the same way as mentally normal ones. But which are the differences that should, and those that should not be taken into consideration? This is the decisive question; and to this question the principle of equality is no answer. In deciding this question, the existing legal orders differ essentially. They all, it is true, agree in ignoring certain differences. But in the differences they do not ignore—the differences they take into consideration in conferring rights and imposing duties on men—there are hardly two legal orders that are completely in harmony. According to one law, only men have political rights, not women; according to another, both, but only men have the duty to do military service; whereas under a third one, the difference of sex has no legal effect in this respect. Which of these legal orders is just? If somebody is indifferent with regard to religion, he will be inclined to consider the difference of religion as irrelevant; if, however, he has a deeply rooted religious conviction, he will certainly consider the difference between those who share his faith—which, for him, is the only true faith—and all others, whether they believe in another religion or are atheists, as more important than any other difference. He will interpret the principle of equality to mean that only equals shall be treated equally. This is indeed the meaning of the principle of equality. Then, the decisive question is: "What is equal?" and this question is not decided by the principle of equality. Hence a positive legal order may make any difference whatever between human beings the basis of a different treatment of its subjects, without getting in conflict with the principle of equality, which is too empty to have practical consequences.

The principle of equality as a postulate directed at the authority creating the law meaning equality in the law, should not be confused with the principle of equality before the law, which is directed at the authorities applying the law to concrete cases. It means that the law-applying organs shall not, in deciding a case, make a difference that is not provided for in the law to be applied, that is to say, they shall apply the law as it should be applied according to its own meaning. It is the principle of legality, of lawfulness, which is immanent in every legal order. It is presented sometimes as justice under the law. But, in truth, it has nothing to do with justice at all.

The principle of equality, if applied to the relationship between labor and product, leads to the maxim: "For an equal quantity of labor an equal quantity of the product." This is according to Karl Marx the idea of justice which is at the basis of the capitalist social order, the allegedly "equal law" of this economic system. It is, in reality, a violation of equality and hence an unjust law. For people who are actually unequal are treated equally. If a man who is strong and a man who is weak get both for the same quantity of labor the same quantity of product, an equal quantity of product is given for a factually unequal quantity of labor. True equality, and hence true, not merely apparent, justice can be realized only within a communist economic system where the principle prevails: "Each according to his capacities and to each according to his needs."[13] If this principle is to be applied within a system of planned economy, which presupposes that the process of production is regulated by a central authority, the questions arise: "What are the capacities of each, what kind of labor is he fit for, what quantity of labor may be expected from him?" It stands to reason that this question cannot be answered by each individual according to his own subjective judgment, but must be decided upon by the competent organ of the community according to general rules adopted by the social authority. And then the next question arises: "Which are the needs that shall be satisfied?" Evidently only those for whose satisfaction the process of production, planned and directed by a central authority, is

13. "Zur Kritik des sozialdemokratischen Parteiprogramms ["Critique of the Gotha Program"], aus dem Nachlass von Karl Marx, *Neue Zeit* IX–1 (1890–1891), p. 567. See my *The Communist Theory of Law* (New York: Frederick Praeger, 1955), pp. 34 ff.

working. Even if, as Marx affirms, in the communist society of the future
the production forces should grow and all springs of social wealth should
pour forth a full flow, the choice of the needs to be satisfied and the extent to which they are to be satisfied could not be left entirely to the subjective wishes of the single individual. This question too, must be decided
by the social authority according to general norms. Thus, the communist
principle of justice—like the formula "To each his own"—presupposes
the answer to questions essential for its application to be given by an established social order. It is true, not by any such order whatever, but by
an order of which nobody can foresee how it will answer the questions
concerned. This fact taken into consideration, the communist principle
of justice—so far as it claims to be such a principle at all—amounts to the
rule: "Each according to his capacities recognized by the communist social order, to each according to his needs likewise recognized by that social order." It is a utopian illusion that this social order will recognize the
capacities of each individual in complete conformity with his own subjective judgment and guarantee the satisfaction of all his needs according to
his own subjective wishes, so that there will be full harmony of the collective and individual interests and, hence, unrestricted individual freedom
within the society constituted by this order. It is the typical utopia of a
Golden Age, a paradise where not only—as Marx prophesied—the "narrow horizon of bourgeois law" but—since there will be no conflicts of interests—also the much wider horizon of justice will be completely
overcome.

   Not very different from the principles of equality and retribution is the
golden rule—to do, or not to do, to others as we would, or would not, have
them do to us. What everybody wants others to do to him, is to give him
pleasure; and what everybody wants others not to do, is to give him pain.
Hence the golden rule amounts to the norm: "Give pleasure to others, do
not inflict pain upon them." However, it frequently occurs that it is
somebody's pleasure to inflict pain upon another. If this is a violation of
the golden rule, then the question arises: "What shall be done to the vio-
lator in order to prevent such violation as far as possible?" This is the
question of justice. If nobody would inflict pain upon another, no problem of justice would exist. It is quite evident that the golden rule, if applied to cases of its violation, must lead to absurd consequences; for
nobody wants to be punished, even if he has committed a crime. Hence,
according to the golden rule, nobody should punish a criminal. Somebody
might not mind at all that others tell lies to him, since he—rightly or
wrongly—thinks himself to be clever enough to find out the truth and

thus to protect himself against the liar. Then, according to the golden rule, he is allowed to lie. The golden rule, taken literally, results in the abolition of law and morality. But its intention is evidently not to abolish, but to maintain, the social order. If interpreted according to its intention, the golden rule cannot, as its wording pretends, establish a merely subjective criterion of the right behavior, the right behavior of the individual being the behavior that he wishes to get from others; such criterion is incompatible with any social order. The golden rule must establish an objective criterion. Its true meaning is: "Behave in relation to others as the others shall behave in relation to you." But how shall they behave? This is the question of justice. The answer to this question is not given, but presupposed by the golden rule; it is given by an established social order—by any such order, whether just or unjust.

VI

If the subjective criterion of the right behavior—implied in the wording of the golden rule—is replaced by an objective criterion; if the meaning of the golden rule is that each individual shall behave toward the others as the others shall behave toward him, then this rule amounts to the principle: "Behave in conformity with the general norms of the social order." It was evidently the golden rule, interpreted in this way, which inspired the German philosopher Immanuel Kant[14] to his formulation of the categorical imperative, which is the essential result of his moral philosophy, and his solution of the problem of justice. It runs as follows: "Act only on that maxim whereby you can at the same time will that it should become a universal law." Its meaning is that one's acts should be determined only by principles that one shall wish to be binding on all men. But which are these principles of which we shall wish that they be binding upon all men? This is the decisive question of justice. To this question the categorical imperative, just as the golden rule—its model—is no answer.

The concrete examples by which Kant tries to illustrate the application of his categorical imperative, are precepts of the traditional morals and the positive law of his time. They are not, as the doctrine of the categorical imperative pretends, deduced from this principle—for nothing can be deduced from this empty formula. They prove only to be compatible with it; and any precept of any established social order is compatible

14. Immanuel Kant, *Grundlegung zur Metaphysik der Sitten* [*Grounding for the Metaphysics of Morals*], I. Abschnitt.

with the principle that says nothing else but that the individual shall act in conformity with general norms. Thus the categorical imperative, just as the rule "To each his own" or the golden rule, can serve as a justification of any social order. This possibility explains why these formulas in spite of—or rather because of—their emptiness, are still, and probably always will be, accepted as satisfactory answers to the question of justice.

VII

Another characteristic example of a futile attempt to define justice in a scientific or quasiscientific way based on reason, is the ethics of Aristotle.[15] He aimed at a system of virtues of which justice is the "chief of the virtues," the "perfect virtue." Aristotle assures us that he has detected a mathematical-geometrical, a scientific, method of defining virtue, and that means the morally good. The moralist, Aristotle maintains, can find the virtue he is looking for just as the geometrist can find the point equidistant from the two ends of a line. Hence virtue is a mean state between two extremes, which are vices (one of excess and one of deficiency).[16] Thus, for example, the virtue of courage is a mean between the vice of cowardice, as too little, and the vice of audacity, as too much confidence. This is his famous doctrine of the mean (*mesōtes*). A geometrist can divide a line into two equal parts only if the two extreme points of the line are given, and if these two points are given, the middle point of the line is predetermined by them. Thus Aristotle can find by his geometrical method the virtue he is looking for only if the two vices are given. But if we know what the vices are, we know also what the virtues are, because a virtue is the opposite of a vice. If deceitfulness (falsehood) is a vice, veracity is a virtue. And indeed the existence of the vice, Aristotle takes for granted. He presupposes as self-evident that vices are what the traditional morality of his time stigmatizes as such. This means that the ethics of the *mesōtes* doctrine only pretends to solve its problem—the determination of what is evil or a vice and, consequently, also the determination of what is good or a virtue, because the latter is implied in the former. It leaves the solution of this problem to another authority—to the authority of the positive morality and the positive law, the established social order. By presupposing in his *mesōtes* formula the given social order, the *Ethics* of Aristotle justifies the positive morality and the positive law, and it is this

15. Aristotle, *The Nicomachean Ethics*, 1129b.
16. *Ibid.*, 1107a, 1106a, 1105b.

positive morality and positive law, not the philosophy of Aristotle, which, as a matter of fact, determines what is "too much" and what is "too little," what are the extremes of evil or wrong, and thereby determines what is the mean, that is, good and right. In this justification of the given social order lies the true—the highly conservative—function of the empty tautology which a critical analysis of the *mesōtes* formula reveals.

In its application to the problem of justice the tautological character of the *mesōtes* formula is still more evident. Aristotle says that "just conduct is a mean between doing and suffering injustice, for the former is to have too much and the latter to have too little."[17] Here the formula that a virtue is the mean between two vices is useless even as a mere figure of speech, for the injustice done, and the injustice suffered, are not two different evils; they are one and the same evil, of which justice is simply the opposite. The decisive question: "What is injustice?" is not answered by the formula. Instead, the answer is presupposed, and Aristotle presupposes as unjust what is unjust under the then existing moral and legal order. The true function of the *mesōtes* doctrine is not, as pretended, to determine the concept of justice, but to confirm the validity of the established social order; and this politically highly important achievement protected it against a critical analysis which proves its scientific futility.[18]

VIII

The metaphysical as well as the rationalist type of legal philosophy is represented in a school of thought which was prevalent during the seventeenth and eighteenth centuries, and which, although repressed more or less during the nineteenth century, has again gained influence in our time. It is the doctrine of natural law.[19] This doctrine maintains that there exists a perfectly just regulation of human relations, emanating from nature—nature in general; or human nature, the nature of man as a being endowed with reason. Nature is conceived of as a legislator. By an analysis of nature we find the immanent norms prescribing the just conduct of men. If nature is supposed to be created by God, the norms immanent in nature, natural laws, are the expression of the will of God. Then the natural-law doctrine has a metaphysical character. If, however, the natural law is to be deduced from the nature of man as a being endowed with reason,

17. *Ibid.*, 1133b.

18. See "Aristotle's Doctrine of Justice," pp. 110ff.

19. See "The Natural-Law Doctrine Before the Tribunal of Science," pp. 137 ff.

if the principle of justice is supposed to be discoverable by an analysis of human reason (in which this principle is immanent), then the natural-law doctrine pretends to assume a rationalistic character. From the point of view of science, neither the one nor the other view is tenable.

Nature as a system of facts, connected with one another according to the law of causality, has no will and hence cannot prescribe a definite behavior of man. From facts, that is to say, from that which is, or actually is done, no inference is possible to that which ought to be or ought to be done. So far as the natural-law doctrine tries to deduce from nature norms of human behavior, it is based on a logical fallacy.

The same holds true with respect to human reason. Norms prescribing human behavior can emanate only from human will, not from human reason; hence the statement that man ought to behave in a certain way can be reached by human reason only under the condition that by human will a norm has been established prescribing this behavior; human reason can understand and describe such behavior but cannot prescribe it. To detect norms of human behavior in human reason is the same illusion as to deduce them from nature.

Hence it is not astonishing that the various followers of the natural-law doctrine deduced from nature, or found in human reason, the most contradictory principles of justice. According to one leading representative of this doctrine, Robert Filmer, the autocracy of an absolute monarchy is the only natural, and that means just, form of government. But another likewise outstanding philosopher, John Locke, proved by the same method that absolute monarchy is no form of government at all, and that only democracy can be considered as such, because only democracy corresponds to the intention of nature. Most writers of this school maintained that individual property, the basis of the capitalistic system, is a natural and consequently sacred right, because it is conferred directly by nature or reason upon man; and that, consequently, communism is a crime against nature or reason. But the propaganda for the abolition of private property and the establishment of a communistic society as the only just social organization was based during the eighteenth and the beginning of the nineteenth century on the same natural-law doctrine.

IX

If the history of human thought proves anything, it is the futility of the attempt to establish, in the way of rational considerations, an absolutely correct standard of human behavior, and that means a standard of human behavior as the only just one, excluding the possibility of considering the opposite standard to be just too. If we may learn anything from the intellectual experiences of the past, it is the fact that only relative values are accessible to human reason; and that means that the judgment to the effect that something is just cannot be made with the claim of excluding the possibility of a contrary judgment of value. Absolute justice is an irrational ideal or, what amounts to the same, an illusion—one of the eternal illusions of mankind. From the point of view of rational cognition, there are only interests of human beings and hence conflicts of interests. The solution of these conflicts can be brought about either by satisfying one interest at the expense of the other, or by a compromise between the conflicting interests. It is not possible to prove that only the one or the other solution is just. Under certain conditions the one, under others the other may be just. If social peace is supposed to be the ultimate end—but only then—the compromise solution may be just, but the justice of peace is only a relative, and not an absolute, justice.

X

What then is the moral of this relativistic philosophy of justice? Has it any moral at all? Is relativism not amoral, or even immoral, as it sometimes maintained? Is relativism incompatible with moral responsibility? On the contrary! The view that moral principles constitute only relative values does not mean that they constitute no value at all; it means that there is not one moral system, but that there are several different ones, and that, consequently, a choice must be made among them. Thus, relativism imposes upon the individual the difficult tasks of deciding for himself what is right and what is wrong. This, of course, implies a very serious responsibility, the most serious moral responsibility a man can assume. If men are too weak to bear this responsibility, they shift it to an authority above them, to the government, and, in the last instance, to God. Then they have no choice. It is easier to obey a command issued by a superior than to be morally one's own master. The fear of personal responsibility is one of the strongest motives of the passionate resistance against relativism. Relativism is rejected and—what is worse—misinterpreted,[20] not because it morally requires too little, but because it requires too much.

20. Thus the relativistic doctrine of justice, essentially connected with legal positivism which does not recognize the existence of an absolute justice, is frequently made responsible for the totalitarian state. The Protestant theologian Emil Brunner says in his work *Justice and the Social Order* (London and Redhill:

The particular moral principle involved in a relativistic philosophy of justice is the principle of tolerance, and that means the sympathetic understanding of the religious or political beliefs of others—without accepting them, but not preventing them from being freely expressed. It stands to reason that no absolute tolerance can be commended by a relativistic philosophy of values; only tolerance within an established legal order guaranteeing peace by prohibiting and preventing the use of force among those subjected to the order, but not prohibiting or preventing the peaceful expression of ideas. Tolerance means freedom of thought. Highest moral ideals have been compromised by the intolerance of those who

---

Lutterworth Press, 1945), the totalitarian state is "the ineluctable consequence" of "a positivism void of faith and inimical to metaphysics and religion" (p. 16). This statement is in open contradiction to the fact that the ideal state of Plato, the prototype of a totalitarian state, is the consequence of his antirelativistic doctrine of ideas which, aiming at absolute values, culminates in the assumption of an absolute good implying absolute justice. See "Platonic Justice," pp. 82 ff. and K. R. Popper, *The Open Society and Its Enemies* (London: G. Routledge, 1945), I, *passim* and pp. 89 ff. If there is a relationship between the philosophy of values and politics, the autocracy of the totalitarian state, political absolutism, is connected with the belief in absolute values, whereas democracy and its essential principle of tolerance presupposes a relativistic view. See "Absolutism and Relativism in Philosophy and Politics" (pp. 198 ff.).

However, Brunner is not very consistent, since he is forced to admit (p. 57): "The Church, which to-day protests, and rightly so, against the oppression it suffers at the hands of the totalitarian State, would do well to remember who first set the State the bad example of religious intolerance by using the secular arm to safeguard by force what can only spring from a free act of the will. The Church should always bethink itself with shame that it was the first teacher of the totalitarian State at nearly every point." This is certainly true; but only because or in spite of the fact that the Church does not teach "a positivism void of faith and inimical to metaphysics and religion" but just the contrary: the belief in absolute justice.

Brunner's work is a justification rather than a refutation of relativism. His doctrine of absolute justice based on "the Christian faith" (p. 8) starts from the thesis: "Either there is a valid criterion, a justice which stands above us all, a challenge presented *to* us, not *by* us, a standard rule of justice binding on every State and every system of law, or there is no justice, but only power organized in one fashion or another and setting itself up as law" (p. 16). Brunner thinks he can find the law of absolute justice in a divine order of creation, which he characterizes as the "Christian law of nature," in contradistinction to the natural law of the rationalistic school of Pufendorf, Thomasius, etc. (pp. 80 ff.). However, after maintaining that the belief in an absolute, divine justice, the recognition of the

fought for them. On the stakes which the Spanish Inquisition set on fire
for the defense of the Christian religion, not only the bodies of the
heretics were burned, but also one of the noblest precepts of Christ was
sacrificed: "Pass no judgment upon others so that you may not have judgment passed on you." During the religious struggles of the seventeenth
century, when the persecuted church agreed with the persecuting church
only in the wish to destroy the other, Pierre Bayle, one of the great libera-
tors of the human mind, said, with regard to those who thought it best to
defend an established religious or political order by persecuting dissent-
ers: "It is not tolerance, it is intolerance that causes disorder." If democracy is a just form of government, it is so because it means freedom, and
freedom means tolerance. If a democracy ceases to be tolerant, it ceases to
be a democracy. But can a democracy be tolerant in its defense against
antidemocratic tendencies? It can—to the extent that it must not suppress

---

Christian law of nature as an order different from and possibly opposite to the
positive law is indispensable in order to stop the disintegration of the idea of justice by the relativistic positivism, he admits—and this is the result of his doctrine
of absolute justice, the Christian law of nature—that all positive law is only "relatively just" (p. 17). That means that he recognizes a relative justice in addition
to the absolute justice. This, however, is a contradiction in terms. If a normative
order does not correspond to the absolute justice it is unjust and, hence, cannot
be just, even not relatively just. There cannot be beside a relative justice an absolute justice, just as there cannot be an absolute justice beside a relative justice. This
is confirmed by Brunner who admits that it is an error to assume "that a law of the
State must be obeyed if it conflicts with the law of nature, and hence is unjust";
otherwise, the law of nature would mean "an intolerable menace to the system of
positive law." "No State can tolerate a competition of this kind presented by a
second legal system. The laws of the State actually obtaining must possess a mo-
nopoly of binding legal force; the law of nature must claim no binding legal force
for itself if the legal security of the State is to remain unshaken" (p. 87). A law of
nature which has no binding force cannot be that "standard rule of justice binding on every State and every system of law" which, according to Brunner's statement on p. 16, is the essence of absolute justice opposed to the relative justice
advocated by legal positivism. A law of nature which has no binding force is no
normative order at all; for the existence of such an order is its binding force.
Brunner justifies this astonishing turn to relativistic positivism by referring to the
reformers, who "in their profound respect for the authority of the State and positive law" "took their stand clearly on the side of positive law, only granting to the
law of nature the function of a criterion" (pp. 87 f.).

   That only the relatively just positive law and not an absolutely just law of nature is legally binding, is exactly the doctrine of relativistic legal positivism. This

the peaceful expression of antidemocratic ideas. It is just by such tolerance that democracy distinguishes itself from autocracy. We have a right
to reject autocracy and to be proud of our democratic form of government
only as long as we maintain this difference. Democracy cannot defend itself by giving itself up. But to suppress and prevent any attempt to over-
throw the government by force is the right of any government and has
nothing to do with the principles of democracy in general and tolerance
in particular. Sometimes it may be difficult to draw a clear boundary line
between the mere expression of ideas and the preparation of the use of
force; but on the possibility of finding such a boundary line depends the
possibility of maintaining democracy. It may be that any such boundary
line involves a certain risk. But it is the essence and the honor of democracy to run such risk, and if democracy could not stand such risk, it would
not be worthy of being defended.

Because democracy, by its very nature, means freedom, and freedom
means tolerance, there is no other form of government which is so favorable to science. For science can prosper only if it is free; and it is free if

---

doctrine, it is true, does not recognize a law of nature even as a criterion, because
such recognition implies the possibility of justifying positive law; and legal positivism, as a science of law, refuses to justify positive law.

In his doctrine of justice, Brunner makes ample use of this possibility. What
he proclaims as the content of the absolutely just law of nature: state, family, individual freedom, private property, are the essential institutions established by the
positive non-communist legal orders of our time. Hence these legal orders are
proved to be, at least in principle, in conformity with the Christian law of nature.
Only communism is according to this doctrine in contradiction to the absolute,
divine justice. However, the communist state which, as a totalitarian state, is declared to be "a monster of injustice" (p. 17), "the acme of injustice" (p. 137), is—
since it is after all a state—finally recognized as "an ordinance of God, a divine
institution" (p. 69). For "even the unjust State is still a State" (p. 174), its legal
order as "a certain order of peace, however brutal," has a certain degree of justice
(pp. 174 ff.). That means: Brunner's doctrine of absolute justice is compelled to
attribute even to the law of the communist state a relative justice. Hence, there is,
according to this doctrine, from the point of view of justice, no essential difference between this law and the law of the capitalist states, since their law too, as a
positive law, is only relatively just.

A doctrine of absolute justice directed against relativistic positivism in view
of the evident contradictions in which it is entangled, cannot claim to be taken
seriously from a scientific point of view, even if it would not declare that its
purpose "is not primarily theoretical but practical, as all theological work should
be" (p. 8).

there is not only external freedom, that is, independence from political influence, but if there is also freedom within science, the free play of arguments and counter arguments. No doctrine whatever can be suppressed in the name of science, for the soul of science is tolerance.

I started this essay with the question as to what is justice. Now, at its end I am quite aware that I have not answered it. My only excuse is that in this respect I am in the best of company. It would have been more than presumptuous to make the reader believe that I could succeed where the most illustrious thinkers have failed. And, indeed, I do not know, and I cannot say what justice is, the absolute justice for which mankind is longing. I must acquiesce in a relative justice and I can only say what justice is to me. Since science is my profession, and hence the most important thing in my life, justice, to me, is that social order under whose protection the search for truth can prosper. "My" justice, then, is the justice of freedom, the justice of peace, the justice of democracy—the justice of tolerance.

13

Vladimir Nabokov,
"About Mira Belochkin,"
from *Pnin*

Vladimir Nabokov was born in Russia in 1899 and, following the Russian Revolution, he lived for some years in England and in Europe before coming to the United States. He taught Russian literature at Wellesley College and Cornell University. He became famous for his controversial novel Lolita *but had already published many enchanting novels and short stories. Nabokov was known for his translations from Russian and also as a chess problemist and a lepidopterist of distinction. He died in Geneva, Switzerland, in 1977.*

Dinner was served on the screened porch. As he sat down next to Bolotov and began to stir the sour cream in his red *botvinia* (chilled beet soup), wherein pink ice cubes tinkled, Pnin automatically resumed an earlier conversation.

"You will notice," he said, "that there is a significant difference between Lyovin's spiritual time and Vronski's physical one. In mid-book, Lyovin and Kitty lag behind Vronski and Anna by a whole year. When, on a Sunday evening in May 1876, Anna throws herself under that freight train, she has existed more than four years since the beginning of the novel, but in the case of the Lyovins, during the same period, 1872 to 1876, hardly three years have elapsed. It is the best example of relativity in literature that is known to me."

After dinner, a game of croquet was suggested. These people favored the time-honored but technically illegal setting of hoops, where two of the ten are crossed at the center of the ground to form the so-called Cage or Mousetrap. It became immediately clear that Pnin, who teamed with Madame Volotov against Shpolyanski and Countess Poroshin, was by far the best player of the lot. As soon as the pegs were driven in and the game started, the man was transfigured. From his habitual, slow, ponderous, rather rigid self, he changed into a terrifically mobile, scampering, mute, sly-visaged hunchback. It seemed to be always his turn to play. Holding his mallet very low and daintily swinging it between his parted spindly legs (he had created a minor sensation by changing into Bermuda shorts expressly for the game), Pnin foreshadowed every stroke with nimble aim-taking oscillations of the mallet head, then gave the ball an accurate tap, and forthwith, still hunched, and with the ball still rolling, walked rapidly to the spot where he had planned for it to stop. With geometrical gusto, he ran it through hoops, evoking cries of admiration from the on-lookers. Even Igor Poroshin, who was passing by like a shadow with two cans of beer he was carrying to some private banquet, stopped for a second and shook his head appreciatively before vanishing in the shrubbery. Plaints and protests, however, would mingle with the applause when Pnin, with brutal indifference, croqueted, or rather rocketed, an adversary's ball. Placing in contact with it his own ball, and firmly putting his curiously small foot upon the latter, he would bang at his ball so as to drive the other up the country by the shock of the stroke. When appealed to, Susan said it was completely against the rules, but Madam Shpolyanski insisted it was perfectly acceptable and said that when she was a child her English governess used to call it a Hong Kong.

After Pnin had tolled the stake and all was over, and Varvara accompanied Susan to get the evening tea ready, Pnin quietly retired to a bench under the pines. A certain extremely unpleasant and frightening cardiac sensation, which he had experienced several times throughout his adult life, had come upon him again. It was not pain or palpitation, but rather an awful feeling of sinking and melting into one's physical surroundings—sunset, red boles of trees, sand, still air. Meanwhile Roza Shpolyanski, noticing Pnin sitting alone, and taking advantage of this, walked over to him ("*sidite, sidite!*" don't get up) and sat down next to him on the bench.

"In 1916 or 1917," she said, "you may have had occasion to hear my maiden name—Geller—from some great friends of yours."

"No, I don't recollect," said Pnin.

"It is of no importance, anyway. I don't think we ever met. But you knew well my cousins, Grisha and Mira Belochkin. They constantly spoke of you. He is living in Sweden, I think—and, of course, you have heard of his poor sister's terrible end...."

"Indeed, I have," said Pnin.

"Her husband," said Madam Shpolyanski, "was a most charming man. Samuil Lvovich and I knew him and his first wife, Svetlana Chertok, the pianist, very intimately. He was interned by the Nazis separately from

Mira, and died in the same concentration camp as did my elder brother Misha. You did not know Misha, did you? He was also in love with Mira once upon a time."

"*Tshay gotoff* (tea's ready)," called Susan from the porch in her funny functional Russian. "Timofey, Rozochka! *Tshay!*"

Pnin told Madam Shpolyanski he would follow her in a minute, and after she had gone he continued to sit in the first dusk of the arbor, his hands clasped on the croquet mallet he still held.

Two kerosene lamps cozily illuminated the porch of the country house. Dr. Pavel Antonovich Pnin, Timofey's father, an eye specialist, and Dr. Yakov Grigorievich Belochkin, Mira's father, a pediatrician, could not be torn away from their chess game in a corner of the veranda, so Madam Belochkin had the maid serve them there—on a special small Japanese table, near the one they were playing at—their glasses of tea in silver holders, the curd and whey with black bread, the Garden Strawberries, *zemlyanika*, and the other cultivated species, *klubnika* (Hautbois or Green Strawberries), and the radiant golden jams, and the various biscuits, wafers, pretzels, zwiebacks—instead of calling the two engrossed doctors to the main table at the other end of the porch, where sat the rest of the family and guests, some clear, some grading into a luminous mist.

Dr. Belochkin's blind hand took a pretzel; Dr. Pnin's seeing hand took a rook. Dr. Belochkin munched and stared at the hole in his ranks; Dr. Pnin dipped an abstract zwieback into the hole of his tea.

The country house that the Belochkins rented that summer was in the same Baltic resort near which the widow of General N—— let a summer cottage to the Pnins on the confines of her vast estate, marshy and rugged, with dark woods hemming in a desolate manor. Timofey Pnin was again the clumsy, shy, obstinate, eighteen-year-old boy, waiting in the dark for Mira—and despite the fact that logical thought put electric bulbs into the kerosene lamps and reshuffled the people, turning them into aging émigrés and securely, hopelessly, forever wire-netting the lighted porch, my poor Pnin, with hallucinatory sharpness, imagined Mira slipping out of there into the garden and coming toward him among tall tobacco flowers whose dull white mingled in the dark with that of her frock. This feeling coincided somehow with the sense of diffusion and dilation within his chest. Gently he laid his mallet aside and, to dissipate the anguish, started walking away from the house, through the silent pine grove. From a car which was parked near the garden tool house and which contained presumably at least two of his fellow guests' children, there issued a steady trickle of radio music.

"Jazz, jazz, they always must have their jazz, those youngsters," muttered Pnin to himself, and turned into the path that led to the forest and river. He remembered the fads of his and Mira's youth, the amateur theatricals, the gypsy ballads, the passion she had for photography. Where were they now, those artistic snapshots she used to take—pets, clouds, flowers, an April glade with shadows of birches on wet-sugar snow, soldiers posturing on the roof of a boxcar, a sunset skyline, a hand holding a book? He remembered the last day they had met, on the Neva embankment in Petrograd, and the tears, and the stars, and the warm rose-red silk lining of her karakul muff. The Civil War of 1918–22 separated them: history broke their engagement. Timofey wandered southward, to join briefly the ranks of Denikin's army, while Mira's family escaped from the Bolsheviks to Sweden and then settled down in Germany, where eventually she married a fur dealer of Russian extraction. Sometime in the early thirties, Pnin, by then married too, accompanied his wife to Berlin, where she wished to attend a congress of psychotherapists, and one night, at a Russian restaurant on the Kurfürstendamm, he saw Mira again. They exchanged a few words, she smiled at him in the remembered fashion, from under her dark brows, with that bashful slyness of hers; and the contour of her prominent cheekbones, and the elongated eyes, and the slenderness of arm and ankle were unchanged, were immortal, and then she joined her husband who was getting his overcoat at the cloakroom, and that was all—but the pang of tenderness remained, akin to the vibrating outline of verse you know you know but cannot recall.

What chatty Madam Shpolyanski mentioned had conjured up Mira's image with unusual force. This was disturbing. Only in the detachment of an incurable complaint, in the sanity of near death, could one cope with this for a moment. In order to exist rationally, Pnin had taught himself, during the last ten years, never to remember Mira Belochkin—not because, in itself, the evocation of a youthful love affair, banal and brief, threatened his peace of mind (alas, recollections of his marriage to Liza were imperious enough to crowd out any former romance), but because, if one were quite sincere with oneself, no conscience, and hence no consciousness, could be expected to subsist in a world where such things as Mira's death were possible. One had to forget—because one could not live with the thought that this graceful, fragile, tender young woman with those eyes, that smile, those gardens and snows in the background, had been brought in a cattle car to an extermination camp and killed by an injection of phenol into the heart, into the gentle heart one had heard beating under one's lips in the dusk of the past. And since the exact form of her death had not been recorded, Mira kept dying a great number of deaths in one's mind, and undergoing a great number of resurrections, only to die again and again, led away by a trained nurse, inoculated with filth, tetanus bacilli, broken glass, gassed in a sham shower bath with prussic acid, burned alive in a pit on a gasoline-soaked pile of beechwood. According to the investigator Pnin had happened to talk to in Washington, the only certain thing was that being too weak to work (though still smiling, still able to help other Jewish women), she was selected to die and was cremated only a few days after her arrival in Buchenwald, in the beautifully wooded Grosser Ettersberg, as the region is resoundingly called. It is an hour's stroll from Weimar, where walked Goethe, Herder, Schiller, Wieland, the inimitable Kotzebue and others. *"Aber warum*—but why—" Dr. Hagen, the gentlest of souls alive, would wail, "why had one to put that horrid camp so near!" for indeed, it was near—only five miles from the cultural heart of Germany— "that nation of universities," as the President of Waindell College, renowned for his use of the *mot juste*, had so elegantly phrased it when reviewing the European situation in a recent Commencement speech, along with the compliment he paid another torture house, "Russia—the country of Tolstoy, Stanislavski, Raskolnikov, and other great and good men."

Pnin slowly walked under the solemn pines. The sky was dying. He did not believe in an autocratic God. He did believe, dimly, in a democracy of ghosts. The souls of the dead, perhaps, formed committees, and these, in continuous session, attended to the destinies of the quick.

The mosquitoes were getting bothersome. Time for tea. Time for a game of chess with Chateau. That strange spasm was over, one could breathe again. On the distant crest of the knoll, at the exact spot where Gramineev's easel had stood a few hours before, two dark figures in profile were silhouetted against the ember-red sky. They stood there closely, facing each other. One could not make out from the road whether it was the Poroshin girl and her beau, or Nina Bolotov and young Poroshin, or merely an emblematic couple placed with easy art on the last page of Pnin's fading day.

Further Readings

Cicero, *On the Commonwealth*, trans. George Holland Sabine and Stanley Barney Smith. New York, Macmillan, 1976.

Emmet, Dorothy, "Justice," *Proceedings of the Aristotelian Society*, supplementary volume 42 (1969).

Goodman, L. E., *On Justice: An Essay in Jewish Philosophy*, New Haven, Yale, 1991.

Hardie, W.F.R., *Aristotle's Ethical Theory*, Oxford, Oxford University Press, 1968.

Hayek, F. A., *The Constitution of Liberty*, Chicago, University of Chicago Press, 1960.

Lucas, J. R., *On Justice*, Oxford, Oxford University Press, 1980.

MacIntyre, Alasdair, *Whose Justice? Which Rationality?* Notre Dame, University of Notre Dame, 1976.

Miller, David, *Social Justice*, Oxford, Oxford University Press, 1976.

Paul, Jeffrey, *Reading Nozick: Essays on Anarchy, State and Utopia*, Totowa, N.J., Rowman and Littlefield, 1981.

Perelman, Chaim, *The Idea of Justice and the Problem of Argument*, trans. John Petrie, New York, Humanities Press, 1963.

Pitkin, Hannah, *Wittgenstein and Justice*, Berkeley, University of California Press, 1972.

Raphael, D.D., *Principles of Political Philosophy*, New York, Praeger, 1970.

Reid, Thomas, *Essays on the Active Powers of the Human Mind*, Essay V, Ch. V, "Whether Justice Be a Natural or an Artificial Virtue," Cambridge, Mass., M.I.T., 1969.

Sandel, Michael, *Liberalism and the Limits of Justice*, Cambridge, Cambridge University Press, 1982.

Walzer, Michael, *Spheres of Justice*, New York, Basic Books, 1983.

Wolff, Robert Paul, *Understanding Rawls*, Princeton, Princeton University Press, 1977.

Woozley, "Injustice," *American Philosophical Quarterly*, Monograph 7, Oxford, 1973.

DATE DUE

The Oxford Book
of American
Literary Anecdotes